Twilight of Press Freedom

The Rise of People's Journalism

LEA'S COMMUNICATION SERIES
Jennings Bryant/Dolf Zillmann, General Editors

For a complete list of titles in LEA's Communication Series, please contact Lawrence Erlbaum Associates, Publishers.

Twilight of Press Freedom

The Rise of People's Journalism

JOHN C. MERRILL
University of Missouri–Columbia

PETER J. GADE
University of Oklahoma

FREDERICK R. BLEVENS
Southwest Texas State University

LAWRENCE ERLBAUM ASSOCIATES, PUBLISHERS
2001   Mahwah, New Jersey   London

Lawrence Erlbaum Associates, Inc., Publishers
10 Industrial Avenue
Mahwah, NJ 07430

Cover design by Kathryn Houghtaling Lacey

Library of Congress Cataloging-in-Publication Data

Merrill, John Calhoun, 1924–
   Twilight of press freedom : the rise of people's journalism / by John C. Merrill,
   Peter J. Gade, Frederick R. Blevens.
      p.   cm.
   Includes bibliographical references and index.
    ISBN 0–8058–3663–2 (cloth : alk. paper) — ISBN 0–8058–3664–0 (pbk. : alk. paper)
    1. Journalism—Social aspects. I. Gade, Peter J. II. Blevens, Frederick R.
  III. Title.
PN4749 .M47 2000
302.23—dc21   00–037639

Books published by Lawrence Erlbaum Associates are printed on acid-free paper,
and their bindings are chosen for strength and durability.

Printed in the United States of America
10 9 8 7 6 5 4 3 2 1

Things fall apart; the center cannot hold;
Mere anarchy is loosed upon the world,
The blood-dimmed tide is loosed, and everywhere
The ceremony of innocence is drowned;
The best lack all conviction, while the worse
Are full of passionate intensity.

—William Butler Yeats

. . . excessive love of liberty destroys democracy and
leads to dictatorship where there is no freedom at all.

—Plato, *The Republic*

Each of us puts his person and all his power in
common under the supreme direction of the general
will, and, in our corporate capacity, we receive each
member as an indivisible part of the whole . . .
whoever refuses to obey the general will shall be
compelled to do so by the whole body.

—Jean-Jacques Rousseau

Contents

Foreword

EVERETTE E. DENNIS
Fordham University

Few scholars have devoted more rigorous attention to press freedom than John C. Merrill. He is joined here by Peter J. Gade and Frederick R. Blevens to issue an ominous warning and thoughtful critique of what they call "the twilight of freedom"—meaning institutional press freedom. This timely and important book is not, in my opinion, quite as pessimistic as its title suggests. Indeed, by exposing and confronting head-on the current embrace of community by many social critics who concurrently offer prescriptions for the media, these authors demonstrate why the public need not be alarmed after all.

Lest this seem tortured logic, it is important to know that adherents of communitarianism and one of its retail products—civic or public journalism—have already diagnosed society's grip on freedom as fragile and flawed. The public journalists offer a treatment program that involves a commitment to community, to the common good through an engaged communication system. Along the way they discard the noble, but not easily attained, model of impartial information long promoted by advocates of libertarian communication. Instead, such critics argue for a *journalism of engagement,* wherein the journalist or modern media worker is not an actor representing an objective ideal, but one who openly takes positions and becomes an active player, rather than an observer.

Merrill and his colleagues trace the evolution of this new journalistic stance from the Enlightenment of the 17th and 18th centuries to the rise of the counter-Enlightenment criticism, through modern flirtations with critical theory, deconstructionism, postmodernism, multiculturalism, poststructuralism, communitarianism, and public/civic journalism. It should be clear to readers who are familiar with Merrill's basic libertarianism that this book is not an endorsement of this communitarian drift to a new paradigm but is simply an attempt to describe it and to explicate its basic philosophical rationale. It can be read both as a description of this new people's journalism and also as a warning to press libertarians that the old institutional-press freedom model is being seriously eroded by a new breed of anti-Enlightenment critics.

There is much support for this notion in the emerging literature of communitarianism and public journalism, but it also changes the role of the communicator from that of independent storyteller to one of community organizer. Although some promoters of public journalism deny they would transmogrify the social worker and the journalist, that is in fact what the system they propose actually does. When confronted with the real consequences of this proposed new regime for journalism and other information gathering, however, they blink and veer away, arguing that they don't want change at all, just good old-fashioned fact-gathering and journalistic integrity. Still, the treatises on the subject say otherwise, and a cowardly retreat in the face of powerful criticism does not wipe out the written word.

This book demands of its readers, before they get to the main event, that they review the several philosophies and axioms of freedom deriving from some of the great thinkers of the ages and connect these with postmodernist critics. Only then, the authors say, can one truly understand the nuances of the restatement of affection for the community, whether a new or old concept. In a real sense, the argument here is summoned up by distinguishing between individualism in the Enlightenment sense and more recent entreaties for accountability, no doubt hastened by this period of media excess and sensationalism. More than anything, poor performance by the news and information media and a blurring of entertainment and opinion with information have fired the current critique. For some, the new community-oriented journalism plan is the best solution to a problem that warrants public concern. Our authors give us their perspectives and the rationale for this new journalistic focus.

As many of the instruments of media criticism have either been ignored or have failed outright—and here I mean press councils, fair trial–free press councils, the journalism review movement, and others—an embrace of community is offered as a quick fix for poor media performance, lack of public interest in associational life, and even declining newspaper circulation. While not clearly defining *community* in an age when all kinds of new communities and interest groups have evolved thanks to the Internet, the critics that our authors discuss focus their attention more on the content of the media's lowest rung practitioners, and more distantly on their owners, than on commingling of social forces, whether economics, regulation, or technology.

Although well-intentioned, the communitarian voices the authors bring to us actually resemble some devotees of community in other parts of the world with whom they would quickly part company. The same critics who call for a community-based communication system, including a more constructive and positive journalism, also decry the "Asian values" argument made by leaders in Singapore and Malaysia, for example, who believe that too much individual freedom and criticism impairs the commonweal. Thus, under this system inspired by Confucianism, the good of the whole—whether the family, the neighborhood, the community, or the nation—must be considered in any communication that leads to conflict and disruption. It is a mirror image with an Asian accent of the communitarian public journalism proposal.

It is easy to see why and how sensationalism and destruction of individuals at the hands of an overzealous press is very much at issue in the United States today. Still, we are not willing to silence such voices for the good of the whole, something that Lee Kuan Yew and other influential advocates of Asian values would do. What is proposed in the postmodernist Western media (mainly in the United States, as the community argument holds little sway in Europe) Merrill, Gade, and Blevens describe in this book.

For my taste, *Twilight of Press Freedom* is too generous in giving the positive appeal of the trend toward community, in laying out the arguments of the contemporary critics of libertarianism, many of which I think the authors feel are fundamentally wrong. It bothers me somewhat that many modern intellectuals are mentioned right along with eminent thinkers of other times—something like comparing a low-wattage newspaper columnist with Thomas Jefferson. In this sense the book is a bit too respectful, too earnest in its assessment, and a bit understated in its own conclusion—perhaps revealed between the lines, but never screamed from the rooftops. This understated view, I believe, is and ought to be that the current antiliberal or antilibertarian view, held by communitarians and public journalists who seem to relish the twilight of press freedom, is simply wrong and contrary to historical evidence. The authors may hint at this but do not say it bluntly.

This personal objection aside, *Twilight of Press Freedom* is a valuable entry into the literature of journalism and the often intolerant debate over community. Without a doubt, it provides the reader the most thorough and best balanced picture yet of the critical shift in thinking away from freedom of expression. An open-minded reader of this volume will have a panoramic journey into the history of ideas and arguments that can, and do, make a difference in the world of public discourse.

Preface

The center, as Irish poet W. B. Yeats said, will not hold, and things seem to be falling apart. Old traditions and ideas are dying. As the 21st century gets underway, that is exactly what is happening in the field of mass communication. Dedication to freedom, a legacy derived from the Enlightenment of the 18th century, has caused the journalistic world to plunge into a frenzy of excessive multifaceted verbal and pictorial gyrations that threaten to vulgarize civilization.

At least that is what modern critics seem to believe. Individualism is running rampant, liberty is morphing into license, communal cohesion is dissipating, a press with a passion for public service is dying out, and humane considerations are nearly nonexistent. That is a common critique of the modern world.

We contend in this book, however, that things have been changing since the mid-20th century. A new social paradigm of order, harmony, and security in community is replacing the old paradigm of freedom and individualism. Social reformers are everywhere on the scene, proclaiming a new day and waving again the flags of populist utopianism.

That is what this book is about: this new paradigm and the reformers (among them the public or civic journalists) who are trying to bring it about. In the world of journalism, manifestations of change are many and varied, and we have tried to isolate many of these, while at the same time attempting to orient the reader with the values of the European Enlightenment against which the new communitarian reformers are reacting.

This book is not intended to be a polemic either for or against public (a.k.a. civic) journalism and other communitarian changes that are taking place. We are simply trying to expose the development and practices of the new public journalism, to introduce the reader to the leaders in the movement, and to predict what impact such populist social inclinations are likely to have on press freedom in the 21st century. We hope that our book will at least stimulate thought and discussion on this vital subject. Writing such a book has not been easy, but we have had much encouragement and help from many quarters in the press, the academy, and the general public.

We want to acknowledge the suggestions, encouragement, and help of many persons—far too many to name here. A few of these, however, must be singled out for special appreciation. First of all, our sincere thanks go to our wives, Dorothy, Susan, and Charly, who have supported us in this project, offering encouragement and valuable suggestions. To them we dedicate this book.

In addition, we owe a great debt of gratitude to Sue Schuermann and Robin Rennison, remarkably efficient assistant Journalism School librarians at the University of Missouri, who went far beyond the normal call of duty in finding many references and other materials that were used in these pages. Especially helpful in reading the manuscript, making suggestions, and supplying additional information and citations from her prodigious files was Kathleen Edwards, director of the School of Journalism's invaluable Freedom of Information Center. We thank all these people and the dozen or so students and faculty members who stimulated our thinking as we discussed with them the topics of this book.

—*John C. Merrill*
—*Peter J. Gade*
—*Frederick R. Blevens*

Introduction:
A New Spirit of Community

The thesis of this book is simple—and controversial: that the press in America and around the world is losing its freedom (its autonomy) and, as it does, is losing its institutional importance. However, a corollary thesis is that with the loss of this freedom, the 21st century will see more social order and harmony and a more cooperative and citizen-based press. In a sense, one might say that journalists' journalism is disappearing and people's journalism is in its ascendancy. At least this is the new gospel being heard in academic and media circles, not only in the United States with the advent of communitarianism and public journalism, but also in many other countries where there is a rising demand for a more human face to be put on the predominant authoritarian media systems.

A new paradigm is evolving: One of order is replacing one of freedom. Darkness is settling in on the 18th-century Enlightenment liberalism that has marked the freedom paradigm. Harmony and cooperation are new watchwords. Public involvement is the new media objective. As the concept of journalistic autonomy fades, so ordered and responsible groupist journalism is arising, dedicated to the public good and not to private interests. The term that covers this new media emphasis or model is *communitarian* or *public journalism.*

This book deals mainly with this communitarianism and its subgenre, public (a.k.a. civic) journalism, in what we hope is a realistic way. The growing loss of journalistic freedom is largely generated by the communitarian call for a more ordered and harmonious community. Those familiar with John Merrill's earlier book *The Imperative of Freedom* (1974) will recognize at once that its strong defense of freedom is exactly what the communitarians are reacting against. In this volume we are reflecting (not endorsing) the shift away from press freedom and toward the more community-oriented and "socially responsible" journalism that Merrill predicted in 1974.

No doubt this book, *Twilight of Press Freedom,* goes against the thinking of many recent authors who see the world heading toward greater personal freedom. They, evidencing a capitalistic optimism associated with the fall of the Soviet Union in 1991 and the promise of individual potential in the new

Information Age of the computer, see an opening of personal freedom and a decline of institutional and state authority. They envision more, not less, pluralism and diversity on ethics and basic social issues, and they see the variety of messages flowing nationally and internationally as greatly increasing.

Taking the opposite thesis to the one we take in this book, these optimistic libertarian individualists foresee a future of increasing freedom and loosening social structure and control. One recent author, Brian McNair, disagrees with us. In his 1998 book, *The Sociology of Journalism,* McNair proclaimed that "the tendency to chaos rather than control is now clear" (p. 166) and projected a more disorderly journalism in the future. If McNair is correct, we are in for long-term disorder and social disequilibrium, and the communitarians will be sorely disappointed. But McNair went on to say that, even though "the consequences for the future conduct of relations between journalism and society are uncertain, watching them unfold in the coming years will be nothing if not an interesting spectator sport" (p. 168). We say "amen" to that.

Since the fall of Communism in the Soviet Union, numerous books have reasserted the values of libertarianism and the free-market economy. Their authors stress what they think is a basic human yearning for freedom and individualism. They are trying to revive faith in the 18th-century Enlightenment. Journalist William Greider (1993) in *Who Will Tell the People: The Betrayal of American Democracy,* while giving a warning about the decline of democracy in America with power increasingly falling into the hands of the few, nevertheless contended that the desire for "individual self-realization, a desire to discover and establish one's own worth . . . is profound and universal" (p. 21). Sociologist Francis Fukuyama, in spite of his alarm at seeing signs of social collapse in his *The Great Disruption* (1999), stood by his earlier prediction in *The End of History and the Last Man* (1992) that the capitalistic, libertarian political system is triumphantfully established until the end of time. History, he wrote, so far as politico–economic systems theory is concerned, has ended and only minor adjustments would be necessary for the world of the future.

Perhaps the most optimistic recent book that sees a new century filled with freedom and individualism is *The Sovereign Individual* (1997) by James D. Davidson and William Rees-Mogg. Although admitting that the new world will see a jump in violence, assorted crime, and other antisocial activities, the authors visualized a less highly structured society that will see increased individual autonomy and meritocracy. They saw the computer as the instrument through which individuals can become real public communicators, conducting almost any informational business anywhere. David Boaz, in *Libertarianism: A Primer* (1997), also presented the computer and the Information Age "as one big reason that the future will be libertarian" (p. 284). Boaz added that governments will find it more difficult to keep their citizens in the dark about world affairs and about government malfeasance, and he predicted that government efforts to block certain messages, spy on computer users, and force them to use government keys (like the "Clipper Chip") will fail. Coercive force, he said, simply cannot be projected across such a vast network.

The communitarians and public journalists visualize, or at least want, a quite different kind of world. They would hate to see the world of the *sovereign individual* come about. They want less individual freedom, more social discipline and order, less pluralism and social atomism, more harmony and cooperation, and increased social predictability. Communitarians see Boaz' prediction that libertarianism is the ideology of the future as extremely naive, given the social harm that personal freedom has done to society for the last few centuries. In spite of the strident and optimistic voices of the previously mentioned libertarians (joined by many others such as Milton Friedman, Murray Rothbard, and Robert Nozick), the communitarians and public journalists, with their assorted social-order colleagues on both right and left, are convinced that they will be successful in what they see as the new Communitarian Century.

There are signs that they may be right. This is the age of insecurity. It is the age of disintegrating family. It is the age of anxiety. It is the age of atomistic persons who have lost their footing in a fast-changing world. It is the age of fitful, gossip-mongering, sensational journalism that shamelessly and arrogantly throws the filth of society in the public's face. Fukuyama (1999) called this period "The Great Disruption" and saw the period from the 1960s through the 1990s as bringing a sharp loss of moral cohesion and threatening the social fabric of liberal democracy.

But things are changing, probably largely as a reaction to the aforementioned chaos. To counter this anomie, this social entropy, this danger and anxiety, Americans are putting more and more faith in government and in social and community institutions to provide some sanctuary against the impending social disintegration. They are stressing cooperation, community solidarity, networking, and other activities and policies that tend to deemphasize atomistic individualism and to enthrone a cooperationist and collectivistic public policy. Gated communities, community watch programs, private security forces, elaborate home electronic warning systems, metal detectors in schools and airports, increased funding of police—all these, and many others, are signs of the newly developing social model of order. Security, not freedom, is the clarion call as the new century begins.

Harmony not competition, the community not the individual, solidarity not autonomous units, altruism not egoism, other-directedness not inner-directedness—all of these antinomies help to explain the paradigm shift that is taking place. In the process, the concept of freedom and individualism is being lost—or at least de-emphasized. So be it, say the new communitarians. Freedom and individualism had their day; they had their chance to bring about a better world, but they failed. It is time for something new, in society generally and certainly in journalism. It is time for consensus building, for social participation, for community solidarity, for political involvement—in short, for positive democratic effort that goes beyond simply voting. It is time to realize that freedom of the press is really freedom of public access to the press, as lawyer and professor Jerome Barron (1973) contended in *Freedom of the Press: For Whom?* Journalists cannot take old ideas and institutions (even the press) for granted; they are "not indestructible," wrote Professor James Carey (1998) of Columbia University. He asserted that journalists "seem to believe that democratic politics, which alone underwrites their craft, is a self-perpetuating machine that can withstand any amount of undermining. They are wrong" (p. 6).

A new parade is forming. Collections of like-minded communities and interest groups in distinctive ideological uniforms are beginning to march. Socially relevant music is being played. Community spirit permeates the ranks. Solidarity and brotherhood enliven and quicken the step. Just over the hill is a new world, and the parade of hopeful and idealistic marchers is moving to the summit. Under an umbrella of inspirational banners, and with smiles on their faces and songs in their hearts, the marchers are moving as one over the hill into the brave, new world of communitarianism.

Their quest for order is really nothing new in the world. Throughout the ages, people have desired order. Established order has dictated all theories of government, from tribal culture and discipline to more sophisticated political systems. When order breaks down, when social expectations become vague, when discipline weakens, when people fragment and disagree, when laws are ignored or broken, when authorities lose their credibility and respect—it is then that we have the genesis of social anomie, of unpredictable activity, of individualism run wild, of social trauma that cries out for structure and order. Without some authority to wield power, to set limits for social activity, to establish social goals and provide for a system to reach them, there can be no order. Order is opposed to freedom. Order is opposed to planlessness. Order is opposed to individual autonomy. Order, in a real sense, is a conformist and comforting result of social planning and social cooperation.

A country can and must have a certain degree of order if it is to have a meaningful pluralism and freedom. However, order is inversely related to diversity, and it is not congenial with maximum personal freedom. Nor is it found in societies where there is a legacy of strong individualism. Since the 18th century, we in America and our ancestors in Europe have had considerable respect for individualism. With it has come ever more freedom, but also with it we have seen the social order become more tenuous, more problematic. States' rights, individual rights, and the fragmentation of government authority have increasingly played havoc with the concept of order. The situation began to change in the mid-20th century, at least in the United States, as social instability and even chaos became rampant. The historic magnet of authority reasserted itself after some five centuries, and people began talking seriously of social stability, public order, and harmonious cooperation rather than freedom and individualism. The spirit of communitarianism (that had hung around on the periphery at least since the days of Plato and Confucius) was reasserting itself, and the individualistic era of the Renaissance and the Enlightenment was slowly fading away.

In this book we have tried to present the case for the new communitarianism and the general shift from individual (and press) freedom to social (and press) responsibility. There is little doubt that there is considerable justification for the many critics who have condemned the capitalistic media. We acknowledge this while still believing that many of the criticisms have been naive or extreme, or both. In spite of this belief, we have reiterated many of those criticisms in this book and have added a few others as we now write from a more balanced—and we hope more realistic—perspective. Our goal has turned from one of missionary zeal (so frowned on by the Third World) to one of description and prediction, still relativistic of course, but perhaps less ethnocentric.

Western media ethnocentrism and capitalistic nationalism are continuing to bind communication cultures to the old Enlightenment paradigm that has undergirded American press theory. However, the social forces pulling ever more complex and growing populations toward order are thrusting media systems into a new and more harmonious communitarianism. As many leaders in the Third World see it, order and discipline are preferable to freedom and competition. Western intellectuals generally, including many journalists, are coming to agree with this position.

As media practices become ever more extreme, especially in areas of sex, crime, gossip, violence, and invasion of privacy, even libertarian journalists in the West are recognizing that freedom must somehow be harnessed. It might just be that public welfare and social stability take precedence over journalists' egocentric and often eccentric escapades of freedom. It is little wonder that a kind of neoauthoritarianism based on increased public authority, order, and a monistic concept of responsibility seems to be developing at this time in history. At least, this is the thesis of our book and the hope of the communitarians, and only time will tell whether or not this new paradigm of order—one that is rather sharply opposed to the free-wheeling and heterogeneous postmodern world view—will emerge as the dominant one for most of the world.

It may be, as many media observers believe, that journalism is becoming more democratized, more people-oriented, and more socially relevant as it responds increasingly to the public's wishes. Polls, surveys of all types, and media-sponsored focus groups and open discussions are providing the media with ever more public opinion. Vox populi has begun to propel the new communitarian agenda. And, say the proponents of the new model, look at the Internet. See how it is actually making journalists of all citizens (at least all computer users). Such expansion of journalism to the citizenry, if definitions are stretched somewhat, may actually bring about a new "people's journalism." If such is the case, however, it simply bears out another thesis of this book: The press as an institution (at least as we understand the term and as it is constitutionally protected) is diminishing in importance. We maintain also that it has been press freedom, in spite of its negative attributes, that has largely given the press its power and its social importance. Without such freedom and the contentiousness that accompanies it, the press would have likely lost its vigor, its excitement, its social impact, and its controversial nature long ago, and would have (as it probably will) become little more than a people's bulletin board of happy notices. However, although it might lose much of its vigor and excitement, it would gain, say the new communitarians, true social significance.

The new communitarianism reminds one of Plato, who might be considered its spiritual ancestor. Plato was the first Western thinker to formulate a systemic view of reality in which the moral standard was the community as a whole. For Plato, the good life was essentially one of renunciation and self-lessness, each person fleeing from personal pleasures and negating individuality in the name of group solidarity. When social allegiances are plural, Plato believed, the result is inevitable and intolerable conflict; therefore, he would ban such diversity in the ideal republic. Unlike his younger contemporary, Aristotle, who was more the libertarian of his day, urging a rational pride in oneself and one's individually developed moral character, Plato saw unity and order as paramount. Since the days of these two Greek philosophical stalwarts, world societies have generally sided with Plato except for the few centuries when Aristotelianism dominated during the Renaissance and the Enlightenment. The communitarians are presently urging their own new Platonic Renaissance.

We must now, say the communitarian media critics, develop the "public sphere"—the community cohering between individualism and statism but with an ordered structure. It is this, said German social critic Juergen Habermas (1991), that will allow for democratic discourse. This public sphere, according to Habermas, would be the "space" independent of both state and business control, permitting citizens to debate on the public issues of the day without fear of either political or economic powers (1996, p. 36). Also writing of the public sphere was Robert McChesney in his *Corporate Media and the Threat to Democracy* (1997), who contended that no institution is more important to this public sphere than the mass media. However, he believed that the professionalization of the media and the development of journalism schools in the 1920s played a big part in the unfortunate depoliticization of American society. With the coming of modern journalism, according to McChesney, social and political issues were neglected and "events" emphasized (pp. 13–14). McChesney and others hope that the new communitarianism will reverse this trend. Only for one brief period in the 1960s and 1970s, McChesney wrote, did the de-emphasis of politics cease. That was when apathetic sectors of the population rose up and demanded a say in political issues.

So, contend the communitarians and public journalists, if the "public sphere" can be activated politically, a new kind of community can come into being that will not simply be passive recipients of media-dominated messages, but will feed community-relevant material into journalism. Indications are appearing in the press of greater citizen participation — news op-ed page essays, more letters, more invited columnists, and more emphasis on public opinion polls and readership surveys. Press autonomy is, indeed, losing its former status, if for no other reason than the impact of stockholders, lawyers, and advertisers. Increasing criticism of press activities, fear of libel actions, and journalistic self-doubt are contributing to the demise of media potency. Press ethics, although increasingly discussed and praised, may be having some effect, though seemingly very little, on order and consensus in the world of journalism.

It does appear that loyalty, obedience, cooperation, and discipline in the media are becoming more common. For instance, team reporting, instead of individual journalistic effort, is a recent innovation in newsrooms, evidencing a more cooperative and group-oriented journalism. Journalism and communication education is growing at a fantastic rate around the world and with it, more standardized and conformist media beliefs and practices. This is a big step on the road to professionalization, a destination that may well improve the social efficiency and solidarity of the media. The downside of this is that it may also solidify the press into a more elite structure and preclude the continued growth of public journalistic participation At any rate, new loyalties are developing — toward order, groupism, harmony, positive news, ethical agreement, community solidarity, and restrained freedom. They are replacing such older libertarian watchwords as individualism, self-enhancement, autonomy, diversity, ethical disagreement, and maximum freedom.

This book attempts to describe this paradigm shift toward order and community and away from freedom and individualism. Although we personally feel somewhat uncomfortable with this new media paradigm of order and harmony, we see it developing in many subtle and not-so-subtle ways that we try to explain on the following pages. Communitarianism is a power concept that must be taken seriously. In America it is invading social consciousness on the coattail of a loss of media credibility, offering to replace an ever-growing media libertinism and arrogance.

A big problem in the new century will be the control of the mushrooming Internet and the new "people's journalism," but this can and will be done in concert with the new spirit of community solidarity. So it would appear that the 21st century will be one of a more orderly and disciplined press, dedicated to social harmony and operating as a thermostat to keep the communal temperature at a comfortable level. It will be a century, as well, that views press freedom somewhat nostalgically—a glorious idea that came and went.

1

The Sunrise of Freedom

I deduce that reason cannot desire for man any other condition than that in which each individual not only enjoys the most absolute freedom of developing himself by his own energies, in his perfect individuality, but in which external nature itself is left unfashioned by any human agency, but only receives the impress given to it by each individual by himself and of his own free will, according to the measure of his wants and instincts, and restricted only by the limits of his powers and his rights.

—Wilhelm von Humboldt

It had been a long night and it looked as if the sun would never rise. But rise it did, the first rays of freedom flickering across Europe during the 15th and 16th centuries, in what we usually call the Renaissance. Essentially this sun was freedom, with a variety of new concepts and accomplishments spinning off of it. At first the light was dim, but it grew brighter during the 17th century—the Age of Reason—and reached its zenith at high noon with the 18th-century Enlightenment. Its rays would stimulate artistic and then scientific endeavors as never before and would create a revolutionary philosophical system of optimism and progress that would spread across the Atlantic and create the United States of America.

Of nearly 2,500 years of Western politics and philosophy, only those four centuries (mid-15th through the mid-19th) stand out as a period of progress, optimism, science, rationalism, and freedom. The genesis of this amazing four-century era of geographical and intellectual discoveries, with its emphasis on individual achievement and value, was the reintroduction of the ideas of Aristotle into European thought by Thomas Aquinas at the beginning of the end of the Middle Ages. Then, during the Renaissance that presaged the Enlightenment, the power of religion faded, the feudal caste system broke up, church authority was challenged, inventions and explorations flourished, and individualism made its debut. In short, sunlight was filtering through the pale and misty world of medieval Europe.

THE PRE-ENLIGHTENMENT SPIRIT

The Renaissance, appearing in the 15th century, became an important part of Western intellectual consciousness and merged into the spirit of the Enlightenment. Referred to at the time by the Italian humanist Ficino of Florence as "this golden century," the Renaissance brought back to light "the liberal arts, which were all but extinguished: grammar, poetry, oratory, painting, sculpture, architecture, music . . . and all this in Florence" (Nisbet, 1980, p. 102). Here we see, emerging from the Middle Ages, the rebirth of Greco-Roman ideas, although some critics see many such ideas also existing in medieval times. And as Nisbet pointed out, all was not light and progress during the Renaissance. For instance, there was the great interest in the occult, magic, and fate or fortune (p. 105). Even in enlightened Florence of the day, according to Nisbet (pp. 105, 107), such thinkers as Machiavelli and his younger contemporary Francesco Guiccardini believed that *fortuna* (chance, fate) has control over a person's life.

During the 17th and early 18th centuries, this early-Enlightenment sunlight was bearing down on Britain and shining into the Italian city-states and Germany. Even more strongly it shone down on France, whose thinkers we observe shortly. Italy felt the intellectual warmth, but to a much less degree. It was actually in England that the Enlightenment was most prevalent. The fundamental and characteristic ideas originated there. As Frederick Beiser (1996) said, "It was no accident that the *Aufklaerer, philosophes,* and *illuministi* [of Germany, France, and Italy] saw England as the source of their inspiration" (p. 4). In Italy, as far back as the 16th century, such Renaissance figures as Copernicus, Galileo, and Machiavelli in their own ways challenged the Catholic Church and veered toward rationalism, setting the stage for the Age of Reason.

Probably the foremost essayist of the Renaissance was the Frenchman Michel de Montaigne (1533–1592), whose idol was Socrates, and it was from him that he appropriated his basic rationalist philosophy. For Montaigne, the greatest evil of the age was fanaticism and, in his original and imaginative style, he assailed it vigorously. Montaigne's essays were extremely varied, thoughtful, and stylishly written, and they evidenced an intellectualism that presaged the later Renaissance and Enlightenment. For a good anthology of his essays, illustrated by the artist, see *Essays of Michel de Montaigne* (Dali, 1942). The scope of his essays is indicated by such titles as these: "Of the Education of Children," "Of Cannibals," "Of Democritus and Heraclitus," "Of Repentance," "Of Vanity," and "Of Experience."

Another Frenchman, René Descartes (1596–1650), is known as the father of rationalism and one of the most brilliant mathematicians of the pre-Enlightenment 17th century. After his education in his hometown University of Poitiers and much traveling in Europe as a soldier, he settled in Holland, where he could have the greatest freedom of expression. He was early obsessed with the question of whether we could know anything for certain. Between 1620 and 1649, he produced his major works, *Discourse on Method* (1637) and *Meditations* (1641). He died in 1650 in Stockholm, where he was tutoring Queen Christina of Sweden in philosophy.

Descartes was, like Montaigne, a superb stylist in his writing. He was the forerunner of the French *philosophes*, and like them was preoccupied with human freedom—from prejudice and from social and political oppression. Although Descartes was vitally interested in other aspects of philosophy, his fundamental concern was with freedom. For him, other traits (e.g., mastery over the passions and progress) presuppose freedom. He thought about, and wrote about, freedom of opportunity, freedom of the will, freedom from prejudice, and freedom from indifference. A firm believer in social progress, Descartes thought that if a person were willing, he or she had the capability of self-determination (Schouls, 1989, pp. 40–48). Such strong Cartesian beliefs as the primacy of human freedom and the possibility of autonomy filtered strongly into the 18th-century Enlightenment and became the core beliefs of press libertarianism.

Also in the 17th century, at the dawn of the Enlightenment, the great Jewish thinker Benedict Spinoza (1632–1677) was championing freedom of expression and was serving as the central figure in a band of freethinkers who were drawn to Holland, where he lived. Long before it was popular to do so, liberal-minded Spinoza suggested that freedom of speech was necessary for public order, an idea that might get a cool reception by the communitarians and public journalists of today. However, freedom was the song being sung by philosophers throughout Europe, and Spinoza and his contemporary, Descartes, added their influential voices to the choir.

THE GERMAN *AUFKLAERUNG*

The 18th century saw the appearance in Germany of the great Immanuel Kant (1724–1804), who honored freedom and reason but, as a Platonic idealist, served as a bridge from rationalism to romanticism. The first to apply the term *Enlightenment* had been the Germans. They referred to the period as the *Aufklaerung* (Enlightenment) and it probably was used first by Kant (Gay, 1973, p. 13). Kant and his follower, Hegel, helped usher in the sentiment-endowed period of romanticism that followed in the 19th century; they are discussed later in this chapter.

Two other German thinkers of the 18th century should be mentioned: Gottbold Lessing (1729–1781) and Wilhelm von Humboldt (1767–1835). Lessing was probably the foremost thinker in Germany to be influenced by the French *philosophe* movement. Censorship being very tight in Germany, the freedom movement never gained much headway. Lessing argued against religious intolerance, and his most important book is *Nathan the Wise*, written in 1779. In it he urged religious tolerance of the Jews, and also maintained that human excellence was in no way related to religion. Lessing was known for his lively writing style. Friedrich Nietzsche, probably the premier German stylist, characterized his fellow writers as long-winded, ponderous, with solemnly clumsy styles. The exception, said Nietzsche, was Lessing. This was because of "his histrionic nature which understood much and understood how to do many things" (Nietzsche, 1966, pp. 40–41). According to Nietzsche, Lessing was influenced by Diderot and Voltaire, two French Enlightenment stylists, but could not compare to Machiavelli, who, writing about two centuries earlier, presented the most serious matters in "a boisterous *allegrissimo* (brisk and lively manner)."

Humboldt's most famous book was *On the Limits of State Action*, written when he 24 years old, 5 years before Mill's *On Liberty*. Humboldt was an educator and most of his writings focused on the problems of German education. He founded the University of Berlin and changed the Prussian Gymnasium to adhere to his own philosophy. A champion of personal rights and morality, his goal was a free, self-conscious, self-determining individual (Humboldt, 1993, p. xxix). He believed with Mill and Tocqueville that the only justification for governmental interference is to prevent harm to others. Although Humboldt's life lapped over into the early 19th century, he largely characterized the Enlightenment in his dedication to individualism, freedom, and reason.

The most influential Enlightenment philosopher in Italy was Cesare Beccaria (1738–1794), who was particularly interested in the European outlook on justice and the penal system. He argued that the judicial system should not be designed for punishment, but for the protection of society. He even thought that training jailed criminals would teach them social values that would keep them from repeating their lawless ways. Beccaria would have outlawed capital punishment at a time when public executions were common, but he did call for vigorous enforcement of criminal laws, and he thought that the threat of punishment would cause people to obey the law. He really had little to say about freedom or individualism, but his book *On Crimes and Punishments* (1764), surely the most influential criminal law book ever written, made a lasting impact throughout Europe (G. W. Carey, 1984, p. 31).

ADVENT OF LIBERALISM

In the 17th century as the sun of freedom rose higher, English scientists (e.g., Newton), writers (e.g., Milton, Bunyan, and Swift), and philosophers (e.g., Hobbes and Locke) stressed rationalism in human affairs. An age of confidence, empiricism, and reason had begun. It should be said, however, that this generally optimistic century did include such an influential writer as Thomas Hobbes, who definitely was not an optimist and who believed that people were inherently evil and must be strictly ruled. The medieval shackles of mysticism, emotionalism, sentiment, and faith that were loosened during the Renaissance were broken, and for the first time a serious respect for reason became the mark of the European culture. No longer was a person's intellect suspect, but something to be respected—a virtue. The spirit of this hopeful, rational, and optimistic period, that reached its zenith in the 18th century, was not to last long (only into the mid-19th century) but it was to make a profound impact.

The Enlightenment brought about many changes, most of all in political philosophy. Perhaps the most notable result of the new philosophy was the establishing of a truly revolutionary political system and country—the United States. It was from the ideas of the Enlightenment thinkers in England (largely Locke, Hobbes, and Hume) and in France (mainly Montesquieu, Rousseau, Voltaire, and later Constant) that the Founding Fathers got the political insights with which they created the new nation. It was a philosophy—with some exceptions, of course—that reified individualism and freedom. Peter Gay (1973, p. 16) described the Enlightenment as "a congenial and informal movement of literary men—of philosophers, critics, playwrights, essayists, storytellers, editors, all of them articulate and prolific men of words."

The American concept of press freedom stemmed from the Enlightenment and bore these main characteristics: the press is free from government control, the press operates in a laissez-faire system, the press is privately owned, the press is a quasipublic service, and the press will seek to find the truth. Additional characteristics were grafted onto these basic ones in the 19th and 20th centuries, such as the press is a check on government, the press presents a pluralism of information and ideas (Levy, 1985), and the press must use its freedom responsibly. The Enlightenment spawned the philosophy of *liberalism*, a concept that began to lose its power in the late 19th century. Listen to James Carey (1977) of Columbia University talking about liberalism and making the point of its outmoded status:

> Liberalism, in its 18th century form, has suffered from sustained and withering attacks, particularly from the Left, and from the corrosive effects of industrialization, urbanization and mass democracy: movements that have destroyed the form of society from which liberalism emerged and to which it was adapted and most pertinent. The effect of this dual attack has been to render liberalism weak and defensive: admired in theory almost to the precise degree it is abandoned in practice. (p. 627)

Carey called 18th-century liberalism "a species of individualism . . . grounded in the proposition that the individual existed before society and . . . was of greater value" (p. 622). Carey, a sympathizer with today's communitarians and public journalists, like many other intellectuals today believes that classical liberalism has outlived its usefulness, and the individualism and freedom that it enthroned should be replaced by a new spirit of community and social responsibility.

We should probably mention Aristotle at this point. His philosophy was basically that of the Enlightenment: the importance of the individual, the dominance of man's secular reason, the affirmation of certainty and objectivity, the reality of absolutes, the value of self-fulfillment and personal happiness, the high value given to intellectual development, and the firm belief in human progress. Aristotelianism greatly impacted the Enlightenment and for a while banished the mysticism and the idealistic philosophy of the Platonic tradition (to be revived by Kant at the end of the 18th century and the Romantics that followed him).

Even earlier than Aristotle, in 6th-century China, a voice for freedom spoke out. It was Lao-tzu, perhaps the first known libertarian. "Without law or compulsion," he said, "men would dwell in harmony." He is best known as the author of the *Tao Te Ching*, presenting the classic Tao (spiritual serenity or Way), the verbal underpinning of Taoism. Here is yin and yang, the unity of opposites, showing that harmony can come about through competition. It offers advice to rulers not to interfere with the lives of the people. By and large, however, Lao-tzu's philosophy was an aberration, and China ever since has followed the communitarian tenets of Confucius. It was in the West, in Europe, that freedom or libertarianism came onto the world stage.

However, it was a long time coming. Languishing for centuries in Europe, it suddenly appeared in the 17th century when the English poet John Milton wrote *Areopagitica* (1644), a powerful tract against official licensing of the press and for freedom of religion. Under the banner of the Anglican Church, the Star Chamber and other authoritarian forces became increasingly repressive, leading to the Puritan Revolution, led by Oliver Cromwell. In 1642 a civil war ensued that swept the Stuart king, Charles I, from power. However, Cromwell's harsh leadership lasted only until 1660 when Charles' son, Charles II, was put on the throne. Milton, according to Altschull (1990, p. 40), played a part in all this, lashing out at all signs of authoritarianism. How ridiculous, Milton wrote in 1644, for the church to license publications to keep people away from evil. How can they know good from evil, how can they apprehend vice without hearing about it? And he said, and this is important to journalistic libertarianism: People must read all sides of questions and issues and not be exposed to a single side. Only then can they understand goodness and decency, or as he put it, human virtue.

The Miltonic concept most appreciated by modern journalists is his *self-righting principle*—the idea that truth will win out over falsehood in the marketplace of ideas. Libertarians everywhere delight in Milton's ringing words describing the value of free expression:

> And though all the winds of doctrine were let loose to play upon the earth, so Truth be in the field, we do injuriously, by licensing and prohibiting, to misdoubt her strength. Let her and Falsehood grapple; whoever knew Truth put to the worse, in a free and open encounter? (Milton, *Areopagitica*, in Altschull, 1990, pp. 40–41)

When it came to religion, however, Milton was not so liberal. While he worked for the Council of State in the Cromwell Protectorate, he muzzled Catholic writings, condemned Catholics generally, and even supported (there is a need to eliminate tyrants) the beheading of Charles I. In spite of Milton's inconsistency, he raised the torch of liberty and believed that it was a means to finding the truth. One should note that, for Milton and for those thinkers who followed him in the 18th century, freedom was not absolute. They generally held that reason would dictate moderation in its use. This was not just a period of freedom but of reason as well. Therefore freedom—and that included freedom of expression—should be used rationally.

Another 17th-century thinker, not nearly as optimistic as Milton about the nature of man, was Thomas Hobbes (1588–1679). He saw men as badly in need of authority due to their intrinsic savage natures and unpredictable actions. People, he thought, are naturally wicked, not good, and need protection from one another. Although Hobbes was an early spokesman of the Enlightenment and had a theoretical love of freedom, he was in many ways akin to the 20th-century communitarians in his belief that people should live orderly lives in community. For Hobbes, there must be a firm government (or "commonwealth") that would rein in the natural excesses of human action. The most important social force, for Hobbes, was order, and "order means regularity, predictability, and system as opposed to randomness, chance, and chaos," according to Wrong (1994, p. 37). For Hobbes, the provider of such order should be an all-powerful leader or monarch. He explained his governmental ideas in his influential *Leviathan*, published in 1651.

Going against popular belief, historian Walter Berns called Hobbes "the first libertarian" and "the founder of the modern liberal state" (G. W. Carey, 1984, p. 28). Berns pointed out that modern Americans are indebted to Hobbes for their appreciation of privacy. "Before him, and for a time after him," Berns wrote that "it was understood that every human activity was subject to public scrutiny and public control, if not by the state, then by the church, and usually by the state as church" (G. W. Carey, p. 28). Hobbes was the first political philosopher to argue that all was private and that the public realm was artificial, being, as it is, made by man.

So for Hobbes, man is a private, not a public, animal, thinking first of himself and only of others as means to a selfish end. This is why he said that life in the state of nature is a "war of everyman against everyman," a war that "ceaseth only in death" (G. W. Carey, 1984, p. 29). This warfare will cease, said Hobbes, only by the individual turning over his natural rights to the ruler created by a social contract. This Leviathan or ruler, however, would confine himself to keeping the peace and would otherwise leave the people alone to pursue their private lives and activities. This kind of state is called a "liberal" state because its objective is to grant the people the greatest range of liberty consistent with peace. Hobbes believed the principal duty of the sovereign was to see that neighbor does not bother neighbor and to guard against foreign enemies—and nothing else. This concept of limited government is, indeed, a libertarian tenet.

So the verdict on Hobbes is really unclear. Was he an authoritarian or a libertarian? Certainly he exhibited signs of being both. He would have people living in a strictly ordered society, but at the same time he would permit a great degree of personal freedom. Those living in such a society, because they fear anarchy and war, are willing to accept this harsh authority. The commonwealth was created by the citizens for their own self-preservation and so that, protected from the anarchic tendencies of their fellows, they could enjoy considerable freedom. For Hobbes, security comes before freedom. As Berlin (1969, p. 19) wrote, Hobbes turns out to have been right and not his contemporary Locke: People really desire above all else not happiness nor liberty nor justice, but security.

It is somewhat ironic that modern communitarians often criticize Hobbes as an Enlightenment thinker when, in one important way, he agreed with one of their basic desires: social order. He believed so much in order that he advocated force if necessary to get it. This, of course, would not resonate well with communitarians who would seek peaceful, discursive ways to achieve an orderly community, but Hobbes' antipathy to disorder was so strong that his philosophy reflected an Islamic proverb—that "sixty years of tyranny are better than one hour of civil strife" (Edgerton, 1985, p. 246).

John Locke (1632–1704), generally considered the leading philosopher of the Enlightenment, set the tone for those who followed him. He believed in natural rights, and on the basis of such God-given rights, he supported freedom of all kinds, especially freedom of expression. Although property rights were Locke's main concern, he was also interested in what he termed the pursuit of happiness, and he felt that government should stay out of personal affairs as much as possible.

Locke, like Milton, worked to end the licensing system in England. In his arguments, he connected a free press to property rights, and this has been an important part of the libertarian press philosophy ever since. His general ideas concerning freedom of speech and religion, natural rights, and the right of rebellion had a great impact on revolutionary thought in both France and America. Locke was also in favor of natural law—the law of reason. He was skeptical of man-made laws generally. These laws, written by governments and legislators (positive laws), are too often irrational. For Locke, the fewer man-made laws the better. Locke also stressed the sanctity of the individual, the need for free expression, the rule of law, checks and balances in government, the rule of reason, and a belief that the mind is capable of knowing the truth.

The stage had been set for the European Enlightenment of the 18th century in which rationalism and freedom became central philosophical concerns. Although it flourished predominantly in Britain and France, it influenced thought in many other places, having its greatest political impact in America and France. Ideas planted by Enlightenment stalwarts such as Locke, Hume, Voltaire, and Montesquieu without a doubt provided the rationale and spark that led to the new American republic. America's Founding Fathers reflected the Enlightenment philosophers' conviction that they lived in the best of all worlds and times. They were optimists; nature seemed good and people rational. Reason was enthroned, as were individualism and freedom. Exactly when the Enlightenment began is arguable, but one writer has given the date as roughly 1720, when the French author Voltaire arrived in England after his flight from French tyranny (Boaz, 1997, p. 37).

BRITISH ENLIGHTENMENT

David Hume (1711–1776) and fellow Scot Adam Smith (1723–1790) were the two most important thinkers of the Scottish Enlightenment. Best known for his philosophical skepticism, Hume also contributed to the development of an understanding of the productiveness and benefits of the free market. Hume was an influential proponent of libertarianism—the constriction of state control and the maximization of individual freedom. He was not only a skeptic, questioning everything and believing in no absolutes, but he was a supreme relativist in ethics, believing that moral action depends on individual cases rather than general principles. As an empiricist like Locke, Hume believed that all we know is based on perceptions, and he spent little time considering abstract ideas. Perhaps his most significant contributions to traditional American journalism are his skeptical disposition, his dedication to freedom, and his belief in relativism.

Other than John Locke and Thomas Hobbes, Adam Smith had the leading role in forming liberalism, or what is now called libertarianism. The idea that people act out of self-interest is usually attributed to Smith. What he did seem to say in his *Theory of Moral Sentiments* is that people sometimes do act from benevolent motives, but that society *could* exist (at least if the family were intact) without altruistic motivations. Justice and not benevolence, he thought, should be the society's main concern.

An important concept that Smith pushed was that of *spontaneous order.* He believed that if people were free to interact with one another—and without any interference from a central authority—a spontaneous order would result. One of the forms of such order, for Smith, was the market economy. This idea of a *free market* became very important in America and was projected to the world of information and ideas, dove-tailing nicely with Milton's earlier principle of differing ideas competing in the marketplace.

Smith describes his concept of *natural liberty* or individual freedom (especially in economics) in his famous *Wealth of Nations* (1776), which had immediate influence on both sides of the Atlantic. It was Smith's belief that human progress meant the steady improvement of life through the increasing wealth of a nation as a whole. His famous book systematically attempts to explain the process of acquiring collective national wealth. Behind his economic philosophy lay an "invisible hand" that guided people in a free society to take the right action. This was his concept of *laissez faire* (allow the people to do as they please): permit people to pursue their own selfish aims, then the total wealth of the nation would increase. The concept of *self-interest* was paramount to Smith's philosophy. In one of the most famous passages in the book, he wrote:

> It is not from the benevolence of the butcher, the brewer, of the baker that we expect our dinner, but from their regard to their own interest. We address ourselves, not to their humanity but to their self-love, and never talk to them of our own necessities but of their advantages. (Nisbet, 1980, p. 188)

So we see the priority that Smith gave to the individual, reflecting one of the chief tenets of the Enlightenment. In many ways he was like Hobbes in his insistence that the government involve itself as little as possible in the public sphere. He saw the only legitimate functions of a government as these: to defend the country from attack, to administer justice, and to oversee a few public works. But individual freedom was his main interest. He even warned against many voluntary organizations and institutions—especially corporations—that would, because of their very nature, restrict personal freedom.

One of the most radical liberals that spoke out for freedom prior to the American Revolution was Thomas Paine (1737–1809). He has been called "an outside agitator, a traveling missionary of liberty" (Boaz, 1997, p. 42). Born in England, he went to America to spur on the revolution. That accomplished, he left for France to help foment another one. His most influential writing was *Common Sense,* which almost everyone in America read. In it he denounced monarchies, justified natural rights and independence, and maintained that civil society was prior to government, and that people can interact in peace to create spontaneous order.

Paine was closer to the French revolutionaries than to the British libertarians, as his celebrated verbal feud with Edmund Burke (1729–1797) made clear. Although he, like Burke, appealed to reason, it was passion that animated Paine's rhetoric. He believed in the General Will and the rights of man that his idol Rousseau was advocating in France. His love of freedom was deep and was pronounced in forceful, often biting, commentary.

At the same time his Irish contemporary, Edmund Burke, was condemning the French revolutionary followers of Rousseau as dangerous and naive, Paine was busy fanning the flames of revolution. Paine sought to smash old institutions, to overthrow them and start anew. Burke, against revolution, saw only the need to reform institutions and governments, not to overthrow them. Whereas Paine was a thoroughgoing democrat and egalitarian, Burke, as a follower of Locke, put his trust in an elite of well-educated, well-informed people; through them a society could have stability. Whereas Paine had little respect for tradition and great confidence in "the people," Burke saw a need to conserve the best of the past, to honor tradition, and to be suspicious of giving too much power to the people. It was to the credit of Jefferson and other Founding Fathers in America that they valued the ideas of both Paine and Burke (and thus the ideas of Rousseau and Locke) and synthesized them in the founding principles of their new nation.

Burke, like Locke, believed that freedom comes from Natural Law, that it is our birthright and is given up only through a departure from reason or through violence. Freedom must comport with order, he said, and order depends on wisdom. Burke also believed that freedom without wisdom and virtue was the greatest of all evils, calling it "folly, vice, and madness" (Attarian, 1997, p. 40) if it is without restraint and orderly use.

THE *PHILOSOPHES* OF FRANCE

The Age of Enlightenment was equally potent across the channel in France. The French philosophers of the period, calling themselves the *philosophes,* were familiar with the thinking going on in England. Some of them (e.g., Montesquieu and Voltaire) had lived and studied in England. And of course, early Americans such as Thomas Jefferson and Benjamin Franklin had been diplomats in France for extended periods during the 18th century. Franklin especially was acquainted with the *philosophes* and their Enlightenment ideas.

French thinkers of the Enlightenment, thriving in the middle of the 18th century, were a heterogeneous mix of people pursuing many intellectual interests. However, they were bound by a few common beliefs—in rational and intentional progress, in tolerating various sects and non-Christian religions, in systematizing intellectual disciplines, and in overcoming human cruelty and violence through social improvements and government structures. Unlike most of their British counterparts, the *philosophes* abstained from speculative philosophy and abstract thinking, and mainly sought the betterment of human beings and society. Their focus was on reform of people and society, making their emphasis primarily practical.

The French philosophers, far more than their prosaic and direct English counterparts, were rhetorically abstract, involved, even passionate. With the possible exception of Rousseau, they were certainly not democrats, any more than were Hobbes and Locke. They were, in spite of their changing social philosophy, still essentially aristocrats. Freedom of expression, for them, was mainly *their* freedom of expression and, as John Stuart Mill reiterated in the next century, did not extend to those segments of society not prepared for it.

The most influential of these French thinkers was Jean-Jacques Rousseau (1712–1778). Much like Hobbes in England, Rousseau is difficult to classify. Is he a free-spirited individualist or is he an authoritarian that encourages individuals to permit themselves to be subsumed into the State? Perhaps he is idealistically the former, and practically the latter. Much of his philosophy stems from his basic belief that people were born good but were corrupted by society. He has been called the first Romantic, meaning that he thought that feeling, not reason, should be our guide and judge in life. Rousseau believed that our natural instincts are good, but so-called civilized society teaches us to frustrate these instincts and repress our true feelings. This, he says, results in alienation of the true self. So it is that Rousseau saw civilization as "the corrupter and destroyer of true values—not, as people seem always to assume, their creator and propagator" (Magee, 1988, p. 127).

In *The Social Contract* (1762), Rousseau declared that "Man is born free, and everywhere he is in chains." He believed that people entered into a social contract, agreeing to surrender all their rights to the community and submit to the General Will—a kind of majority declaration. Government, a necessary evil, was set up by the people to carry out the General Will. If government fails to do this, the people have the right to overthrow it. One can see the influence of Rousseau on Thomas Jefferson and the Founding Fathers in America. What he was arguing for was popular sovereignty—the people as ruler—and his idea helped in the development of democratic ideology.

Rousseau's idea is readily adapted to dictatorships of all kinds to justify their totalitarian rule. Stalin, for example, in 20th-century Soviet Union, claimed that the Communist Party determined and spoke for the General Will that all citizens must obey. Adolf Hitler and many other dictators were also influenced by Rousseau. At any rate, Rousseau's ideas have had tremendous influence. His idea of democracy is the forcible imposition of the General Will. This is quite different from—in fact, almost the exact opposite of—that of Locke, whose objective was to protect and preserve individual freedom.

The individual, according to Rousseau, has no right to deviate from the General Will. This means that Rousseau's type of democracy is not compatible with personal freedom. For the first time in Western thought, a concept of *democracy* denied individual rights and allotted a key role to charismatic leaders (Magee, 1988, p. 129). The modern British historian Paul Johnson (1988, p. 25) believed that Rousseau's political philosophy is not only authoritarian, but totalitarian "since it orders every aspect of human activity, thought included." Under Rousseau's social contract, wrote Johnson, the individual must "alienate himself, with all his rights, to the whole of the community" (p. 129). Rousseau's insistence that the individual desires to escape the constraints of reason and give expression to feeling and instinct presaged the death of rationalism and individual freedom, and it harmonized with the many writers and artists of the 19th-century Romantic period that followed, whose works overflowed with sentiment and emotion. One might wonder why we have Rousseau in this chapter with the freedom lovers instead of with the communitarians later on. Perhaps it is because he is a democrat, although his democracy is a kind of collectivistic democracy with the emphasis on the General Will and not on the individual citizen. History will have to assign him his proper place.

Montesquieu (1689–1755) was born Charles-Louis de Secondat as heir to the title of Baron de Montesquieu. He was a great admirer of the British political system and did what he could to bring about a constitutional monarchy in France. In 1748 he wrote a book proposing that governmental powers be separated among three branches—executive, legislative, and judicial. This would end the old French system of having power concentrated in one person, the king. This proposal was made part of the United States Constitution as well as the French Constitution of 1791. Under such a system, Montesquieu believed that the maximum degree of political and economic freedom would be available to the general public. He called this system of distribution of power *checks and balances,* and it was probably the single most important idea adopted by the founders of the American republic.

With the possible exception of Rousseau, Francois-Marie Arouet de Voltaire (1694–1778) is usually considered the most fiery writer of the French Enlightenment. Certainly he was the most prolific (more than 50 volumes) and perhaps the most witty and eloquent stylist. He was the most journalistic of the French thinkers; certainly none of his countrymen cared more about human liberty and the right to freedom of expression. Although he was an aristocrat and for most of his life cared little for democracy (people were a stupid and barbarous rabble), when he found the government oppressive in the years before the Revolution, he began to feel some affinity with the masses. However, he was no Rousseau; in fact, he criticized him for his revolutionary zeal. Voltaire's opinion of Rousseau was very similar to that of Edmund Burke in England. Even though Jefferson and other American revolutionaries did not agree with Voltaire's disdain for the public, they delighted in his rationalism and his advocacy of a free press.

Altschull (1990, p. 80) gave us a good view of Voltaire's ideas on journalism, noting that they have a remarkably modern ring to them. Voltaire urged journalists to be skeptical about the information they receive, not to trust anything they hear unless it can be confirmed by independent examination, and to adopt disciplined and scientific methods of reporting. Of course, he urged journalists to treasure their independence and express themselves freely.

Probably Voltaire is best known (at least among journalists) for his defense of his friend and fellow philosopher, Claude-Adrien Helvetius, a utilitarian, who angered many Frenchmen for writing that morality is determined by customs, common conventions, and a desire to seek pleasure, not by God. Helvetius had brought such ideas back from England where he had been greatly influenced by British utilitarians, especially Hume, and in 1758 had incorporated them in his highly controversial *Essays of the Mind.* Although Voltaire did not agree with Helvetius, he fired off his famous words to Helvetius: "I disapprove of what you say but I will defend to the death your right to say it" (Torrey, 1960, p. 185).

18TH-CENTURY AMERICAN VOICES

Benjamin Franklin called the 18th century in America the *age of experiments,* meaning that it had less to do with ideas than with the practical use the Americans made of them. According to Meyer (1976, p. vii.), the American counterpart of the French *philosophe* of the Enlightenment was the self-taught tradesman seeking education along with fame and fortune—the preacher or the lawyer, or the statesman trying to establish a new nation. The Americans not only spoke out for liberty as did their European brothers, but their new land became, in James Madison's words, the "workshop for liberty" (p. vi).

The Founding Fathers—Jefferson and his colleagues—thought the essential freedoms were those that had been the most commonly denied. Of these, there were three main ones: "freedom of opinion in order that the truth might prevail; freedom of occupation and economic enterprise in order that careers might be open to talent, and freedom from arbitrary government in order that no man might be compelled against his will" (Becker, 1945, p. 15).

Although a love of freedom was a common denominator, the American Enlightenment differed in many ways from that in Europe. For example, in America far more emphasis was put on the emotions (sentiments, affections, and passions) than in Europe during the same period. In fact, an Enlightenment American, John Adams, called his time the "age of frivolity" and said he would not object if it were called the "Age of Folly, Vice, Frenzy, Fury, or Brutality" (Meyer, 1976, p. xii). In spite of such remarks, the 18th century in

America was a period of imagination and generally good taste. It was certainly an age of political rhetoric and a critical spirit. The idea of natural rights, largely inherited from John Locke, permeated the thinking of the American liberals of the Enlightenment. There was also a concern with human decency and an awareness of the evil of suffering.

Donald Meyer (1976) summed up Enlightenment America with these words:

> The eighteenth-century world in which the United States of America was born was morally and intellectually a fiercely exciting one. It marked Western culture's coming of age—a dawning of philosophical maturity, a struggle for moral autonomy, an awakening of political consciousness. (p. xix)

A number of Enlightenment thinkers in America stand out. It should be remembered, however, that the country was small in the 18th century, and the population was mainly found along the eastern seaboard in a few big cities. The center of intellectual culture lay some 3,000 miles across the Atlantic. In a way, it is amazing that so many thinkers were to be found in the new country. Chief among them were Jonathan Edwards, Jonathan Mayhew, and Benjamin Franklin, focusing mainly on religious and moral issues. In political philosophy there were stalwarts like Washington, Jefferson, Madison, Adams, and Hamilton, plus lesser figures like Richard Henry Lee, Patrick Henry, and Samuel Adams.

Perhaps we should look briefly at several of these American thinkers. All were serious Enlightenment persons with intellectual roots in France and England, but they were quite different in their views of freedom and its place in society. However, each in his own way believed in the basic Enlightenment concepts of freedom, rationalism, and individualism.

James Madison (1751–1836) might well be called the father of the Bill of Rights as well as the father of the Constitution; he was convinced that a bill of rights would limit governmental powers, preventing legislative and executive abuse of power, and would thwart the majority from taking advantage of the minority. There was very little enthusiasm for the Bill of Rights, and according to Levy (1985, p. 266), "but for Madison's persistence the amendments would have died in Congress." The question that arose at the time (and was not answered) and that has come down to us today is: What did the congress mean by "freedom of the press"? Levy, an authority on the First Amendment, said (p. 268) that nobody knows what the Framers had in mind about press freedom; it is probably true that they themselves did not know what they had in mind. At any rate, the First Amendment states clearly that there shall be *no* law abridging press freedom. Madison, it seems, was a strict constructionist and meant precisely *no* law.

In the 20th century, philosopher Alexander Meiklejohn, another noted free press advocate and prolific writer on the Constitution, rendered a Madisonian interpretation that the Framers meant exactly what they said—that the First Amendment imposed "an absolute, unqualified prohibition" on the Congress (Meiklejohn, 1948, p. 17). Meiklejohn stressed the message and not the speaker; for instance, he did not believe that it was necessary that "everyone shall speak, but that everything worth saying shall be said" (p. 25). Just why he thought this is not clear. Obviously in his day, as in ours, there must certainly be some things that are worth saying that are not said. Therefore, it is obvious that it is not necessary that they be said. Maybe he meant "desirable," and not "necessary."

Madison, although he was in favor of free expression, did not have a strong belief in the people's desire to seek the truth, agreeing with Benjamin Franklin that the people mainly desired to reinforce their own beliefs and to seek the company of those who shared those beliefs. What was, to Madison, important in society were factions, groups of like-minded people who desired social control so as to maintain their own value systems, even at the expense of other freedoms. Madison was thereby led to a different view of press freedom and of the press's main social role. He thought the press should provide accurate and comprehensive information, but he thought factions would try to influence the press for their own advantage. So the press was in a kind of adversarial relationship, not only with government, but with the multitude of social factions.

It is generally believed by historians that only Madison, of the leaders of the Republican Party (Madison, Albert Gallatin, and James Monroe) can stand in historical significance along with Jefferson. As Jefferson's Secretary of State, Madison played a critical role in the President's diplomacy, often supplying a clear direction when Jefferson himself was helpless with indecision (Tucker & Hendrickson, 1990, p. 5). His thinking generally ran parallel to that of Jefferson, although in his thoughts on press freedom he was much closer to his fellow Virginian, George Hay.

Now we come to Thomas Jefferson (1743–1826), who is usually held up as the great paragon of press freedom in early America. However, it was Madison, not Jefferson, who was the great libertarian. Jefferson was a firm believer that human beings were rational and perfectible, and he undoubtedly was the prime example of an intellectual formed by the Enlightenment ideas of 18th-century Europe. This perfectibility, he believed, was contingent on the people's being exposed to a wide variety of information and ideas. In this belief one can see the influence of Milton, Locke, and Mill, and, like them, Jefferson would put strings on freedom. For example, he thought the press was obligated to provide dependable, accurate, and comprehensive news and opinions—sounding much like the Hutchins Commission some two centuries later. He believed that if the press failed in its responsibility, the people should force the press (he never said how) into a more responsible mode.

Jefferson was more like the communitarians and public journalists of the 21st century: He had a "responsibility" view of press freedom. Certainly it was a limited view of press freedom, far more limited than Madison's. The essence of Jeffersonian freedom was doing as you ought, not as you please. Jefferson's ideas about freedom have been shared by many Americans and were especially important to Abraham Lincoln, whose love of liberty was surpassed by his love of virtue. Today's public journalists claim to be in this tradition.

Ever ambiguous about his true opinion of newspapers, Jefferson poured scorn on them at times and at other times he seemed to feel they were indispensable to the new republic. At one point, he noted that the basis of the government was public opinion, for which he saw the press essential. "If it were left to me to decide whether we should have a government without newspapers or newspapers without a government, I should not hesitate a moment to prefer the latter" (cited in Commission on Freedom of the Press, 1947, p. 13). But, it is important to note, Jefferson added, "But I should mean that every man should receive those papers and be capable of reading them."

Jefferson would be distressed to see what has happened in America: an expensive and standing military; skyrocketing debt and high taxes; the gigantic complex of banks, financial markets, and corporations; the subordination of state governments to national power; and the exalted status of the federal judiciary. For Jefferson, it would indicate the victory of Alexander Hamilton's vision of American life, and that would cause him great sorrow. Hamilton (1757–1804) was a kind of economic "nationalist," a position alien to Jefferson's mindset. It was Hamilton who pushed for external and internal taxes, the creation of a national bank, and the development of a manufacturing infrastructure (Tucker & Hendrickson, 1990, pp. 33–40).

Specifically, Hamilton supported trade with Britain, which Jefferson and the Republicans opposed, and he dedicated himself to making America a progressive economic power in the world. Jefferson could see in Hamilton's policies the incipient danger of fostering the power of the national government and the enlargement of the executive branch; Jefferson believed such policies might lead to war, and this he was firmly against. Hamilton, who perhaps could not be called a hawk, was a realist, believing that war was an inescapable fact of political reality. Therefore, he believed America should have strong military forces. Jefferson's attitude toward England and France was the opposite of Hamilton's. Whereas Jefferson feared and hated England, Hamilton was sympathetic and friendly. Jefferson supported and sympathized with the French Revolution; Hamilton considered it with horror and had no sympathy for the violent successive governments that came to power in postrevolutionary France (Tucker & Hendrickson, 1990, pp. 42–44).

Assuming the virtue of the people, Jefferson believed that an innate moral sense resided in every person and this precluded the exercise of great power over the people by the government. He believed that this moral sense naturally led people to seek the common good and to live justly in society. Government, for Jefferson, did not have the great importance that it did for John Adams. Jefferson saw government being absorbed into society, whereas Adams saw society absorbed into government. This difference in perspective clearly marked the difference between these two Enlightenment figures (Peterson, 1976, pp. 20–21). John Adams (1735–1826) was significantly influenced by the Scottish and English political thinkers of the radical Whig tradition, who represented for him sound judgment and sanity. Not all 18th-century philosophers of the Continent impressed him; some were too skeptical and irreverent for his taste. Their thought could, and did (in the case of the French Revolution), lead to social chaos (Meyer, 1976, p. 137). The British thinkers, on the other hand, provided Adams with a commitment to republican government. Adams always desired a government that was carefully engineered so that human passions could be controlled. Always an advocate of law and order, he wanted a well-balanced and law-bound social system that would serve the public by producing what he called "social Happiness" (p. 137).

The state, according to Adams, must maintain the balance of power between the aristocratic and democratic elements of society—between "the few and the many." Not a democrat like Jefferson or Madison, Adams believed that man's ambition, lust for power, and passions must be controlled by government. This involves setting up instruments of "order and subordination" that would inculcate feelings of esteem, sympathy and admiration in the public. Adams saw rank, status, nobility as natural and necessary parts of an orderly society. It was Adams, according to Peterson (1976), who was the first political theorist to speak of "the tyranny of the majority" (p. 40). This theory created quite a stir among Americans who saw in the American Revolution the chance to emphasize the majority and dispose of aristocratic notions, and the Republican press, especially during the last decade of the 18th century, attacked Adams as a monarchist and an apologist for privilege.

Unlike most thinkers of the Enlightenment in America, Adams did not understand what was meant by the perfectibility of man. Nor did he believe that the masses—the public—really knew enough or cared enough to be entrusted with the reins of government. Life, for Adams, was "a continual moral struggle, a fight for rational self-control" (M. Peterson, 1976, p. 40). Given this view, it is understandable that Adams would care little for those who glorified and flattered human nature and championed the perfectibility. A realist and a pessimist, Adams would not dignify his age as the Age of Reason; in his view it was not represented best by Voltaire or Diderot, but by Tom Paine, the rascally, alcoholic journalist whose superficial writings had a profound impact on the society. Pessimist that he was, Adams in 1816 could write to Jefferson that the age had not been so bad, and that it had marked the awakening of the political intelligence of Western civilization (M. Peterson, 1976, pp. 146–147).

THE AGE OF SENTIMENT: 19TH CENTURY

As the ideas of Adams, Jefferson, and Madison in America and the Enlightenment philosophers of Europe trailed off in the 19th century, a period emerged that is most commonly known as the Romantic Era, its main characteristic being a slow rebellion against reason and a tendency toward instinct, emotions, and feeling. In short, it was an Age of Sentiment. This change did not come all at once, and many thinkers of the early 19th century were still concerned with reason and freedom. Whereas Germany had participated only marginally in the Enlightenment in the 18th century, it was well represented by the philosophers of the Age of Sentiment.

Two figures who created the new movement, welding the growing mystic stirrings of the late 18th century into a new intellectual voice, were Immanuel Kant (1724–1804) and Georg Wilhelm Friedrich Hegel (1770–1831), neither of whom was a full-fledged Romantic. At the heart of Romanticism was the idea that existence and reality are unknowable to the mind. This led naturally to the idea that in journalism there could be no objectivity. It was Hegel, an early disciple of Kant, who popularized this central idea in all phases of his philosophy and spread it across Europe and into America.

First let us look briefly at Kant, and then at Hegel. Kant was born and lived all his life in the East Prussian town of Koenigsberg. He was one of the first academic or professional philosophers and is generally regarded as probably the greatest philosopher since the ancient Greeks. Kant believed that we could know only a small portion of reality—what he called the phenomenal world that we can detect by our senses. Beyond that was what Kant called the noumenal or transcendental world to which we have no access (Magee, 1988, pp. 134–135). So for Kant, as for many modern journalists, objectivity is out there (and in here), but a verbal depiction of it (e.g., a newspaper story) cannot be anything but partial and representative, never objective.

Kant believed in free will. If this were not so, then there would be no reason to complain when someone treats us badly, because it would have been impossible that it be otherwise. Therefore, Kant would say that a journalist can do the kind of journalism he or she likes, or exercise free will and refuse, and even leave the job if necessary. In Germany during the period, Kant was one of the very few (Humboldt was another) to stress individual freedom in the sense that it was valued in France, England, and America. In ethics, Kant indicates his rationalism. For instance, he says that only a rational creature can be thought of as ethical or unethical because what is needed is the capacity to make a choice between or among alternative positions. Such considerations led Kant to form his famous Categorical Imperative (Magee, 1988, pp. 136–137) as the fundamental rule of morality: "Act only according to maxims which you can will also to be universal laws." Kant was not an ethicist who, like John Stuart Mill, believed that a consideration of consequences should guide ethical action. On the contrary, he thought that when people acted on the basis of projected consequences, they could not be ethical. What was necessary was acting out of a sense of duty—duty to a principle (such as telling the truth) that could serve as a guide a priori. Such principles or maxims should be formed by testing them against the master guide: the Categorical Imperative.

Georg W. F. Hegel (1770–1831), a philosopher who taught at Heidelberg and Berlin and who had been a newspaper editor, developed ideas that substantially impacted the new American nation. This influence manifested itself mainly in the 19th century when swarms of Americans went to Germany to study at Heidelberg, Berlin, and other universities. He did much to spread the philosophy of Kant. The influence on Hegel of Thomas Paine and Edmund Burke was profound.

His philosophy reveals several other important influences—the early Greeks, Kant, Spinoza, the New Testament, Fichte, and Schelling (Collinson, 1987, pp. 98–99). Another influence was Rousseau, from whom Hegel borrowed the idea of the General Will, which he modified somewhat in that he conceived of it as the Idea, God, or the World Spirit. He claimed to detest abstract writing in others, while indulging in it himself. Rousseau's romantic, mystical style bothered him and he criticized the Frenchman for being too abstract. Unlike Rousseau, Hegel rejected democracy (Altschull, 1990, pp. 136–137) and had little concern for the revolutionary rights of man.

A good example of Hegel's abstractness and mysticism is his conception of what he called *Geist,* which is something akin to spirit or mind. *Geist,* for Hegel, was the essence of reality, the very substance of existence. The historical process was the development of *Geist* toward self-knowledge and self-awareness. When this process is completed, what is left is complete harmony —what Hegel called the *absolute.* Marx took over this idea (Magee, 1988, p. 159) but claimed that the historical process was not mental or metaphysical, but material.

Hegel's philosophy bears a close resemblance to that of the modern communitarian and public journalist. The ideal state will be reached, believed Hegel, when a community of individuals is functioning harmoniously, with every person serving the interest of the whole. He believed that such a society is much superior to the values of liberal individualism. Advocates of state authority, from both left and right, were quick to adopt this idea. Those Germans advocating a distinct form of nationalism and state worship were called

Right Hegelians, and those (following Marx) who wanted to revolutionize and democratize society were called Left Hegelians. It can be fairly said that Hegel espoused the most intellectually based antiliberal political thinking in the modern world. Departing from the Enlightenment thinkers that came before him, he insisted that individualism and freedom are unrealistic and shallow. What is needed, according to Hegel, is for the individual to be subsumed by the group, the community, or the nation. Only then can a person achieve self-realization, security, and happiness.

The door had thus been opened by Kant and Hegel to such German Romanticists as Herder, Fichte, Schlegel, Schelling, Schopenhauer, and Nietzsche. We should also add the name of Karl Marx (1818–1883), a rather typical Romanticist hiding behind a veil of reason and science. Although he called his system scientific, many deny that this was really the case. Johnson, for one, in his *Intellectuals* (1988, p. 69), said that Marx did not understand capitalism because he was unscientific, and he evidenced (especially in his *Das Kapital*) a disregard for truth "which at times amounts to contempt." He also rejected the idea of journalistic objectivity and was hostile to the atomistic individualism of the Enlightenment. Freedom he saw mainly as "people's freedom"—freedom to support the collective, freedom from capitalist exploitation, and freedom from gross inequality. Anticipating the 20th-century communitarians, Marx saw the need for a journalistic system that would support social progress and the collective safety and harmony. For him, the journalist's and the citizen's responsibilities were more important than their freedom.

The Romanticists thought that reason cannot penetrate to true reality, only see a very superficial surface world. A person's true source of knowledge is intuition or feeling. Sentiment: that was the answer. According to this view, a person is an emotional being, not a rational one. The Romanticists prided themselves on their more intuitive insights into the world, insights that lay below the level of appearances. Quite commonly these sentiment philosophers (along with their fellows in literature) condemned the Enlightenment and admired European medievalism and Oriental mysticism. They were the first real Counter-Enlightenment writers and have been followed by a series of such thinkers, right up to the current existentialists, postmodernists, communitarians, and public journalists. Like the communitarians of today, the Romanticists saw the individual as atomistic and narcissistic, unrealistic and harmful in complex society.

One of the most original and powerful writers of this Romantic Era was Friedrich Nietzsche (1844–1900), usually considered one of the founders of existentialism. Certainly he was among the most ardent individualists of this increasingly communal period. If he were living today, he would be one of greatest critics of the communitarians. Also a great advocate of freedom and the will to power, he scorned what he saw as the trend toward conformity and weakness in the society. He talked of two main types of morality (Durant, 1966, p. 420): the *Herren-Moral* (the morality of the masters, which he admired) and the *Herden-Moral* (the morality of the herd, which he despised). The former, he contended, was the standard in classical antiquity, especially for the Romans, and has led to strength, masculinity, and individualism. The latter, stemming from Asia and the Middle East, stressed humility, altruism, and peace. Nietzsche thought this herd morality (he also called it "slave morality") had led to weakness, femininity, democracy, utilitarianism, and socialism. It was not his cup of tea, or better, his glass of beer.

He lamented (Durant, 1966, p. 421) the fact that the morality of the herd was dominating society. It had, he thought, been largely popularized by Jesus—the ideas of equality, self-sacrifice, and pity. For Nietzsche, pity was for the incompetent, the defective, the vicious, and the criminal. Unfortunately, said Nietzsche, no longer are the strong permitted to exercise their strength; they must simply become as much as possible like the weak. Violence, war, danger, and severity, he believed, are as valuable to society as peace and kindliness, and great individuals come on the scene only in times of danger. Nietzsche believed (Durant, 1966, p. 423) that the best thing in a person is strength of will, passion, and a love of power. And if evil were not good, he said, it would have disappeared. Unlike the thinkers of the Enlightenment before him, Nietzsche had no hope for the improvement of mankind, for social regeneration. He saw society as only "an instrument for the enhancement of the power and personality of the individual; the group is not an end in itself" (p. 425).

Nietzsche rejected the conclusion of Arthur Schopenhauer (1788–1860) that we should turn away in disgust from the world, that we should reject it, and try to withdraw from it, that we should eliminate our will—for power, to get material things, to covet. Far more than Nietzsche, Schopenhauer represented the mystical spirit of the Renaissance. Schopenhauer maintained that compassion, not rationality as Kant had believed, was the foundation of ethics. He developed a deep understanding of Oriental philosophy and incorporated its ideas into his writing. A great influence on creative artists of his period and since, he especially had an impact on Wagner and Mahler, Tolstoy, De Maupassant, Zola, Hardy, Conrad, and Thomas Mann. Nietzsche thought we should be very much "in the world" (Magee, 1988, p. 172) and should live to the full, confronting the anxieties and difficulties of life head on and getting all we can from life. The main question for him was how best to do this in a godless and meaningless world.

Although most thinkers of the 19th century had begun to devalue personal freedom and individualism, there were some like Alexis de Tocqueville in France, Soren Kierkegaard in Denmark, and John Stuart Mill in England who still revered the Enlightenment values. However, even they, in many ways, were veering away from the rationalism and strict libertarianism of the preceding century and were exhibiting many of the characteristics of the Age of Sentiment to which they belonged.

Tocqueville (1805–1859) came to America from England in 1831, traveled from New York to the western limits of the country at that time, and from Quebec to New Orleans. Sent by the French government to study prisons, his observations went beyond that assignment, and when he returned to France he wrote his classic two-volume *Democracy in America* (1835 and 1840), the first critical appraisal of the new country's sociopolitical system. He wrote that as equality increases among a people, the individual becomes of less value, whereas the society gains in value. Being an aristocrat himself, Tocqueville was reminding the Americans of what might result from a democratic society. In fact, he questioned whether people really want to be free to shape their own values and destinies. Here he anticipated Erich Fromm's *Escape from Freedom,* written in the next century.

He was quite critical of the American press, saying that it consisted largely of coarse appeals to the passions, assaults on the character of individuals, of invasions of privacy, and the stressing of negative social aspects (Merrill, 1994, p. 180). Here Tocqueville was saying what the Hutchins Commission, in its criticism of the press, would report in the middle of the next century. As for press freedom, he saw it as mainly preventing evils, as being a kind of check on government.

In Denmark, Søren Kierkegaard (1813–1855) was indulging in a kind of passionate or emotional writing that typified the Romantic Age. He is usually considered a forerunner, along with Nietzsche, of 20th-century existentialism. As such, he continued the emphasis that had been placed on freedom and individualism from the 18th century over into the new century of sentiment. He stressed the importance of personal choice and the taking of personal responsibility for actions, but he departed from the liberals of the 18th century in his de-emphasis of rationalism and the scientific attitude. Like his Romanticist colleagues, he did not believe in objectivity, believing that subjectivity is inevitable in journalism and that inwardness and the expression of opinion and sentiment is actually a good thing (Merrill, 1994, p. 80).

Now we come to John Stuart Mill (1806–1873), undoubtedly the foremost 19th-century philosopher of freedom. A social reformer and defender of personal and political liberty, his tract *On Liberty* (1859) is probably the foremost declaration on freedom ever written. In it he declared that the "only freedom which deserves the name, is that of pursuing our own good in our own way, so long as we do not attempt to deprive others of theirs, or impede their efforts to obtain it" (Merrill, 1994, p. 84). He did not conceive of liberty for everyone, however, believing that people in all "backward states of society" should not have freedom. He also excluded "barbarians" and children from freedom's realm. Only those who could use it for the betterment and happiness of society should have it, Mill thought. Thus it had a utilitarian rationale for Mill, unlike that for John Locke, earlier, who viewed freedom as a natural right.

Like Milton before him, Mill wanted a free marketplace of ideas and opinions. He was, in a way, a bridge from the Enlightenment to the Romantic Era. Although he praised freedom, he reflected the Romanticist's concern with feeling, social concern, and altruism, and like the communitarians of today, he advocated "a feeling for humanity." One should act, according to Mill, so as to promote the general interests of society (Albert, Denise, & Peterfreund, 1969, pp. 244–250).

Today Mill is still one of the darlings of the press libertarians. He is seen as the great champion of the freedom principle: that personal freedom is the end-all of human existence. This is really unfair to Mill, who was more cautious in his discussion of freedom. However, Mill did believe that freedom was basically good—except, of course, for certain types of people. James Fitzjames Stephen, a legal scholar and a contemporary of Mill's, was probably the first to seriously criticize *On Liberty*. He did that in *Liberty, Equality, Fraternity*, published in 1873, in which he blasted Mill unmercifully. For example, he said that liberty was like fire—neither good nor bad, but dependent on how it is used, and it is folly to tolerate every variety of opinion (as Mill suggested we do) out of devotion to an abstract "liberty." Why? Because expression soon results in action, and the fanatics whom we tolerated will not tolerate us when they get into power. Russell Kirk noted that many 20th-century events have served to prove Stephen's case. He posed this question: Was the world improved by free discussion of the Nazis' belief that Jews ought to be treated as less than human? It is order, discipline, morality —not freedom—that Kirk says must be established today (G. W. Carey, 1984, p. 116). So although Mill symbolizes the dedication to freedom still declared by most American journalists, his rationale for it and his often exaggerated benefits of it are increasingly being questioned. Certainly they are by the communitarians and public journalists.

DIMMING OF ENLIGHTENMENT FREEDOM

In this chapter we surveyed the rudiments of Enlightenment liberalism— the principal philosophy that today's communitarians and public journalists are anxious to consign to historical obsolescence. Press freedom, in particular, seems to be a thorn in the communitarians' side, and they see it as their mission to remove it. In the next chapter, we try to show how press libertarianism is being eroded and a new kind of community-based freedom is taking its place. The communitarian spirit is suspicious of so much power (press freedom) consolidated in so few hands.

Although America's Founding Fathers incorporated many of the ideas of the 18th-century European Enlightenment philosophers into their new country, they had concerns about press freedom, even if it is not evident from the wording of the First Amendment. Such a press run by elites, say the American communitarians, is incompatible with democracy. It should be noted, however, that the Founding Fathers were also wary of democracy, so much so that the word *democracy* does not appear in the Constitution or the Declaration of Independence. James Madison, especially, thought that democracy could lead to tyranny, and his words on this subject are instructive:

> Democracies have ever been spectacles of turbulence and contention, have ever been found incompatible with personal security or the rights of property, and have in general been as short in their lives as they have been violent in their deaths. (Kendall & Carey, 1966, Federalist Papers, No. 10)

It was largely due to Madison's kind of caution, and drawing on the ideas of Montesquieu, that checks and balances were built into the American Constitution. The people, and not only the government, were not to become too strong. Even the First Amendment and its press freedom provisions faced much debate, many of the country's founders feeling that the amendment was too obscure and would lead to problems. Benjamin Ginsberg, professor of government at Cornell University, insisted that there should be limits on press freedom, and said that when someone suggests this, he or she is seen as bigoted and arrogant. He noted, however, that the "chief proponents of free communication can generally be found among the most powerful producers of ideas and among those groups that believe they can increase or expand the popularity of their views." For example, he says that "in international affairs it is the western nations and their news media that advocate the free flow of ideas" (Ginsberg, 1986, p. 104; Hamelink, 1983; Mattelart, 1979; Tunstall, 1977).

Reflecting the communitarian critics of the modern news media, Ginsberg stated that the so-called marketplace of ideas is dominated by the social elite. This elite forces its views on the lower classes, especially those more exposed to the mass media. He said it is ironic, that in the name of freedom of expression, the West has sought to remove "all impediments—legal, technological, social" to the communication of ideas. This gives the elite, contended Ginsberg (p. 148) "the complete freedom to spread their views around; the poorer sectors of society have no such possibility." So if Ginsberg is to be believed, the strongest support for freedom of the press today comes from upper income cosmopolitans who have sufficient resources and access to the media to effectively promote their ideas in the marketplace.

What this means is that freedom of the press really belongs to the upper income elite and therefore the total community cannot be well served. This is basically what modern public journalists and communitarians are saying.

Something must be done about it, they say. What this something will be, and what the consequences will be, is what this book is about. Freedom, for one thing, must be restricted for the press and spread to the public. Individualism must be tempered and community must be enshrined. Order and social harmony must be inculcated, with community solidarity stressed, and the whole realm of mass communication must be democratized so as to promote civic participation.

We have seen, in this initial chapter, the rise of the freedom problem with the coming of the European Enlightenment. As the book's title indicates, press freedom's sun has begun to set as the 21st century begins. In this chapter, we described the nature of the Enlightenment in order to show what the antiliberal critics of the present day are ready to reject. Freedom of expression and the enthroning of the individual have been seen by many of late as a dangerous experiment, opening the door to all kinds of excesses and socially harmful speech and acts.

Such a reaction to the Enlightenment gained force during the 19th century, ushering in a new intellectual milieu of mysticism, emotion, and sentiment that has largely denigrated the philosophy of rationalism, freedom, and individualism. What these new critics value—feeling, responsibility, and groupism—and what this book is about, is a new social model (or theory) that would stabilize society and bring about brotherly love and harmony. This emphasis on sentiment grew throughout the 20th century, and today what appears to be standing in the twilight of freedom, ready to move in as the force of the future, is *communitarianism*—a spirit of community and a desire that people be free from the excesses of freedom.

2

Freedom From Freedom

When the individual is thrown back upon his own inner resources, when he loses the sense of moral and social involvement with others, he becomes prey to sensations of anxiety and guilt. Self-destruction is frequently his only way out. Such sensations . . . are on the increase in Western society. For, in the process of modern industrial and political development, established social contexts have become weak, and fewer individuals have the secure interpersonal relations which formerly gave meaning and stablity to existence.

—Robert Nisbet

Now that we have had a look at the Enlightenment philosophy that spawned the great impulse toward freedom, let us turn to a new social worldview that would consign those "obsolete" values to an early grave. What is needed, say community-oriented social reformers (in and out of journalism) at the start of the 21st century, is quite simply a new model based on *community authority* that substitutes the people for the elites that have been setting the agenda.

Participation in power: that is what the communitarians want for the public. For the public journalist, public participation in press power is what is desired. This participation in social power is also what would confer freedom—not personal, autonomous freedom of the Enlightenment kind, but community freedom to influence society. Just as government needs to be concerned with the people's power and freedom, the same is true with the press. It needs to change to a community-based press that serves as an instrument of public power. The press's autonomous freedom needs to be handed over to the public for use in the public interest, not in the narrow interests of profit-making private interests. In the libertarian press, the public was virtually powerless; in the communitarian press, the public would have the power and also the positive freedom to use this power

People's freedom to use authority is a difficult concept to grasp. In fact, democracy itself is increasingly suspect. How does the public will get expressed? How is it found? Such questions point up the age-old problems with democracy. There are, of course, implicit problems with democracy. It does not always secure the most rational solutions, nor does it guarantee human happiness. It is, as Yugoslav philosopher Mihailo Markovic said (1974, p. 242), "solely a form of social organization which offers optimal *possibilities.*" Whether these possibilities will be reached will depend on the imagination, strength of will, creativity, and intellectual and moral power of those assuming political responsibility. Regardless of such optimistic theorizing, in actual practice the democratic ideal is a very real problem.

In the 18th century, Rousseau faced it with his General Will, which he warned was not the mere "will of all." For him it was more elusive and fundamental. Such a will was often not even apparent to the people themselves, but what was certain was that it could be inferred by community (or national) leadership devoted to the welfare of the people and concerned with the people in their collective reality and their political unity (Nisbet, 1990, pp. 153–154). Modern communication scholars have the same problem with the concept of "public opinion," which must mean about the same thing as Rousseau meant by the General Will.

At any rate, the time has come when the voice of the people seems to mean more than it has in the past. Elections, in which at least half the people do not even vote, are recognized as not enough. What is needed is continuous checking on public opinion, or the General Will; we can see that this is being done increasingly through polls and all kinds of public surveys. The public journalists, too, are giving up some of their former freedom by engaging in focus groups, polls, surveys, and conferences with public representatives. At long last, journalism is slipping out of its Enlightenment mode and is willing to share at least some of its power and freedom with the public. This undoubtedly will continue well into the 21st century until all the press is brought, however reluctantly for some hearty individual journalists, into the Communitarian Era. Community interest is the new social mantra.

NEEDED: A NEW PRESS CONCERN

To achieve this community emphasis, the press, according to communitarian proponents, must take the lead. Listen to Clifford Christians, a communications theorist and researcher at the University of Illinois and a leading communitarian (Christians, Ferre, & Fackler, 1993, p. 12): "Despite the conundrums and the far-reaching ramifications, community cannot be resuscitated without the leadership of the press." And he goes on to say that his book (written with Ferre and Fackler) would "attempt to demonstrate that bringing community to the forefront is impossible *without a distinctively new theoretical model to undergird the press's role*" (emphasis ours).

One should note that Christians did not simply want to reform the older, libertarian theory of the press, but proposes a "distinctively new theoretical model." He made it clear in the book's introduction that he and his co-authors recommend a communitarian model that "features the dialogic self, community commitment, civic transformation, and mutuality in organizational culture." Basic to this new model is the elimination of individual autonomy which, the authors said, has been since the Enlightenment in the 18th century "the West's cultural core and the defining feature of that cultural activity we call reporting" (p. 13). Christians et al., although they discussed communitarian journalism at great length, did not really get to the core of their "new theory." But it seems to us that its basic features are these: a need for community, a need for journalism to invigorate community, a need for social order and discipline, a need for less personal freedom, and a need for a new authority, a politically active citizenry.

For communitarians (the antiliberal advocates of community) the chief problem in journalism (and in society generally) today is the problem of reconciling human freedom with social order. The Enlightenment tried to solve it, but could not. Can it be done? Perhaps not, but the communitarians hope they can do it without going so far toward social order as to completely wipe out human freedom. Some social technique will be required that will both restrain and permit, limit freedom but give it some play in society. If it is to succeed, what the new communitarian model must do is to replace individualism and its "rights" with what Christians et al. called the "integrating norm" of the "social whole" (p. 13).

Universal solidarity is an important concept for the communitarians; for Christians et al. it is the "normative core of the social and moral order" (p. 14), and the journalist, instead of "drowning audiences with data and fattening company coffers," must help to engender a "a like-minded world view among a public still inclined toward individual autonomy." When the Enlightenment concept of pluralism is enthroned and the individual reified, the communitarians believe, it is difficult if not impossible to mold a "like-minded world view." Thus, for communitarians, journalistic freedom that leads to a barrage of conflicting and dissonant messages pouring over mass audiences encourages social chaos and psychological trauma.

Libertarians, for their part, are convinced that market-driven journalism will naturally root out the socially irresponsible content and bring the press to a more ethical level. Communitarians do not believe it, saying that it has failed to do this during the last few centuries. John H. McManus, in *Market-Driven Journalism*, a report of research he did in California in the mid-1990s, concluded (1994, pp. 162–164) that four interlocking rules govern market-journalism, at least in television: (a) seek images over ideas, (b) seek emotion over analysis, (c) exaggerate, if needed, to add appeal, and (d) avoid extensive news-gathering.

In spite of what McManus saw as the dismal state of today's journalism, he ended on a hopeful note, saying that market journalism can respond to consumer demands, unlike journalism controlled by the state or by a few media barons. Ending his book on a "public journalism" theme, he referred to Jay Rosen and others who are trying to respond to the public. What Rosen said (Rosen & Taylor, 1992, p. 10) is that the news media should adopt a "public bias," in that they should produce "a discussion which the polity learns more about itself, its current problems, its real divisions, its place in time, its prospects for the future."

If journalists do not assume such a public bias, they will continue doing what they have been doing. Walter Cronkite had this to say in a speech at the University of South Dakota on October 22, 1989: Journalists are "producing a population of political, economic, and scientific ignoramuses at a point in time when a lot more knowledge rather than less is needed for the survival of democracy." These are strong words, but the public journalist would agree with them.

Many writers, and certainly not only communitarians, have warned that the press had better get a new concern, or it will indeed find its freedom endangered. Carl L. Becker, former professor of history at Cornell and a respecter of human freedom, wrote (1945, p. 122) that "what we need most of all, is a heightened sense of individual and collective responsibility—less insistence on negative rights and the unrestrained pursuit of individual self-interest, and a more united and resolute determination to concern ourselves with the public good and to make the sacrifices that are necessary for it." And he warned (p. 37) that if the individual (journalist) will not assume an honest stance, "the government must assume the responsibility of restraining his freedom."

ESCAPING FREEDOM'S LURE

The legacy of modern journalism in America comes to us in a colorful package, promising journalists great personal opportunity to excel, to develop to their greatest potential, to be themselves, to do their own thing, to fulfill their dreams, to operate largely unrestrained in their presentation of the world to their audiences. This legacy, spawned by the Enlightenment and strengthened by existentialism, has enshrined press freedom and has considered it both a natural right (from Locke) and a utilitarian right (from Mill). It is God-given and it permits us to ascertain and transmit the truth, and for the existentialists, the use of this freedom actually makes us what we are. Therefore, for libertarian and existential journalists, such freedom is necessarily good and must be protected at all costs.

Not so for the communitarians. Individual freedom, as a blanket concept, cannot be considered good. Injected into journalism, it does more harm than good. It too easily becomes a plaything for the egocentric journalist who somehow believes that following his or her own whims and beliefs, without consideration of responsibility to others, results in worthwhile journalism. For the communitarian, this Enlightenment freedom concept leads unerringly to extremism, vulgarism, licentiousness, narcissism, egoism, and pluralism of values. Such freedom in journalism (and in society generally) must be harnessed and replaced by a community-oriented order and a normative, consensual ethics.

Freedom must be considered only a minimal and tangential part of journalism. Communitarians seek to limit its social impact and to escape its superficial lure. Even Seidenberg, who does not like to see such a limitation, predicts it in his seminal book *Posthistoric Man.* "Freedom and liberty . . . must be recognized as tangential ideals," he wrote (1974, p. 85), "projections of an individualistic and transitional philosophy silhouetted against a background of events moving in an opposite direction." He went on to say (pp. 86–87) that the 20th century has been the supreme era of individualism and freedom, and "once past will never again return." He believed that journalism of the future will reflect the basic attitudes of a people rather than the individualism of the journalist. In what must stir the souls of communitarians, he saw the future journalist becoming "a vehicle of expression for the people, a voice, an articulate artisan, whose creative impulses will demand the suppression of his personality as the condition of his craft."

Many social observers believe that the dominance of the collective aspects of society and of journalism is virtually assured, along with a de-emphasis of personal freedom. Seidenberg is certainly one of the chief among these observers who sees the individual with personal freedom being gradually converted into a cooperating member of the organization and community. "The process," said Seidenberg (pp. 112–113), "is irreversible and implicit: history moves in only one direction—inert and unerring, she flows toward her goal." Psychologist Carl C. Jung also noted (1924, p. 95) society's gravitational pull toward community and observed that the individual's worth is increasingly based on collective contribution and cooperation.

A viable and progressive community can exist not only if the individual contributes and cooperates, but as one writer said, there must be "a sense of common interest" among the community members. Bull went on to say (1977, p. 46) that order can be maintained in a community only if everyone stands "in awe of a common power." Maintenance of such order (at least in a democratic community) means that everyone pays allegiance to the common power of democratic dialogue and decision-making. Bull added (p. 53) that a community's members must have "a sense of *common interests* in the elementary goals of social life." And there must be, he added, "rules which spell out the kind of behaviour that is orderly."

Erich Fromm, a leading psychiatrist who warned often about the trauma associated with individual freedom, believed that it is quite natural for society to evolve toward groups and communities. It is also natural that individuals, ultimately weighted down with the heavy responsibility of making a multitude of decisions, become ready to give up their freedom for the comfort of being free from freedom. Paternalism is a luxury for the citizen. Delegation of daily decisions to a leadership is understandable. In addition, said Fromm (1941, p. 19), there is a basic drive to escape from freedom and a "need to be related to the world outside oneself, the need to avoid aloneness."

Surely the journalist, whose job has always been the chronicling of events and interrelationships among people while at the same time being told to respect their freedom and autonomy, senses this Frommian desire to escape from freedom into the cool comfort of indecision. Journalists low in the hierarchy of the institution can avoid the pangs of personal decision making by passing the buck to an editor, a news director, or some other superior. Also, the special place in society of the news medium itself and the rather tightly knit community that it forms gives the journalist a sense of security to a limited degree. However, always with the journalist, even the more libertarian one, is the haunting question as to whether or not he or she is working as a public servant for the community or for the private interests of the medium. It is a knotty question, one that perhaps will bring journalism into a larger "public" community and cause it to share power with nonjournalists, as communitarians desire and predict.

NO GLOBAL EMBRACE OF FREEDOM

The world is paternalistic. Throughout vast regions of the world there is no tradition of freedom. Group identification and tribal loyalties have for centuries dominated. Allegiance to strong or religiously ordained leaders and long-standing, common traditions is deeply ingrained. However, during the last century the concept of individual freedom, inherited from the West, has infiltrated many traditional societies and has led the press, at least, to the frustration of knowing about freedom and not being fully able to practice it. It seems that most journalists, in the Third World at least, are willing to sacrifice journalistic freedom for a stake in building nationhood.

Journalists appear to be aware that a contentious, pluralistic, and competitive press is a barrier to social harmony and respect for authority. They intuitively recognize, although some of them fight against it, that individuals want a group-confirmed status and want to escape from the freedom of individualism. They realize that the Western contention of a free press's compatibility with democracy is an illusion.

At least Third World journalists are undecided and questioning. Zhao (1998, p. 9) saw some advantages in the Western concept of press freedom grounded as a privately owned, profit-making commercial enterprise, but was skeptical. For he saw this model, which he called the "press market model of editorial freedom," as equated "to the property rights of media owners." He wrote (pp. 9–10), "While I am critical of the fundamentally undemocratic nature of Party journalism and sensitive to the liberalizing impact of commercialization, I do not equate democracy with the market." For Zhao, what was needed was the democratization of journalism.

He mentioned the new Western tendency toward communitarianism that would provide for such democratization. In fact, he said that recently a "democratic participant" model has been growing in the West "to take into account emerging democratic media theories and practices." He referred specifically to the theory of Picard (1985) that, drawing on the Nordic press experience, calls for a "social democratic" journalism. It would, said Zhao (p. 183), provide legitimization for public intervention and collective ownership to ensure media independence from various vested interests."

In similar vein, Spanish communication scholar Santiago Sanchez Gonzalez pointed out (1992, p. 8) that journalists in many countries recognize that American-style press freedom is not democratic. This is because, he continued, "Democracy relates to participation in the decision-making for the whole communities and . . . is foreign to the streams of constitutionalism and liberalism, either political or economic." In most parts of the world, journalists seem to recognize this problem with press freedom, seeing it as a narrow antiliberal concept that benefits only a small segment of society—the press.

In Latin America, although the term *press freedom* is heard in every country, the reality of the situation is quite different from the rhetoric. Jorge Fascetto, chairman of the board of directors of Argentina's *El Dia* and president of the Inter-American Press Association, in a speech in Columbia, MO (1999), pointed out that the average Latin American was little concerned about press freedom. He noted that what the people wanted was food and security; that they had little inclination to worry about freedom of the press and other esoteric concerns of the rich and powerful.

As Nisbet said (1990, p. 26), it is hard to deny the fact that increasingly, not only in the Third World but in the West also, individualism is on the defensive. "New imperatives are the order of the day," he wrote, "and these are not confined to the ranks of the intellectuals." It is true that in the Third World (but to some degree everywhere) what is being developed is not a unitary community but a pluralism of ethnic and religious communities. And just as an individual person can disrupt the harmony of a single community, an individual community can bring disorder to a larger community. One has only to note what is going on in various African countries and in the former megacommunities of the Soviet Union and Yugoslavia.

American-type press freedom meets strong criticism in every developing nation. At least, it does from the governments. In all the "developing democracies," there are pressures against the development of such freedom. Feinstein (1995, p. 16) pointed out in *IPI Report* that such pressures "range from new press laws against journalists who 'spread panic' or harm the 'public interest' to blatant decrees closing publications, to threats and trials, to more subtle economic leverage, to requirements for 'licensing' of journalists." Shuster (1995, p. 19) noted that the situation in the developing world in terms of press freedom is getting worse. Many spokesmen for their countries' press contend that their media blur opinion and information and always exaggerate and lack sensitivity. In Russia, as the 20th century ended, the population has "fallen prey to the mental junk food on which Westerners have fed for decades," wrote Williams (1995, p. 23). And in Egypt, wrote Alaily (1995, p. 25), the press that was once "free to bark, but not to bite" now has to even stop barking. Alaily, an Egyptian journalist working for the BBC Arabic Service, said that the government is determined to make the press more orderly and helpful to national development. This would mean, in part, that the press should not show "disdain for the country's institutions" or "incite or cause harm to the public interest or the national economy."

Not all global journalism observers agree with us that there is an antipathy toward American-type journalism in the world today. For instance, William Hachten, a long-time international communication scholar at the University of Wisconsin, contended (1996, p. 174) that since the demise of the Communist "second" world (presumably with the breakup of the USSR), the Western concept of journalism and mass communication has become the "dominant model throughout the world and is widely emulated."

Even if we agree with Hachten (but we don't) that the communist "second" world has fallen, it is doubtful that the Western concept of journalism has become the model for world press systems. Perhaps technologically it is true, but so far as press freedom and individualistic journalistic practices are concerned, the world is still far from the American pattern. Although Hachten maintained that journalists in the developing world today are seeking autonomy and freedom from government interference, we think (considering reports by New York's Freedom House) that such seeking is virtually nonexistent. In fact, most signs are that they are gravitating more and more to a conformist and predictable press that de-emphasizes autonomy and emphasizes social stability.

We must be careful not to think that all nations despise authority, order, and discipline. We can look at South Africa to see that one autocratic and apartheid government was simply replaced by another (of Nelson Mandela), perhaps just as rigid. A similar situation occurred when Rhodesia became Zimbabwe and British authority was transferred to the Africans. People in many parts of the world may not want a certain kind of authority, but they are lost without some authority.

Calling itself a democracy does not mean that a country has freedom of expression. Many of the countries, for instance, in Francophone Africa began having multiparty elections in the early 1990s, thus becoming "democratic"; but as Diamond (1996, p. 73) pointed out, freedom there is no better than before. In most of the 45 sub-Saharan states where elections have been held since 1991 (18 in 1996 alone), "there have been setbacks for freedom" in most of the countries. Diamond added that the same pattern holds generally for Latin America, the Middle East, and Central and South Asia. In the so-called democracies of the Third World, he said, elections have resulted in strong executives and weak legislatures and judiciaries.

ISLAM: A RELIGIOUS PERSPECTIVE

It appears today that about the only force that can forge a unity among smaller communities is religion, and even religion cannot do this in many places (e.g., Northern Ireland). However, in the sprawling Muslim world's various national communities, Islam, through the leadership of Allah (God) and his prophet Mohammed, has harmonized the groups to a large extent, although splinter groups often do not get along too well. Certainly in the province of journalism the theory of *tawhid* (implying the unity, coherence, and harmony of all parts of the universe) has stood—throughout Islam— for exclusive servitude to Allah and is opposed to any intellectual, cultural, or political forces that take away from this transcendental authority (Mowlana, cited in Cooper et al., 1989, pp. 141–142).

Negated by *tawhid* is any right of guardianship or authority of anyone except Allah over human activity. Certainly this would preclude Western-style journalistic freedom with its propensity to set standards (or to deny them) and would tempt minions of the press to develop an arrogant egoism. Allah's authority is *the* authority, delegated to religious leaders.

The purpose of journalism in the Islamic world is to work within the limits of *tawhid* to restrain individual freedom, to diminish democracy, personal achievement, and success—at least as they are prized in the Western world. The press in the Muslim world is viewed as an instrument to develop the community (the *umma*). For the Islamic journalist, working within *tawhid,* the term *freedom of the press* has no meaning when there is no social accountability on the part of the individual journalist or the press institution. In other words, the Muslim must be responsible to society—and *the society is defined by religious authority along with the concept of responsibility.* A concept like Western free-press theory coming from European Enlightenment is not only alien to Islam, but anathema to the religious principles of *tawhid.*

The Islamic sense of community is very strong, as is the necessity of people to have an authority and discipline, in this case the authority and discipline of Allah. Mowlana wrote (pp. 143–144) that the term *Islam* comes from the Arabic *sulama,* meaning surrender and peace "or the peaceful submission to the Will of Allah." It is thus that community is developed and sustained. Islamic community (*umma*) transcends borders and political ideologies. It is a religio-economic concept and is found only where it is nourished and governed by Islam. Such an *umma* is required of the society at large and by each individual member. It must be exemplary, setting the highest standards, avoiding excesses and extravagancies, be consistent and steadfast. For the Muslims, the sovereignty of the state belongs to Allah, not to a ruler or to the people themselves. No individual or class should dominate, exploit, or corrupt the state.

Muslim countries respect social order, although the world's press often fails to emphasize this. The Islamic world, maintained Orientalist Michael Cook (Gellner, 1996, p. 17), combines the theocentrism of Christianity with Judaism's legalism, resulting in a legal blueprint for social order "which stands above mere power and political authority." British philosopher Ernest Gellner, writing about Islam in the middle 1990s (1996, p. 22) pointed out that when in Islamic societies citizens want to confront their leaders, they do so by "applying religious norms of sacred law, rather than the secular principles of a Civil Society." Other than their fastidiousness about sacred prescriptions, Gellner continued, they are "not otherwise over-sensitive about the internal organization of political authority."

So we can see that the Muslim countries have a deep reverence for *umma* and the social order that it represents. Arkoun in *Rethinking Islam* (1994, pp. 52–53), said that such a Muslim community is based on a deep-seated religious belief, a respect for leaders, and it draws its energy and cohesion from a spiritual quality that permeates all Islam.

Not only in the Muslim countries are press systems gravitating toward authority and order. In the realistic world out there where people in many regions live on the borderline of starvation, it is the struggle for food, shelter, and community, not press freedom, that occupies their waking hours. When they can achieve these ends, they feel free from a sense of futility.

Most have no special interest in such esoteric concepts as press freedom; they mainly want a feeling of belonging to a microcommunity, having no particular concern for the complexities of even a national community. The history of, and concern for, such ideas as free expression is beyond them, unimportant in all its intricacies. They seem to realize that even if they had a free press, their concerns and activities would not be published.

As Eric Hoffer, the longshoreman philosopher, said (1956, p. 29), "The game of history is usually played by the best and worst over the heads of the majority in middle." We could modify that easily by saying the game of *journalism* is played by the richest, most powerful, and most celebrated over the heads of the vast multitudes of average and poor people. But these "average and poor" seem to be relatively satisfied, usually because they have the support of community. Hoffer wrote (p. 44) that a "vivid feeling of solidarity, whether racial, national or religious, is . . . an effective means of preventing (social) unrest." And he further believed (p. 36) that a "sense of liberation comes from having escaped the burdens, fears and hopelessness of an untenable individual existence."

WESTERN DISENCHANTMENT

Although the concept of "democracy" is under attack from some quarters today, it holds a major place in the hearts, if not the minds, of communitarians and public journalists. Public journalists believe that modern-day Platonists, the elitist antidemocrats in and out of the press, do not want to lose their special power and it is natural for them to disparage any desire on the part of the people for involvement, and like Plato before them, these press elitists continue to believe in the general apathy and ignorance of the masses.

Even though a devotee of Plato, philosopher Jay Newman wrote (1989, p. 107) that, even if Plato's "elitism is more reasonable and less maleficent than others, it shows an unwarranted and dangerous disrespect for the judgment of the common man." Public journalists would certainly agree with Newman that today's Platonists have an unwarranted disrespect for the common person. It may well be that generally the masses are apathetic—especially in Third World countries, where hopelessness is common and opportunities are limited, the people desire little freedom and much paternalism. In the advanced countries of the West, where there is no such hopelessness and where the press and the individual journalists have obtained much autonomy, there has been no rush by journalists to escape from freedom. However, here and there in varied areas of the Western world, there is developing a realization among journalists that all is not well and that their special position is antithetical to democracy and a sense of community.

This sense of the need for community is growing in spite of the view of such psychologists and sociologists as Sigmund Freud, Gustave Le Bon, and Robert Park that all groups are essentially authoritarian and their collective behavior is easily channeled by emotional contagion into irrational and socially harmful acts. Freud, especially, looked at groups as socially dangerous. His view is similar to that of Niebuhr (1932, p. 272), who believed that the "selfishness of human communities" is inevitable, and that the group "permits all sorts of actions that individuals would refrain from undertaking on their own initiative." Modern advocates of community would contend that, even if Niebuhr's observations are true, individualism causes far more social harm than does collectivism and that journalists need to give up their freedom (their power) for the public good. If there are to be power holders and power brokers, they should be of the people, and not of the elite.

CRITICS OF PRESS ELITISM

In spite of moral pressures to do so, the press is understandably reluctant to give up power. During its history in America, it has been in control. It has set the public agenda for news and discussion. It has created the operational reality for the people. Unrestrained by laws or public opinion, it has run freely over people and institutions, and under its self-proclaimed "watchdog" function, has demeaned the dignity of political institutions and leaders. This authoritarianism of the media elite is coming to an end. The advocates of the community and its authority are speaking out and acting to try to change the long-prevailing situation.

Journalists can either play a part in changing this long-time situation or they can play it safe and go along with the old Enlightenment-fed journalism. Fallows (1996) wrote that journalists can continue entertaining the public or they can engage it. At least, he said, they can choose. He added:

> Concentrating on conflict and spectacle, building up celebrities and tearing them down, presenting a crisis of issue with the volume turned all the way up, only to drop that issue and turn to the next emergency. . . . But if journalists should choose to engage the public, they will begin a long series of experiments and decisions to see how journalism might better serve its fundamental purpose, that of making democratic self-government possible. (p. 267)

Since the 1970s, Chomsky and Herman have argued that an American power elite has conspired to control the news agenda and suppress or marginalize any threat to the established social paradigm. They believe that journalistic media are in the hands of the ruling classes of the West that use the media for their own interests. The two critics, one a linguist and the other an economist, emphasized (especially in their 1979 *The Political Economy of Human Rights*) the limitations of press freedom in the United States and elsewhere, arguing that such freedom never leads to challenging the bases of economic and political power. Therefore, they maintained (McNair, 1998, pp. 84, 111) that the media are no more than propaganda instruments of what they term the *national security state*. Chomsky noted (McNair, 1998, p. 5) the power of the government and corporations over the press when he wrote:

> The media serve the interests of state and corporate power . . . [and] not only allow the agendas of news to be bent in accordance with state demands and criteria of utility, they also accept the presuppositions of the state without question.

One way to break this hold by the state on the press is by widespread use of the computer by the public. At present, at least, there seems little the state can do to control the Internet. A great pluralism of information is possible.

The computer is aiding in giving individuals (in and out of communities) a public forum. For the first time in history, the average (or nearly average) citizen can, in effect, become a journalist. "At the beginning of the 21st century it is estimated that online services span nearly every country and that at least 50 million people use online services daily to deliver and gain access to all kinds of information" (Packard, 1998, p. 1).

There are some, however, who feel the computer will make only a limited and marginal contribution to community-building. Theodore Roszak, chairman of general studies at the University of California–Hayward, for example, is one of the leaders of these dissenters. He wrote (1986, p. 167), "Certainly the snippets and summaries its [the Internet] so-called new services offer (such as the Compuserve Information Service and The Source Newswire, edited from the United Press International) are inconsequential for anything that goes beyond weather and stock market reports."

According to Roszak (p. 167), America's "mainstream public" would be better off if it were "actively in touch with a few good journals of opinion (left, right, and center) than if we had a personal computer in every home." In spite of such doubters as Roszak, there is general agreement that the Internet will increase the citizen's view of the world and offer the chance for community-building dialogue.

Other than the mammoth changes being brought about by the computer, there is a change going on in the institutional press as well: Public journalism is rapidly recognizing the needs of the community. In later chapters, we describe exactly what steps the public journalists are taking to resuscitate the communities, to give them power, and to get them more involved in politics and public life. Whereas the computer is but an instrument in such a change, the public journalists are proposing a general attitude change for journalism.

CONTROL BY COMMUNITIES

Future society—perhaps a society of communities—will be one, according to linguist and social critic Noam Chomsky, that will be under control and orderly. "That means," said Chomsky, "control through communities, through workplaces, through works councils in factories or universities, whatever organization it happens to be" (Achbar, 1994, p. 36).

At present, according to Chomsky, the media set the agenda "in all sorts of ways by selection of topics, by distribution of concerns, by emphasis and framing of issues, by filtering of information, by bounding of debate within certain limits. They determine, they select, they shape, they control, they restrict—in order to serve the interests of dominant groups in the society" [p. 55]. The media, believed Chomsky, do not want active, involved audience members. What they want, he said, is "a passive, obedient population of consumers and political spectators—a community of people who are so atomized and isolated that they can't put together their limited resources and become an independent, powerful force that will chip away at concentrated power" (Barsamian, 1994).

Such statements by Chomsky, earlier considered extreme criticism of the press, are now rather typical of media criticism and reflect the disillusionment of the public with media authority. According to Chomsky, journalism basically wants to divert people from serious matters, things that affect them and their neighbors. Media want to get people to watch football and other sports, to worry about "mother with child with six heads," or to look at astrology, or to "get involved in fundamentalist stuff or something or other." Along with getting people away from things that matter, Chomsky (Achbar, p. 90) believed the press feels "it is important to reduce their capacity to think." What is needed, he said, is organization among people to develop communities of interest and sharing. In the U.S. "each person is sitting alone in front of the tube," said Chomsky (Achbar, p. 195), "and you can't fight the world alone, you know . . . The way to do it is through organization."

It is through these organized communities of trust and sharing that the concept of freedom takes on a new meaning. Freedom, like power, stems from the community needs, desires, and aspirations. The communities will set their own agenda, and as Etzioni said (1993, p. 133), each "community— whether residential, work-related, monoethnic, or 'integrated'—needs to work out its own agenda, depending on local circumstances and needs." There must be moral order, said Etzioni, for there to be freedom. If not, he believed there will be ever-increasing reliance on the State.

HABERMAS' IDEAL SPEECH SITUATION

Juergen Habermas, perhaps Germany's premier current philosopher, would endorse Chomsky's and Etzioni's insistence on communities of interest. He would insist (1975, p. xiii), however, on one of *communicative competence,* as he calls his theory. This includes what he terms the *ideal speech situation* and the *consensus theory of truth.* Participants in Habermas' community would be free from restraint, equal in their capacity to express their ideas and ask their questions. The goal: a consensus on values and actions. The community, then, could develop maxims and principles that would lead them in ethical action. This seems somewhat similar to Kant's rational determination of ethical maxims by universalizing them, except that Habermas would have these maxims formulated by the group-in-discussion instead of solely by the individual person. In a sense, with Habermas we have a consensus truth emerging from group conversation and debate that will be used to guide the community.

Kant would have the individual test his or her maxim or principle against his Categorical Imperative by asking: Would I want this principle to be accepted and acted on by everyone? For Habermas, the test would be more focused and consensual: Would all of us in community agree that this ethical maxim or this action is correct? It is important to note what Habermas would want the ideal speech situation to obtain in order to come to this consensus.

This ideal speech situation of Habermas' would be one that would insure unlimited discussion and discussion free from all constraints of domination, "whether their source be conscious strategic behavior or communication barriers secured in ideology and neurosis" (p. xiii). Habermas believed that several things are needed for this ideal speech situation: rationally motivated discourse, understandable utterances, truthful propositional content, sincerity of those discoursing, and participants who desire to understand other positions and reach a consensus.

POSITIVE FREEDOM IN COMMUNITY

It should be made clear that the communitarians do not disdain freedom. They, like Habermas, simply redefine it as *community freedom* or monistic freedom of the group to seek a consensus and pursue a common goal. It falls within what Isaiah Berlin, Britain's foremost modern philosopher, called *positive freedom*. Positive freedom, said Berlin (Gray, 1996, p. 16), is a rational freedom to control one's life—in Habermasian terms, to control the life of the group.

In other words, positive freedom is freedom used; it is not enough to be free of interference by others (Berlin's *negative freedom*) or to be free from external control or coercion. One problem with negative freedom, insist the communitarians and public journalists of today, is that most people are not using this freedom to do positive, socially responsible things. Persons in a community must freely use their community-derived potential to contribute positively to the progress, order, and harmony of the group. Active participation for the good of the community: that is the objective, and the basis of freedom.

Positive freedom assumes that citizens have the ways and means to participate and communicate in their communities. Many point to technology as offering these ways and means. They see the new electronic age (especially the computer and the Internet) as opening up individual freedom and extending the libertarian theory into the 21st century. This, to some extent, may well be the case. At the same time, the new technologies should provide for more community dialogue, more interpersonal communication, and thereby strengthen the ties of communities of interest. Listen to Ithiel de Sola Pool: "A panoply of electronic devices (e.g., the computer) puts at everyone's hand capacities far beyond anything that the printing press, radio, and television could offer." Writing at last can become dialogue, said Pool (1983, p. 231), and such dialogue can undoubtedly help in the formation of new communities.

Habermas would prefer the face-to-face communication of his "ideal speech community" to the technological community mentioned by Pool, but he would agree with the importance of information to the establishment of a normative community with participatory practical discourse. According to Habermas, the "validity claim of norms is grounded not in the irrational volitional acts of the contracting parties, but in the rationally motivated recognition of norms, which may be questioned at any time" (Habermas, 1975, p. 105).

The ideal situation of Habermas may never really materialize, but we know the impact of technology will, and with it will come a multitude of content-oriented problems. What about reaction to the new technology's potential for placing antisocial messages before the public? As with older technology such as television, surely there will develop social restraints on the Internet. How can we permit complete freedom (with no gatekeepers) for the Internet when we are, at the same time, insisting on more and better restraints on the traditional media? In the short term, the Internet may increase freedom (and with it informational anarchy), but in the long term it will be subjugated to the will of the people and harnessed for the benefit of the community. Undoubtedly there will be more and more voices, like that of Walter Cronkite who, speaking in 1998 at the National Press Club in Washington, DC, made a strong call for legislation to control Internet users.

THE CASE FOR FREEDOM'S DEMISE

The bright sun of freedom that has prevailed to a considerable degree since at least the 18th century has finally begun to set. We are now in the twilight hours, and as the night approaches, it is with relief and not sorrow that people can rest from the frenzied and competitive activity of the day. It is evident that the day of personal freedom is ending. Many reasons exist for the communitarians' disdain for personal freedom, a freedom that they believe would grow ever more extreme without restraints. A few of these reasons, gleaned from a number of their books, indicate that freedom:

- Depreciates the rights and needs of others
- Harms the sense of belonging, of association, of community
- Develops into egoism and arrogance
- Disregards the wishes of others
- Leads to narcissism

- Militates against order and social stability
- Brings about psychological trauma
- Causes alienation, anxiety, and ennui
- Narrows the perceived scope of the world
- Leads to, or stimulates, social entropy or anomie.

Let us at least take a brief look at the last one: Personal freedom, especially atomistic individualistic freedom, so beloved by many modern journalists, leads to a loss of energy and potency in human societies and basically causes social disorder. At least, this is what communitarians believe. This process is often referred to as *entropy* (or, in sociology, anomie), derived from the 2nd Law of Thermodynamics—the tendency of a system to run down, to lose energy, to fall apart. Needham noted (1943, p. 224) that man has always had the tragic sense that all was falling apart, that the universe was dying, and that disorder was increasing. Communitarians today see this entropic process increasing in America and around the world.

The drift toward social disorder is seen everywhere. One way to postpone final extinction and social breakdown is through establishing order, organization, cooperation, and community—making a solid front against the natural entropic tendencies. Entropy, then, must be fought by increasing order. Wrong (1994, p. 242) defined *order* thusly: "Order consists of the predictability of human conduct on the basis of common and stable expectations. This approach is primarily concerned with the shared meanings that make possible stable, recurrent, and cooperative social interaction."

There is little doubt that social disorganization is rampant. Nisbet noted (1990, p. 8) that "innumerable studies of community disorganization, family disorganization, personality disintegration, not to mention the myriad investigations of industrial strife and the dissolution of ethnic subcultures . . . all serve to point up the idea of disorganization in present day social science." Nisbet also bemoaned (p. 9) the "alienation of man from historic moral certitudes," which has "been followed by the sense of man's alienation from fellow man." Hobbes very early, it should be remembered, depicted autonomous individuals as a danger to society. He saw them as "relentlessly pursuing their own interests at odds with one another . . . [and as] a theoretical reflection of the erosion of medieval and feudal ties and the rise in the numbers of 'masterless men" (Wrong, 1994, p. 21). The solution to this situation for the modern communitarian, of course, would not be a powerful leader ("leviathan") but a politically astute citizenry acting from a community, not a personal, interest.

One of the most significant reasons for the prospective demise of freedom was discussed (1955, p. 270) by psychologist Erich Fromm who saw belonging to a group or community as an escape from the burden of freedom. Fromm gave as a solution to the problem of the anxiety of freedom the implementation of what he called *democratic communitarianism.* In order to escape this freedom that causes a person to be insecure, dissatisfied, bored, and anxious, Fromm proposed a "sane society" where there would be justice, group solidarity, and a sense of community. The journalist in America, protected by the Constitution and stimulated by the competitive market forces, continues a style of journalism that increasingly is seen by critics as harsh, uncaring, and socially harmful.

No doubt America's journalists are greatly impressed with their importance. Narcissism is prevalent in the press, perhaps more in the electronic than in the print media, but prevalent nevertheless. Dartmouth researcher Robert Lichter and his colleagues (1986. p. 123) noted that the late Joseph Kraft, a highly respected journalist, complained of the "new narcissism" in his profession. Kraft wrote that "those of us in the media have enjoyed an enormous surge in status and power in recent years . . . But while we have acquired confidence and self-assertiveness, there is no security. . . . We are prone to the disease of the times—narcissism."

THE FIRST AMENDMENT PROBLEM

The First Amendment to the U.S. Constitution is rather blunt: Congress shall pass no law abridging the freedom of the press. Through the years legislatures have tried to abide by this, in spite of the fact that they have not really known what "freedom of the press" means. They have, by and large, simply stayed away from laws related to the press, especially a priori directive laws that guide press actions prior to publication. Those who would like to eliminate press excesses and irresponsible actions see the First Amendment as a primary and insurmountable stumbling block. This Enlightenment-inspired press protection gives a special place to the press, making it the only profit-making institution in the country that really has no law to control it.

A good example of a great absolutist champion of press freedom is Alexander Meiklejohn, one-time president of Amherst College. He wrote (Mayer, 1969, pp. 50–51) that the First Amendment is uncompromising, admitting no exceptions. He, speaking for many others, believed that press freedom is inherent and inalienable and, even in the name of security, cannot be touched. It will be difficult, if not impossible, for the communitarians and public journalists of tomorrow to get very far in depreciating press freedom while there is a First Amendment. Such an amendment granting freedom, although undefined, to the institutional press stands squarely in the way of press reform. The amendment seems to give unlimited rights to the press to freely determine its editorial contents. Certainly it restrains Congress, and state legislatures by extension, from abridging freedom of the press. It still remains, however, a nonabsolute freedom clause because it only restrains *law-making* and says nothing about restrictions on the press that might be instituted by the executive or judicial branches of government.

However, public opinion has traditionally limited press restrictions by the courts and by the president. A breakdown of order in the society (or social *anomie*) if not caused by the press, is certainly facilitated by the mass media's constantly sensationalizing events, digging into socially taboo areas, invading privacy, demolishing reputations, ridiculing heroes, deriding religion and the court system, promoting the equality of values, enthroning the importance of material things and money, and otherwise demeaning basic stabilizing social forces such as police and the military.

Order, to put it mildly, is not what the libertarian press tries to instill in society, and for good reason: Stability does not fit its concept of news. The press promotes excitement, and along with it the eccentric, the atypical, the strange, and the deviant personalities. In fact, it detests the definition of "news" that is built around typical people, the socially integrated, happy and loving relationships, the well-adjusted child, the stay-at-home mother, the hard-working and dependable father, and the religious family. Order, harmony, predictability, cooperation—these are simply not newsworthy for the modern journalist. Most modern journalists probably like the First Amendment just as it is, absolute in its provision of freedom to the press. But Mayer (1969, p. 53) pointed out that even the so-called "absolutists" with regard to the First Amendment are not "absolute absolutists." Judge Oliver W. Holmes, for example, believed that the First Amendment "while prohibiting legislation against free speech as such, cannot have been, and obviously was not, intended to give immunity to every form of language." For example, Justice Holmes said that nobody is free to cry fire in a crowded theatre, or to counsel murder, or to hand a small child a strychnine pill and tell him it is candy (Mayer, p. 53).

Most countries would go even further than Justice Holmes in limiting freedom. For instance, even in Britain, the First Amendment's unconditional prohibitions on government constraints of expression have no sympathetic acceptance in law and, as Kirtley pointed out (1997, p. 54), it is likewise throughout Europe. Article 10 of the European Court of Human Rights recognizes a right to freedom of expression, but such a right is subject to "necessary" restrictions to protect public morals, national security, and the rights and reputations of others. Also such "freedom" can be abridged to prevent crime, disorder, or disclosure of confidential information. For Europeans, free expression is just one fundamental right among many and laws can be passed to protect other rights—like privacy. Discussing and conversing, for European lawmakers, is not the same thing as inciting violence or invading privacy.

James Carey, to whom we referred earlier, has been prominent in providing the public journalists with one of their main rationales—the essentiality of public conversation. The main purpose of the First Amendment, he contended, is to stimulate this public conversation, making us a society of public conversationalists who talk with one another to resolve differences (Munson & Warren, 1997, p. 218). According to Carey, the press is grounded in the public; it exists to serve the public, is the guardian of the public interest, and protects the public's right to know. Although we may wonder where Carey gets these obligations of the press (especially the protection of the public's right to know), certainly we concur that the press is grounded in the public, as are all social institutions.

The public journalists of today, as we see in chapters 7 and 8, have as a main purpose Carey's stimulation of public conversation and the bringing of the public increasingly into the business of journalism. They would wholeheartedly endorse Carey's belief that "the press maintains and enhances the conversation of the culture, becomes one voice in that conversation, amplifies the conversation outward, and helps it along by bringing forward the information that the conversation itself demands" (Munson & Warren, 1997, p. 219).

Disorder and lack of public conversation, in the Enlightenment legacy of journalism, is what sells newspapers and glues people to their television sets. Crime, sex, racial tensions, religious fanatics, burning buildings, terrorists in action is what journalism thrives on. Disorder symbolizes crisis and social disintegration, which generates anxiety, social friction, and violence. And such journalistic emphases are protected by the First Amendment.

Even before the 20th century ended, there was considerable criticism of the First Amendment. University of North Carolina journalism professor Philip Meyer called the First Amendment "such a powerful and integral part of our basic law that [the journalist's invocation of it] is a little like invoking Holy Scripture to avoid taking out the garbage." Meyer contended (Cohen, 1992, p. 111) that the press has used it as a rationale for doing all sorts of unethical practices. For instance, journalists have invoked it to rationalize publishing names of rape victims, for not allowing persons who have been disparaged to reply in their columns, and for revealing "the circumstances of people which, if known, would make them potential victims of crime." Ben Bradlee, former editor of the *Washington Post,* thought (Flink, 1987, p. 45) the people have lost faith in the free press and "the Bill of Rights wouldn't pass, if they voted today."

In fact, in the summer of 1999, a survey by the First Amendment Center at Vanderbilt University found that a majority (53%) of the American public believes the press has too much freedom, an increase of 15% since 1997 ("Survey: First Amendment Taking a Beating," 1999). Paul McMasters, the center's ombudsman for the First Amendment, analyzing the survey, wrote, "Those who follow such things know that the First Amendment is under incredible assault on a daily basis, whether from adverse court decisions, proposed laws, scholarly studies or citizen initiatives." By notable majorities, he added, Americans said journalists should not be allowed to endorse or criticize political candidates, use hidden cameras for newsgathering, or publish government secrets.

James Carey, weighing in on the First Amendment and press freedom, (Summer 1999, p. 18), maintained that the First Amendment increasingly refers simply "to a property right, establishing ground rules for economic competition." He noted (p. 18) that a politically free press, as in the United States, does not follow from an economically free one, and he emphasized that "for democracy and social justice, press freedom must mean something more than freedom from government." Proponents of public journalism would say "amen" to that.

If in the 21st century public journalism wins a firm foothold, we can expect to see some kind of revamping of the First Amendment free-press clause. Laws will be needed to keep the press responsible. Individual media self-determination, spawned by the Enlightenment, had its chance. It failed, contend the communitarians.

TOWARD A PRESS UNDER LAW

The public journalists and communitarians see the press as needing more than independent journalistic desire to make the press relevant and helpful to the people. Why should the press not be checked by laws? Other social institutions are so controlled. We are a country of laws, and laws control almost all we do in a public way. The press, however, seems to be above and beyond usual expectations of other institutions, able to communicate any harmful, distasteful, untruthful, and scurrilous material it desires. If the press in America is too free, and the public seems to think it is, then is it unthinkable that the social anomie caused by the press be thwarted by a revamping of the First Amendment?

Here is the way the free press clause appears now in the First Amendment: "*Congress shall make no laws . . . abridging the freedom of the press. . . .*" For the sake of community, local and national, would it be best if Americans in the 21st century see to it that the First Amendment is revised to give some order and morality to the new communitarian epoch? We present a possible revision simply as an example of what might be done in a communitarian society. Undoubtedly many other versions would accomplish the same thing, providing a journalism *under law* that would give stability and harmony to the public sphere. Here is one suggestion: *Congress shall make laws regarding the press only when such laws are deemed necessary by the Congress and state legislatures to protect national security and community and civic morality, and to maintain a responsible and truthful flow of information of a socially helpful nature. The subjectivity inherent in the above sentence is self evident, but the determination of such necessity for press laws will be made by representatives of the people and not by businessmen or a politically appointed court.*

Perhaps we are not speaking for communitarians and public journalists when we propose such a First Amendment change, but it seems to us that, based on their basic feelings about press irresponsibility, we are in sync with their thinking. Communitarians mistrust press freedom, believing that it has caused untold damage to the social fabric and has de-emphasized democracy by placing too much power in an elite and arrogant press. A revised First Amendment such as we presented would eliminate press autonomy and shift power to the legislature (the people), thereby enlarging the scope of democracy.

As long as the present language is in the First Amendment, the press elite will do about whatever it desires, regardless of the social harm that might result. A journalism without laws is an unchained institution, free to lie, misinterpret, invade privacy, give away state secrets, cause social dissention and even violence. Of course, there are libel laws to provide some press accountability (after publication), but it is obvious that these have done little good in curbing press excesses. We must remember that a press restrained by no laws is a press free to be as socially irresponsible as it likes. It is hard to be a country "under law" if arguably the most powerful institution of all—the press—is not under the law.

3

Order Out of Chaos

People today are in a period of transition. The individual finds himself in the grip of forces . . . forces that drive him, irresistibly into ever more rigorous orbits of collective procedure. The traditional freedom of the individual, thus narrowed by the organized patterns of collectivized society, no longer sustains a sense of inward autonomy; as the wells of inward values are drained, the nuclear sense of the person as the source of free choice and values must likewise vanish.

—Roderick Seidenberg

The Renaissance or the Enlightenment person might be astounded to find the collectivist spirit, quite prominent in earlier ages, flourishing today, and it promises to get stronger as the 21st century progresses. From the localized cooperative communities of the 1800s to the Marxist-inspired "national" communities of the 1900s, the concept of social harmony and order has persisted in the minds (and in some cases, the actions) of social reformers. From the warrior chieftain of the ancient world to the religious authoritarianism of the Middle Ages to the royal absolutists and socialist plutocracies of the modern age, the spirit of social control and order has maintained a firm hold on social and political philosophy.

Seidenberg, whose words begin this chapter, highlighted this powerful trend in his important book, *Posthistoric Man* (1974), that explored the causes and ramifications of this steady drift toward order. The organizational trend of the masses of humanity toward solidarity and security, he said (p. 207), has shaken the world of the Enlightenment individualism, not as though by "a wind in the treetops, but at its roots by an earthquake!" Seidenberg (p. 113) saw this shifting social paradigm as an "emerging historical determinism," where the "dominance of the collective aspects of man is inherently assured and the gradual conversion of the individual into a frictionless member of the community" is just around the corner.

Robert Bellah, a conservative communitarian, and his associates, in their influential *Habits of the Heart* (1985, p. 25), also saw the coming of a complex society dominated by giant corporations where interdependence is essential in the people's "collective future." Such giant entities, formed and run by business interests, are not really what the communitarians want. Although the profit motive may well bring people together and prompt some coopera-tion, it does little to instill any kind of lasting sense of community where non-material considerations create common values, deep concern for one an-other, and a willingness to struggle together for the good of all. We saw in the last chapter that there is a growing tendency to be free of the kind of freedom that breeds anxiety and a sense of loneliness and to escape into a communal haven where there is order, companionship, and harmony.

What it seems communitarians do want is a kind of community modeled on the family. Instead of blood relationships, however, certain bonds would unite the members into a genuine community, rather than a mere group of persons living under the same roof. Such bonds would usually be derived from common aspirations, a shared philosophical worldview, or religious convictions. Such a community, like a family, would be united not by coer-cive power, but by mutual respect and love. Rules in such a community would resemble custom more than law and would be similar to manners adopted for harmonious relationships.

There is no chaos here. Such a community, as is true in a family (at least most of them), provides a safe, stable, orderly environment. For such order to arise in community, there must be full participation, cooperation, shared values, and a sense of loyalty to the group. This is, of course, the way it gen-erally works in the smallest community—the family.

The family as the ideal community is said to have originated with the Chi-nese sage Confucius (Kung Fu Tzu, or Great Master Kung) in the 5th cen-tury B.C. It is generally believed that Confucianism, largely articulated by his disciple Mencius (Meng Ke), fostered the community—first the family, then the village, then the province, then the country. Individualism and personal freedom were not considered important. Rather, a deep respect for author-ity and a spirit of cooperation were at the center of the Confucian doctrine. The concepts of *jen* and *yi* were basic Confucian principles, the first meaning benevolence, goodness, altruism, and humanity, and the latter signifying righteousness. *Jen* is more basic and for Confucius meant the totality of moral virtues; therefore, *yi* is actually found within *jen* (Lau, 1970, p. 12).

Born about a century after Confucius, Mencius explicated and elaborated on the sayings of his master. It was he and the other principal early Confu-cian, Hsun Tzu, who lived about half a century later than Mencius, who spread the teachings of Confucius throughout China. Their emphasis (Lau, p. 15) was on morality (moral thinking)—thinking about moral duties, pri-orities, and the purpose of a person in the universe. For Mencius, especially, intellectual thinking was an insignificant part of thinking. The main differ-ence in the teachings of Mencius and Hsun Tzu was that the former believed that human nature was good and the latter thought it was bad. Thus Hsun Tzu emphasized rules, believing that morality was an artificial way of behaving (Lau, pp. 20–21).

One other Chinese philosopher should be mentioned as one who contributed greatly to the idea of community and brotherly love. His name was Mo Ti, and he was known widely as Mo Tzu (Master Mo). He appears to have lived some time between the death of Confucius in 479 B.C. (?) and the birth of Mencius in 372 B.C. He studied under Confucian masters, but later in life he attacked some of the ideas of Confucius. He traveled among the feudal rulers of the time and tried to get them to live in peace and to accept his main doctrine of universal love — for Mo Ti, *the whole world was community*. Besides his doctrine of universal love, Mo Ti spoke out against fatalism, offensive warfare, and excessive expenditures. He advocated honoring the worthy (meritocracy), loyalty to one's superiors, and communal cooperation. In later life he criticized Confucianism for teaching fatalistic doctrines and for encouraging music and elaborate and expensive funeral rites (Lau, p. 6).

A good example of group-oriented society today, said Alasdair MacIntyre, can be found in Japan, where moral judgment and action are prompted by the established values of the family, the workplace, and other groups, rather than within the individual. Japanese, according to MacIntyre (1990), see the purpose of individual lives as serving institutional needs and objectives, and cooperating harmoniously in their communities (pp. 489–497).

This Japanese model is quite different from that of American society today. Instead, say the communitarians, in the United States the unfeeling, competitive, scientific attitude that has hung on since the Enlightenment has unleased a spirit of rebellion and contentiousness and individualistic atomism on the Western world. In other words, the 17th and 18th centuries with their spirit of the individualism and freedom brought a temporary halt to Seidenberg's collectivistic or communitarian determinism. The communitarians believe such an individualistic spirit is fading away, and the 21st century should see a revitalization of a sense of sentiment, empathy, and collective cooperation. Feeling and sentiment will replace rationalism and this will lead to greater order, for the communitarians would agree with Gellner (1996, p. 139) when he wrote that "reason leaves almost everything unsettled, and so only irrational pressures can give us a stable and habitable world."

ROMANTICISM AND EXISTENTIALISM: RISE OF SENTIMENT

Precursors of the communitarians were the Romanticists of the 19th century, who departed from the Enlightenment sense of science, certainty, and order, and instituted a renewed interest in sentiment and subjectivity. Hostile to the "cold" objectivity of the scientific method, they indulged in subjective fantasies and took refuge in the inner world of intense feeling. The true source of knowledge, they maintained, is feeling—intuition, passion, and faith. Rationality was downgraded, and the person was seen as an emotional being. Having contempt for the "static" world of the Enlightenment thinkers, a world of stable, ordered, enduring entities, the Romanticists saw everything as constantly changing. They saw the world, and society, as a wild, chaotic flux—something they felt the Enlightenment mind could not grasp. So, for a brief time Romanticism threatened to uproot rationalism and push society into an early form of existentialism, a freedom-loving philosophy that would grow out of it. In many ways, the Romantics were precursors of those known today as postmodernists, who also attack the Enlightenment rationalism and the concept of objectivity.

Peikoff (1982, p. 63) wrote of the Romanticists' view of objectivity:

> Objectivity, they said, like reason itself, is futile—and harmful. The would-be objective man, they said, is "detached," "bloodless," and the like, whereas man should instead be "warm," "committed," "vital." He should live and function under the guidance of a flow of "spontaneous" passion, uninhibited by facts, logic, or concern for external reality.

This concept, of course, is reflective of the later existentialists (Nietzsche, Kirkegaard, Sartre, Jaspers, et al.), whom we deal with later in this chapter. However, although it took issue with many tenets of Enlightenment thinking, Romanticism (as well as postmodernism later on) was not completely averse to the spirit of the Enlightenment. For instance, it idealized the individual and bemoaned "mass-thinking." Its main departure from the Enlightenment was its enthroning of subjectivity and its refusal to accept the idea of certainty or truth.

Romanticism, existentialism, postmodernism, and presently communitarianism have all contributed to the weakening of the Enlightenment emphasis on rational individualism. The social philosophical thinking has shifted from freedom to responsibility, from chaos to order. In journalism this shift is being manifest in "public" or "civic" journalism that deprecates editorial self-determination and attempts to place much decision making in the hands of the public or the community. The libertarian or Enlightenment-spawned media, prizing their own freedom to invade privacy and indulge in all kinds of antisocial activities, have largely brought this new call for basic journalistic change on themselves.

Laquer (1996, p. 232) predicted the coming of a new authoritarianism and a stepping away from freedom and gave some early signs of a neo-authoritarian society. These, he said, can be seen not only in many Third World countries, but also in developed countries in the West. Here are Laquer's main signs:

- The denunciation of corrupt and inefficient politicians.
- Threats of a breakdown of public order.
- Inflation, unemployment, and economic stagnation.
- A social *angst* and feeling of social disaster.

What most countries need, according to Laquer, is a strong authority that will be able to develop an ordered society and eliminate chaos. He pointed to the Middle Eastern and African countries (pp. 233–234) that have stagnated or declined as those where populations have grown rapidly, where tribalism has flourished, where centralized authority has weakened, and where great numbers are very poor and unemployed. This, he said, has generated frustration and hatred and could easily turn into a political system such as clerical fascism. He went on to say that, even in the West, order seems to have eroded, and there is threat of chaos. Some of the reasons for this: a weakness or absence of leadership, moral and cultural relativism, and the fragmentation of society. Laquer said there is a new questioning about the benefits of freedom and individualism and the concepts of the European Enlightenment. As a result of all this, maintained Laquer (p. 235), "the pendulum is swinging back in strange ways to the mood of an earlier age, with the emphasis on the good of the collective rather than on that of the individual, from permissiveness to discipline, order, and authority."

POSTMODERNISM: ALLY FOR CHANGE?

Postmodernism, since about the end of World War II, has been making inroads into almost every area of society, not completely replacing Enlightenment-based modernism but growing simultaneously with it. And this postmodernism has done nothing to restore order to society. It is a multifaceted skeptical philosophy, providing something for everybody but nothing absolute and universal for anybody. Although it takes issue with the rationalism of the 18th century Enlightenment, as did Romanticism of the previous century, it gives comfort to many libertarians as it promotes relativism and individualism. In many ways, postmodernism is the antithesis of the Enlightenment, but it cannot be counted on to subvert the individualistic and chaotic tendencies that the West inherited from the libertarian and rationalistic philosophy of the 17th and 18th centuries. The solution to contemporary chaotic journalism must go beyond postmodernism and reside finally in a more ordered, groupist, disciplined, and community-based philosophy.

Postmodernism negates formalism, absolutism, and certainty, and proposes little more than an experimental progressivism overlaid with a vague kind of transcendental mysticism. As Wilson wrote (1998, p. 38), the main difference between postmodern thinking and that of the Enlightenment is this: "Enlightenment thinkers believed we can know everything, and radical postmodernists believe we can know nothing."

Tending toward chaos or anarchy, postmodernists challenge modernist (traditional) philosophy and science. No objective truths exist outside one's mental activity, they say. As communications scholar Paul Grosswiler saw it (1998, pp. 158–159), whereas modernism prefers simplicity, uniformity, order, and rationality (still mired in Enlightenment philosophy), postmodernism breaks with the past to advocate a tradition of the new, valuing novelty and originality. As one postmodernist (Wilson, 1998, p. 53) saw it, no ethics can be firmly grounded except in the relativistic contexts of each society. What this means is that every society, culture, or community is as good as any other in its concept of truth and morality. By extension, one can say the same thing about every individual. Each is right in his or her special way.

Wrong wrote (1994, p. 242) that postmodernism "signals the loss of faith in redemptive secular social and political ideologies" and considers science and reason as "simply possible perspectives on the world among many others." Like other versions of Counter-Enlightenment philosophy, postmodernism considers possibilities open-ended and directions for social development pluralistic and basically equal in their worth. The postmodernist is a repudiator of most of the Western values of the 20th century and one who dips here and there in search of new insights, largely instinctual and even mystical. A searcher for new social formulations as well as for fresh ideas and philosophies, the postmodernist is suspicious of the Enlightenment-derived worldview. Reason and science, freedom and individualism—all have had their chance and have failed. Something different and better must be out there somewhere and the postmodernist is looking for it. Arguably, in the realm of journalism, postmodernism has spawned *public journalism* and a new emphasis on democratization and the use of public discourse to form and solidify communities.

It should be noted, however, that postmodernism has not wiped away modernism; it simply is coexisting with it at present. However, it has been rapidly piling change on top of change and providing us with a complex and confusing world, thereby unintentionally reinforcing many of the individualistic tenets of the Enlightenment that it criticizes. In other words, it is the impact of postmodernism on modernism that has nudged society in the direction of disorder and chaos, and it is to this disorder that the new communitarians and other neoauthoritarians are reacting in their desire to restore more order to society and reestablish communities. Postmodernists themselves cannot agree about the nature of postmodernism, its origins and history, but they do agree (Jameson, 1988, p. 92) that by and large "modern times are now over" and "that some fundamental divide . . . or qualitative leap now separates us decisively from what used to be the new world of the mid-twentieth century."

Don Corrigan, a professor of communication at Webster University outside St. Louis, believed (1999, p. xvii) that public or civic journalism is an outgrowth of "a certain academic mentality" that has been termed "post-modern." He sees postmodernism, like public journalism, as abandoning objectivity and neutralist empirical investigation, and believing that all truth is relative to the particular social context. Rather paradoxically, its rejection of scientism, objectivity, and rational solutions to all problems has made postmodernism a precursor of a new "sentiment morality." Yet, at the same time, somewhat in the mode of Romanticism, it seeks to restore what it envisions as a sense of order through a kind of spiritual or mystical harmony in society through a repudiation of Enlightenment rationalism.

This tendency toward sentiment, of course, was not really new in the 20th century. Freud recognized its power, as did Max Weber in Germany and Henri Bergson in France. It was a strong current, this rebellion against rationalism. Freud, although himself a rationalist, was certainly the most influential of such thinkers. He gave currency to ideas that could "be interpreted as meaning that human life, both individual and social, was unalterably beneath the sway of non-rational, and possibly irrational, impulses" (Bottomore, 1968, pp. 128–129).

So we can say that postmodernism, although joining forces with communitarianism and public journalism in repudiating many Enlightenment ideas such as objectivity, does not really provide an antidote for the ills of an irresponsible and individualistic modern journalism. In fact, if taken very far, many postmodernist ideas would simply add to the cacophony of activities that threatens the media's stability and even viability and would lead to further social chaos. For these ideas do represent a revival of an earlier Romanticism. In spite of this, wrote Wilson (1998, p. 59), "as today's celebrants of unrestrained Romanticism, the postmodernists enrich culture. . . . Their ideas are like sparks from fireworks explosions that travel away in all directions." Even though postmodernism "menaces rational thought," and is "jargon-prone and elusive," Wilson added, it provides a healthy skepticism needed for social criticism and change.

As a reaction to Enlightenment rationalism with its belief in evolutionary and scientific perfectibility of society, postmodernism reintroduces a kind of romantic and pluralistic concept that further fractionalizes society and splinters communities. It leads to a sense of personal identification with New Age mysticism and nonscientific or metaphysical sense of community largely based on sentiment, not reason. Postmodernism, difficult as it is to pin down neatly, is a small step toward order, but order conceived as a spiritual or aesthetic blueprint for community building and social integration. What many critics see, instead, is a movement that largely destroys social order and, under the guise of opposing the Enlightenment, actually contains many kernels of Enlightenment weaknesses within it, especially its celebration of pluralism, fragmentation of cultures, and individual self-interest.

Enlightenment thought spawned the idea of enlightened self-interest; the assumption was that individuals would behave in a socially responsible manner because it is in their best interest to do so. Postmodernists have repudiated such an idea, pointing to the many excesses and irresponsible activities of individuals who claim enlightened self-interest. Although in some ways postmodernism is compatible with the Enlightenment (such as placing importance of pluralistic thinking and action), it has largely repudiated the earlier rationalism that gave society at least some cohesion and predictability. Modern societies are splintered and chaotic, and as British political scientist Robert A. Dahl said (Nelson, 1955, p. 8), there is "no sense of national integration in the face of ethnic, religious or regional conflicts." Also, he noted (p. 10) that democratic stability is threatened if a society has "ingrown subcultures focused on religion, ethnic groupings, race, language, or ideology." Dahl predicted (p. 9) what is probably in store for countries in the 21st century:

> In a disorderly social climate, the green and shallow roots of democratic culture needed to sustain democratic political institutions may shrivel and die. New . . . ideologies, probably with a strongly populist and pseudodemocratic rhetoric, will surely arise. Persistent economic hardship accompanied by corruption and public disorder may even make the discredited alternative of military rule seem more appealing.

Communitarian Amitai Etzioni concurred with Dahl's emphasis on the lure of order, as he wrote (1996, p. 12), "Almost any form of social order may seem attractive to people engulfed by social anarchy whether it stems from violent crime, tribal warfare, gangs, or widespread moral disorientation." Etzioni would not, however, agree with Dahl that military rule need be in the offing, or that communitarianism would permit political institutions to "shrivel and die," but he would agree that societies naturally seek order.

So we can see that postmodernists, in spite of their reaction against modernism (based on Enlightenment thought), are not really allies of public or civic journalists. While postmodernists reject what has been termed (Best & Kellner, 1997, p. 255) "unifying, totalizing, and universal schemes in favor of new emphases on difference, plurality, fragmentation, and complexity," public journalists are insisting that we have just such unifying schemes. What public journalists and communitarians generally want is solidarity and a certainty that comes with community, whereas, Best and Kellner maintained (p. 256), postmodernists stress indeterminacy, uncertainty, and contingency. Critics of modern journalism find this openness and social contingency the source of many of the current weaknesses in the communication media, and they desire to give the press more structure with a moral foundation.

Leslie (2000), in a recent book on communication ethics in postmodern culture, substantially sums up the public journalists' concern with these words:

> Clearly, postmodern America confronts important challenges. Can we restore continuity and consistency to life? How do we go about applying clear moral standards to discrete events? Can we learn to accept personal responsibility for our actions, thereby reversing the trend toward victimhood? Is it possible to reduce the social and communication gaps that separate us as individuals and as members of groups? (p. 11)

TOWARD "RETRIBALIZATION"

Marshall McLuhan, the Canadian communications scholar, visualized society as proceeding (or some might say, retrogressing) into "tribes"—a kind of what might be termed *"premodernism."* This retribalization, for McLuhan, discussed in his popular *Understanding Media* (1965), was largely due to what he saw as the more primitive and uncivilized nature of the electronic media, but he was optimistic. An antiindividualistic process, that of reestablishing a community, would help to avert social anarchy largely brought about by the individualizing "hot" print media.

This new tribalization is closely related to communitarianism in that it negates the importance of the individual and stresses the dominance of the group, or the community, or the tribe. On the other hand, many scholars see McLuhan's works as an aspect of postmodernism, illustrating in itself a tendency to fly off in all directions with little rational order. As we see it, communitarianism, like McLuhanism, conceives of society as a collective largely held together by a kind of "cool" (more subjective and emotional) information cement, a place where the individual is valued not for his or her own worth, but for membership and contributions to the tribe or community. This does, indeed, resemble postmodernism.

For the postmodernist, there are many communities and the skeptic may reasonably ask, will not the disorderly specter of membership in antisocial communities raise its head? Community membership and loyalty can, of course, be negative and socially harmful, but it is seen by the communitarians as socially healthy; they see the true community as one built on a moral foundation. Clifford Christians, a leading communitarian and communication scholar, wrote (Christians, Ferre, & Fackler, 1993, p. 45) that the Enlightenment's elevation of the individual has devolved into "narcissism and special interests" and should be given up for a "politics of the common good." But again, the "common good" of one community may mean bad times for other communities. Perhaps, however, Christians is thinking about the community ultimately as a *world community* or as a localized *moral* community, and it may well be that socially evil communities will be marginalized by the overpowering impact of moral communities that surround them.

Whatever communitarians mean by *community,* one thing is certain: In community, the negative impact of the individual on society will be minimized by peer pressure; at least, the interest of the group will be maximized. This is definitely a step toward order, and an example of what Riesman (1959) called "other-directed" society.

Communitarians would probably say of postmodernism that its insistence on constant specialized and often esoteric dialogue will create a new elite that would act against the development of helpful and viable communities. German communications scholar Juergen Habermas (1991, p. 34) maintained that community building can occur only *if discourse is taken away from the elite* [italics added] or professional castes, the academics and artists, and returned to the public. This is exactly what the public journalists of today argue when they say that the community, not the media elites, should decide what news it needs or wants.

A MORE DEMOCRATIC AUTHORITY?

At first glance, this public emphasis seems a retreat from traditional authoritarianism and a step toward democratization of the communication process, but what it very well may mean is simply a substitution of the "authority"— the people replacing the press and/or government elite. This potential democratized authority is what we mean in this book by neoauthoritarianism. The traditional journalism of media elites that still dominates in our society, detached basically from the people, results in increased chaos and irresponsibility and serves as a deterrent to social or community cohesion and cooperation. In short, it is seen as a threat to order and a symptom of increasing social chaos.

This all has the reverberant sound of Wiener's concept of social entropy (1950), borrowed from the 2nd Law of Thermodynamics, where a system is seen as having the natural tendency to run down, to dissipate, to become more chaotic. Media systems everywhere tend to become increasingly disorganized, undisciplined, unruly, and unpredictable, therefore socially irresponsible. What is needed is a concerted effort to restore order to the systems, at least to slow down this tendency to fall apart and lose energy. Modernism, with its basic attachment to and support of the Enlightenment, has done little to stem the entropic tide, and postmodernism, while expressing a kind of metaphysical or spiritual reaction to Enlightenment rationalism, has contributed little if anything to combat this message entropy.

Vertical-authority societies, and that includes such so-called democracies as the United States, have failed to stop entropy and to restore order. Perhaps what is needed, say communitarians, is a horizontal people's authority (what we are calling neoauthoritarianism) in cooperating communities dedicated to replacing disorder with order. Communitarianism generally, and public journalism specifically, have been the most effective opponents of media and societal entropy thus far.

They, like the public journalists who follow them, have proposed the *order of community* to replace the disorder and chaos of Enlightenment individualism and freedom, and, as is seen in later chapters, public journalism has not just talked about what should be done, but has actually put remedial programs into practice in American journalism. The disorder of pluralistic elites in the press will, in the 21st century, be replaced by a more community-oriented, democratized neoauthoritarianism that will bring order to journalism and harmony to communities and societies.

Order in itself, however, is not necessarily good for a society or a community, but if this order is tempered with a spirit of cooperation and progress, it will bring about social stability. Common values and morality must be present. Otherwise the community would likely return to 20th century bickering, competition, and social unrest. The cooperating and constantly discoursing community of the future must be built on a solid normative moral base of mutual respect and agreement. Obviously such communities must be relatively small and largely homogeneous. Although some communitarians may talk of a global community largely built on discourse provided by technology, most feel that such community (this McLuhanesque "global village") is an unrealistic dream. Today, as was true throughout the 20th century, the guiding slogan of America was pragmatics and egoistic materialism; in the new century, this must be discarded and replaced with ethics and a sense of altruistic realism. Democracy is not enough—even if we had democracy.

At this point in any discussion of this topic, the Internet and its potential is usually brought up. Although the computer can have a great impact on interactive communication, the nagging problem of ethics will remain. The Internet can, however, aid in democratizing a community (or communities) of users and can, to some extent, help to overcome the problems of democracy associated with large geographical expanses. In fact, the Internet can, said Fishkin (1991, pp. 21–24), help to change the country from a republic to more of a democracy by permitting mass direct participation in political decisions. Fishkin suggested (p. 21) that in the future we might have what he called a *teledemocracy,* formed by a system that would enable people to vote from their homes by television or by the Internet. Such a possibility, he said, might not be available to everybody, but might be available to representative samples of the electorate.

COMMUNITY AS AUTHORITY:
A WORD OF CAUTION

Communitarians realize that as important as communities are, they can lead to problems—that they are not necessarily good quality communities. The concept of community connotes democratic operations, participation of people in governance. But like democracies, communities are neither good nor bad. Actually, they are what Kaplan (1997, p. 60) called "value neutral." He noted that both Hitler and Mussolini came to power through democracy, and he told (p. 56) of being in the Sudan in 1985 when the country's newly elected democracy led immediately to anarchy, resulting in the most brutal tyranny in the Sudan's postcolonial history. He hastened to point out that the lesson from such examples is not that dictatorship is good and democracy bad, but that successful countries simply cannot rely on democracy to make them successful and moral. Morality must come first and be infused deeply in the society. Adding to Kaplan's concern about American-type democracy being pushed for Third World countries, Parenti (1995, p. 72) in his *Against Empire* posed a rather blunt question: "Are our leaders trying to impose a Western style democracy on people who are not ready for it?"

Kaplan helped answer the question by giving the reality of Singapore and South Africa as examples that "shred our democratic certainties" (1997, p. 68). "Democratic South Africa," he said (1997, p. 69), has become one of the most violent places on earth that are not war zones (according to the security firm Kroll Associates), having "a murder rate six times that in the United States, five times that in Russia." In the country, there are ten private security guards for every policeman, according to Kaplan, and the currency has declined dramatically, educated people are fleeing, and the real unemployment rate is about 33%. This has all occurred since the end of apartheid and the establishment of a real "democracy."

Communitarians are aware of the potential problems with democracy and community. This is why they stress moral values and normativity based on ethical common denominators. When someone like Kaplan (1997, pp. 71–72) talks about the huge corporations being the important communities of the future, evolving into the new world political–economic entities, even replacing nation–states, communitarians know that he is referring to a different kind of community than they have in mind. Citizen participation, the sharing of traditions and values, the possibility of continuing dialogue, common ethics, and a sense of order and harmony: that is what communitarians think is community. The desire for community, for order, security, and stability is not one attached to modern ideological labels. Communitarians are really found across the political spectrum.

NAME GAME:
NEOLIBERALS AND NEOCONSERVATIVES

It seems, although it is not always admitted, that this spirit of postmodernism (desire to change, feel, and create) and communitarianism (desire to collectivize or tribalize), along with the rising subgenre of public journalism, is largely in tune with what is sometimes called *neoliberalism* (not to be confused with classical or Enlightenment liberalism). Such a neoliberal stance, enthroning allegiance to government or a central authority while appreciating grassroots opinion, is similar to the practices of European social democracies. In such systems, said Nerone (1995, p. 51), the state takes on more and more responsibility for the general welfare of its people, who are thought to be preyed on by corporate capitalism. The public interest, rather than private rights, is the basis for political decisions, say the neoliberals.

Neoconservatives are not to be left out of the "order paradigm." Unlike their more Enlightenment-inspired classical liberal cousins, the neoconservatives are not against a strong central authority. In fact, they welcome the state's help in establishing social order. They are basically "social conservatives," and, like the communitarians, want to see a restoration of social stability and harmony. One of their branches is "the religious right" or the Christian fundamentalists, one segment that many of them might not want to claim. However, this religious group, too, wants to purify society and establish communities of order. Or, in some cases, they want to inject secular society with their own social and moral concepts. At any rate, they would hope that the new communities would be built on religious foundations, would enthrone cooperation and brotherhood, and would at least slow down the process of entropy.

So we can see that communitarians are not only on the political left, but are found among conservatives also. A strong aversion to what appears to be a lack of authority is what brings the two groups together. Nisbet, a conservative, is a good example of a leading sociologist who sees the establishing of human communities as the salvation of society. His *The Quest for Community* (1990), one of this country's most important social critiques, explored how individualism and statism have flourished while the primary human communities—the family, the church, voluntary organizations, and the neighborhoods—have grown progressively weaker.

What postmodernism, communitarianism, neoliberalism, public journalism, and other splinters of anti-Enlightenment thinking have in common is this: *The just society results when the good of the community (or public, or state) is assured, even if it means that the good of individuals is suborned to the good of the whole.* What leads to a smooth-functioning and ordered society is good; what leads to a disordered, fractured, contentious society is bad.

NEOAUTHORITARIANISM

Although the term *authoritarianism* has a generally negative connotation, when it is coupled with "the people" or the "public," the sting of the term is dissipated. It then becomes a kind of democratic authoritarianism, where the authorities are the communities themselves or the national community itself. There is regular and rather constant "discourse" policy—determination by the communities themselves, almost in the nature of the old New England town meetings but more spontaneous and unstructured. Moral decisions also, said German communication theorist Juergen Habermas, would be made via social deliberation rather than by individuals themselves. Habermas' *discourse ethics* is based on the principle that a norm can be considered moral if everyone who will be affected by a decision agrees to it. This is somewhat similar to Kant's Categorical Imperative, wrote Reddin van Tuyll (1998, p. 14), except that the principle is established through community consensus rather than by an individual using his or her own rational discernment.

Moving away from institutionalized press freedom appears to be the direction in journalism for the 21st century. What is not so obvious is the kind of system that will evolve to take the place of the Enlightenment-oriented press that has marked American journalism history. One thing is, however, predictable: The American press will still be mainly immune to government control and sanctions. The First Amendment free-press clause will probably remain intact, although there will be movements to revise or eliminate it. Press freedom will drain from the system, but the reason will be largely internal, not external. The press, the institutionalized journalistic media itself, will voluntarily hand over much of its editorial autonomy to the people and will increasingly become an instrument of not the state but various factions in society.

Rupert Wilkinson (1972, pp. 173–176) offered us a useful differentiation between authoritarianism and neoauthoritarianism. The first (or traditional) authoritarianism is characterized by punitive aggressiveness, hostility, concern with strength, and is rigid, moralistic, defensive, and sees threat all around. On the other hand, neoauthoritarianism seeks maximum citizen participation in the establishment of order and social stability; it also pays some lip-service to individualism and supports voluntary cooperation and unforced loyalty in the leadership. Like the older authoritarianism, it supports some censorship of media material that harms group solidarity or endangers the society.

During the final years of the 20th century, as we have seen, this trend to order had already begun as communitarianism, with its emphasis on the press's role in reestablishing the community and enlarging the sphere of public discourse, had made its impact. The model had begun to change from the basic emphasis on the press's freedom to a growing concern with the press's responsibility to society. The whole spirit of postmodernism had, to some extent, played its part in loosening the bonds that held the American press to the principles of the Enlightenment. Public or civic journalism came on the scene with its opposition to individualism and other principles of the Enlightenment. It further fostered the idea that the public should participate more actively in the determination of media content. Increasingly, editors and news directors were turning over much of their decision-making to polls, surveys, and focus groups. So a community-oriented impact was being felt on the media, added to the already substantial power of advertisers, media consultants, and lawyers. The traditional editors and publishers and news managers were receding into the background of journalism, becoming little more than public functionaries for a new kind of "people's journalism."

Publishers and owners, of course, would not disappear, but they would increasingly be cogs in large corporate wheels, extending their ownership to megamarkets and international cartels. However, their status would be mainly managerial and profit-making for their shareholders, no longer really concerned with the older concept of editorial self-determination and journalistic autonomy. Give the people what they want. This would be the journalistic motto of the 21st century. The media, of course, would still have some freedom, but the shadows were lengthening, and twilight was at hand.

With the loss of institutionalized press freedom, a new kind of authoritarianism is ready to dominate in the new century. This is the authoritarianism of the people, who will have increasing power, obtained from a guilt-ridden press that has succumbed to constant criticism for its socially irresponsible activities. The days of media competition, contentiousness, and pluralism are coming to an end. Of course, as always is the case, the people generally will not be the true authority for press action. Rather it will be powerful, vocal, politically active segments or factions within society that will wield real power. These segments or factions will be closer to the people than has been the centralized government. One thing is clear: The press will increasingly bow to the wishes of social factions, and the pluralism that remains in American journalism will be the pluralism of factional desires dictated by the people, not the older pluralism of editorial desires dictated by journalistic elites.

Many critics think that this communitarian ideal is far from the case at present. Edward Said, for example, maintained (1981, p. 47) that the American press at present bows only to the policies of the government. Said stated it rather bluntly: "Leaving aside CIA use of journalists working abroad, the American media inevitably collect information on the outside world inside a framework dominated by government policy." He continued:

Every American reporter has to be aware that his or her country is a super-power with interests and ways of pursuing those interests that other countries do not have. Independence of the press is an admirable thing, whether in practice or in theory; but nearly every American journalist reports the world with a subliminal consciousness that his or her corporation is a participator in American power which, when it is threatened by foreign countries, makes press independence subordinate to what are often only implicit expressions of loyalty and patriotism, of simple national identification (p. 47).

THE WORLD TURNS TO ORDER

This new century of neoauthoritarian journalism will not only pervade American journalism, but will have its related systems throughout the world. In fact, the world's media scene is already largely authoritarian under the heavy hand of national leaders—secular and religious. But even these systems are under fire, not from freedom-loving citizens so much as from the increasing impact of market economies with promises of profits. Business-oriented journalism, as can already be seen in China and other authoritarian countries, left and right, is seeping into these societies and lessening their rigidity.

Increasingly, business factions of all kinds are putting more pressure on the authorities for a greater share of power. This means that the people and their desires will begin to make their way into the press systems of these countries, diversifying the content substantially. Added to this is the natural desire, especially in the Third World, to mold the tribalized societies into nation states, to give the societies some social cement, to have a time of peaceful development, and to foster the idea of community. This, of course, means that Enlightenment-type press freedom is anathema because it is fractious and contentious and generally harmful to nation-building. It is the collective—the country and the community—not the individual that must be supported and honored. Leaders in the Third World know this very well and are beginning to see that neoauthoritarian journalism, with its emphasis on the people's solidarity and welfare, is a natural transition from a vertical to a horizontal authoritarianism.

The majority of Third World countries at present simply do not want a Western model for their press systems. They do not worship the concept of freedom as do Westerners of the more economically advanced countries. They do not readily accept the assumptions of traditional first principles ingrained in the West. They do not think that government direction (even control) is necessarily bad. In fact, those considered more insightful among them realize that freedom is a danger to their society at their particular stage of development. In general, they trust the government more than they do individual media owners, seen generally as greedy elitists or government henchmen.

They see Western libertarian journalism as harmful to social stability and nation-building, and they see the Western journalism model as arrogant and based too solidly on economics or profit-making motivations. In short, they want the media to be more, not less, stringently controlled for the good of society. At the same time, people in the Third World do want their voices taken seriously by the media managers. They want order, not chaos. They want more of a monolithic utilitarian press, not a pluralistic and egocentric press. They believe that their leaders should see to it that the press serves the people, the communities, and the nation. They feel closer to their political leaders (a kind of tribal legacy) than they do to independent media owners; it is little wonder that they look to these leaders for direction.

Many of these Third World countries (and even some that are not typically Third World, such as Mexico, Argentina, Saudi Arabia, Iraq, and Iran) respect authority and really want a stabilizing, monolithic press. They feel that social order is more important than individual freedom and pluralism. They feel that libertarian journalism is irresponsible, biased, greedy, imperialistic, and harmful to community building. They are repelled by the chaotic inclination of most Western journalism, and they gravitate toward a press–society model or paradigm based on order. They surely do not see freedom as an unqualified good. If it were, then the ideal societal state would be nothing but an anarchical one—people living together without any coercion, laws, or norms whatsoever. Such a state would be literally one of lawlessness, and the Third World countries already have more lawlessness than they want. What they value more than freedom is order and security, and they do not see an American-style free press as helping in that respect.

Asia offers several examples of this new authoritarianism that is rising in the Third World. Building on a Confucian heritage of family and community, a new Asian authoritarianism will likely not be the harsh totalitarian police state, according to Fukuyama (1992, p. 243). Instead, the "tyranny would be one of deference, the willing obedience of people to higher authority and their conformity to a rigid set of social norms." Fukuyama (p. 241) noted that this kind of paternalistic authoritarianism (that is growing, for example, in Singapore) "is mild by the standards of the twentieth century" and is distinctive in two ways: It is accompanied by economic success, and it unapologetically sees itself not as a transitional arrangement, but "as a system superior to liberal democracy."

Countries like Singapore point to social abuses, press arrogance, and cultural indulgences in the West as evidence of a flawed individual rights policy that contrasts with the Confucian emphasis on family and community. The former prime minister of Singapore, Lee Kuan Yew, stressed order as a cultural sine qua non, and insisted that the American system with its free press would not work in East Asian countries. He foresaw an erosion of the moral underpinnings of society and the lessening of personal responsibility in the

West. He believed that Westerners, following the outdated precepts of the European Enlightenment, "have abandoned an ethical basis for society" (Zakaria, 1994, p. 109).

Australian professor of economics Eric Jones adds a cautionary note to this new Asian belief in neoauthoritarianism. He wrote that "the use of un-democratic means to achieve desirable ends may leave human beings richer in everything but freedom" (Henry, 1996, p. 15). In spite of such warnings, the trend against Western democratic values—including press freedom—appears to be spreading. Already, of course, people in only a third of the world's 187 nations enjoy a free press (in an American libertarian sense), according to a World Press Freedom Committee report (Oct. 2, 1998). According to the report, people in the freedomless two thirds of the world seem satisfied with their press situation. If anything, criticism of U.S.-style freedom is growing in the non-Western (as well as the Western) world. Both authoritarian and neoauthoritarian countries are veering further away from press freedom and are embracing some type of controlling or restricting sanctions on the press in order to make it more responsible. In late 1998, the report continued, Greece, for example, was considering a law that would subject journalists to as much as 2 years in jail for publishing or broadcasting "slanderous or insulting matter." The World Association of Press Councils at their 1998 Istanbul meeting decided to draft an international code of ethics for news media and to consider how a world press council might be created to enforce it.

Undoubtedly in the 21st century there will still be some older traditional authoritarian states, but they will be fewer and will be pressured by other nations to moderate into the neoauthoritarian mode. DiNunzio has written (1987, p. 156) that Hitler and Stalin of the 20th century were "aberrations of authoritarianism," manifesting absolutism without the moderating influ-ence of religion and tradition. Hopeful though he is that the world will resist the pull of authoritarianism in the face of a multitude of problems, he added these ominous words (p. 159) for the new century:

> As the century [20th] draws to a close the totalitarian challenge persists and the threat from a kind of corporate plutocracy stands as an additional danger to the survival of democracy as we know it. In the new century America and the world must decide nothing less than whether the noble experiment will survive as a legacy to future generations or as the memory of a failed dream. (p. 159)

DiNunzio termed authoritarianism the ever-present magnet in social his-tory. Writing about the "Search for Order" in his book (p. 6), he noted that actually for 4 centuries European governance has been authoritarian and elitist. Even during the Enlightenment, he says, what was really applauded was "enlightened despotism, not republican egalitarianism" and the most progressive thinkers of Europe "yearned for reasonable government, not democracy." Order, according to DiNunzio, was valued over freedom.

Many of America's social critics today are endorsing such neoauthoritarianism. For example, theologian Carl Henry (1996, p. 17) wrote that many Latin American spokesmen think democratic regimes too weak to achieve necessary structural changes; they see them as "simply postponing the day when more aggressive reform movements relying on authoritarian methods take over." It has been noted that Muslim fundamentalists in the Middle East champion absolute Islamic authority and strenuously oppose moderates who believe that the Koran and democracy can be reconciled. Henry pointed out (p. 16) that a vocal cadre of American Judeo–Christian religionists also view democracy as a kind of heretical option and believe that Mosaic law is what is universally and timelessly valid in order to obtain social order and harmony. These religionists consider democracy a lamentable defection from the biblical tradition, and would like to see all Jews and Christians following the Mosaic law.

Another Christian writer with an affinity to the ideas of the Mosaic law advocates is Thomas Molnar. He, like many others, was in favor of a kind of neoauthoritarianism, with the Church being the authority. He deplored democracy as largely a Protestant liberal innovation (Molnar, 1967, p. 171) and believed that the Church should withdraw and establish a culture on her own premises. In another place (1998, p. 103), Molnar wrote that the kind of democratic society America exemplifies "has no arbiter other than self-interest." What he was expressing is communitarianism, the community being the Church. This would resonate to some degree with the public journalists who are insisting that people give up their self-interests and dedicate themselves to the good of the community. What we have, said Molnar (p. 110) in our Enlightenment-oriented society is a social pluralism with little cohesion in which the resulting lack of consensus leads to discord and anarchy.

So we can see that voices, foreign and domestic, are growing louder in their skepticism toward American or Western concepts of individualistic democracy. The idea is taking hold that unbridled journalistic individualism and competition is leading to social irresponsibility and is no longer a viable model for an increasingly complex and dangerous world. A pluralistic and autonomous press, ruled by journalistic elites, appears to have had its day and is disappearing slowly into the approaching shadows of night. The new century will see journalism depart from its Enlightenment roots in the West and veer toward order, social integration and responsibility, and increased predictability. In the rest of the world, the maturing media systems will build public foundations of solidarity, communities that will permit individuals to further escape the traumatic effects of freedom so that they might live in the safe neoauthoritarian enclaves. The chaos of the Enlightenment-inspired press will be gone, and a new democratized journalistic order will have its chance on the world stage.

THE ORDER PARADIGM

The Order Paradigm, a model still in its infancy and as yet not readily accepted in economically advanced Western countries, is popular in less developed cultures where tribalism, community, family, and respect for authority have a long history. In such countries centralization of power is important, and some form of Machiavellianism is accepted—even expected—from the leadership (Merrill, 1998). There is a desire for homogeneity of the national culture, a carry-over from the microethnic or tribal cultures. One notes that Puritanism is implicit in the Order Paradigm, and one will find religious overtones in some of its manifestations. Cooperation is very important, and the true voice of the people is greatly honored; and although the leader may still be the leader, he or she is more intimately connected to the people than is true in a libertarian society. Harmony and socialization, a sense of comradeship, and regular community dialogue will undergird the new ordered societies. Undoubtedly there will still be some kind of hierarchical leadership, but it will be listening to, and following, the vox populi.

Kaplan chronicled well (Feb. 1994, pp. 44–76) the way Third World countries have become symbols of disorder and how scarcity, crime, overpopulation, tribalism, and disease are rapidly destroying the social fabric of most of the world. It is true that most of the countries (Kaplan stresses those in Africa) have had more than their share of traditional authoritarianism, and tyranny is almost synonymous with their societies. What is needed is order and discipline (and money, of course), but this order, as the communitarians or neoauthoritarians would say, needs to arise from stable, communicating communities. In the Third World, the communities (where they exist at all) are far from stable, but the call for order is being heard more frequently, and groups in the society are wielding greater influence on their governments.

Etzioni (1996, p. 12) pointed out the attractiveness of order for those countries having severe problems, and noted that "a good society requires an order that is aligned with the moral commitments of the members." He went on to say that almost "any form of social order may seem attractive to people engulfed by social anarchy whether it stems from violent crime, tribal warfare, gangs, or widespread moral disorientation." Alasdair MacIntyre, a moderate social conservative, viewed social order as the primary good. He sees the institutions of the Enlightenment crumbling. "The modern world," he wrote (1984, p. 68), "obsessed with liberty, has slain virtue, leaving us morally bereft, in a world of darkness." George F. Will, another social conservative who recognized the need for strong order (1995, p. 32), believed in the promotion of virtue as people need a strong government "that censors their desires, refusing to fulfill many of them."

It seems that authority is needed to establish order and control freedom. It should be stressed that the communitarian concept of order is not traditional tyranny. It is the authority of the community where a kind of equality (even if it is an equality of economic poverty) is reified. Authority and informed social direction and discipline are seen as necessary to social order; social responsibility is considered far more important than individualism and freedom. Those countries espousing the Order Paradigm are not looking for atomistic journalistic activities that may lead to social upheaval. Rather they are seeking social stability and harmony that really can come about with orderly and predictable media control. In short, such societies basically find freedom traumatic and psychologically and socially disruptive. So they naturally have a deep aversion to the Enlightenment permissiveness, which they characterize as leading to social disintegration and to cultural chaos. The reader will note that the world society has been moving or evolving since the Enlightenment of the 17th and 18th centuries, always in the direction of order, social control, and loss of press freedom. At least, that is our thesis in this book.

VOICES FOR THE COMMUNITY

Out of a long-time but recently explosive rebellion against libertarianism, relativity, and pluralism, a new paradigm of order is developing. The individual is increasingly looking for peer-confirmed status and is giving primary allegiance to the group. Nisbet, a leading modern sociologist, heralded this trend toward order and the community in *Quest for Community,* first published in 1953. He pointed out that fading quickly is the terminology of the Enlightenment and libertarianism—terms like *individualism, autonomy, competition.* These, he said (1990, p. 28), are being replaced by the influential vocabulary of the communitarians—*integration, membership, cooperation, norm, group,* and *solidarity,* concepts that promise more social order and harmony. Nisbet believed (p. 28) that individualism is being destroyed by what he calls the "rage for order, that is, the devouring search for the conditions of security and moral certainty." Individualism will not be tolerable in the future, wrote theologian Paul Tillich (1957, p. 246), as people attempt to escape "feelings of anxiety, uncertainty, loneliness, and meaninglessness."

Michel Foucault, the postmodernist guru from France, argued that Western civilization since the beginning of the 19th century has been moving toward a more ordered society. This does not particularly please Foucault, for he prizes privacy from state surveillance, but he sees individual autonomy and privacy disappearing (Revel, 1978, p. 215). Even Nobel Laureate

Friedrich A. Hayek, in contrast to his usual conservative (classical liberal) tone, proposed in his influential *Road to Serfdom* (1944, p. 220) that there is little hope for international order or lasting peace "so long as every country is free to employ whatever measures it thinks desirable to its own immediate interest, however damaging they may be to others." He added that it is true that the great majority of people are willing to accept views ready-made for them, and that they will be content if "born or coaxed into one set of beliefs or another, and that in any society freedom of thought is of significance only to a small minority." So we have been warned by voices on the right and on the left that individualism is dying and a new paradigm of community, public dialogue, and order is developing.

Can this trend toward community and social order be stopped or reversed? The communitarians and public journalists, of course, would hope not, and they will likely not be disappointed. As societies get to the stage where social friction is minimized and an ordered society allows the people increasing freedom from chaotic tendencies, they will be hard pressed to revert to the modernist individual atomism and irresponsible press actions that have increasingly defined our traumatic society.

It would seem that Communitarian Man will replace Individualized Man in the 21st century. Seidenberg's prophetic words (1974, p. 113) seem an appropriate way to end this chapter: "The dominance of the collective aspects of man is inherently assured; and with it the gradual conversion of the individual into a frictionless . . . member of the community. . . . The process is irreversible and implicit: history moves in only one direction— inert and unerring, she flows toward her goal."

4

The Communitarian Alternative

In an age of real or supposed disintegration, men will abandon all truths and values that do not contain the promise of communal belonging and secure moral status. Where there is widespread conviction that community has been lost, there will be a conscious quest for community in the form of association that seems to promise the greatest moral refuge.

—Robert Nisbet

Even the most egocentric individual, unless mentally incapacitated, has a desire to socialize and find comfort in group activities. This desire varies rather widely, but we may safely say that there is a natural tendency for people to seek community, to be a part of a group. The current concept of communitarianism, then, is nothing new. In ancient China, as we have seen, Confucius advocated it, as did his disciple, Mencius. The family, the group, and loyalty to leadership—this concept permeated Chinese society and still does. In classical Greece, Socrates and Plato promoted community, although in somewhat different ways. All through history, strong voices have spoken out in favor of some type of collectivistic society that would avoid the problems of individualism and social contention.

Although the term *communitarianism* is new, the concept behind it is not. The concept probably goes back to the days when prehistoric men and women congregated in caves for protection from the elements and wild animals. Tribal societies were communitarian, as were various experiments with communal or communistic societies. Altschull (1995, p. 195), pointed out, "Few movements have been more intensely dedicated to a communitarian ideal than early Christianity." Then, of course, came Marxism in the early 20th century, which was, according to Altschull (p. 197), the "most highly developed form of communitarianism yet to have been practiced." All forms of communitarianism have reflected a natural inclination of people to gather together, to belong, to have a common morality and lifestyle. Social order is what really defines a communitarian society. This is true with all types of communitarian societies—those that seek to gain order through vertical power elites with strong central leadership, and also those like the current communitarians who seek order by relying on normative means, wise leadership, consensus, education, peer pressure, moral role models, exhortation, and community opinion. Thus, as Amitai Etzioni, a professor of sociology at George Washington University, said (1996, p. 13), the "social order of good [communitarian] societies is a moral order," and not a politically established order.

It is clear that Etzioni and other modern democratic communitarians recognize that there can be "bad" communitarianism—those communities that use some type of force or autocratic coercion to establish public order. The establishment of social order, however, is a complex operation and often there is considerable difficulty in determining what methods are coercive and which ones are voluntary. Bringing about community opinion and consensus through peer pressure and education, for example, can slip rather easily into a sophisticated coercive mode hardly distinguishable from authoritarianism. This the communitarians recognize and are trying to prevent by stressing democracy, egalitarianism, and morality.

NEW MOVEMENT RISING

This communitarian movement has been rising with amazing speed. It began only in the mid-1990s, pioneered largely by Etzioni. Communitarians simply believe that Americans must realign the balance between the rights of individuals and the responsibilities members of a society have to one another. There is a kind of religious overtone to communitarianism. The Associated Press (Jan. 16, 1994) quoted from Etzioni's *The Spirit of Community:* "To take and not to give is an amoral, self-centered predisposition that ultimately no society can tolerate." Communitarians, who have been supported by William Jefferson Clinton and many others on both the left and the right, advocate sacrificing individual rights for the collective good. Since the late 1950s and through the 1960s, social institutions have been under attack—the family, church, unions, universities, and government. By the 1980s and into the 1990s, America was gorging itself on self-interest and greed. Etzioni wrote (Denton, 1994, p. 6) that "moral transitions often work this way: Destruction comes quickly. A vacuum prevails. Reconstruction is slow. This is where we are now. It is a time to reconstruct."

Through books, articles, lectures, teach-ins, and conferences, the communitarians are trying to spread their gospel of good news throughout the country—and abroad, also. The communitarian movement, narrowly considered, is still quite small. Even in America, where it has made its greatest inroads, it does not command broad support. Thus far it is simply an informal association of academics, journalists, and commentators, with some politicians thrown in (e.g., Al Gore and William Galton of the Clinton administration and British Prime Minister Tony Blair and his advisers). Its basic ideology has drifted over into journalism where it has taken root in the new public (or civic) journalism that, like communitarianism, seeks to reestablish community, encourage social cooperation, and downgrade individualism and freedom.

There are, of course, a whole complex of characteristics of communitarianism. Many of them are brought out in the brief profiles of several of its prominent writers presented later in this chapter. However, there are three main areas of communitarian concern—the establishment of community, combating classical liberalism generally, and depreciation of individualism and freedom specifically—that we take up in the next three sections.

RESTORATION OF COMMUNITY

Just what is communitarianism? Like any complex concept, it is many things to different people. The word itself sounds like a cross between communism and some kind of evangelical religious group and, on close inspection, one can detect elements of both. It is definitely, like early Marxism, a humanistic movement, one aimed at placing more power and responsibility in the hands of social groups or "communities." It is a movement of sentiment, as we pointed out in chapter 3, of feeling instead of reason, and of brotherhood and group loyalty. It is suspicious of elitism, of individualism, of an emphasis on rights. It is a strong advocate of responsibilities. The question for the communitarians is not what can I get, but what can I contribute?

Communitarians talk about "restoring" communities. This implies that western societies were once bound together in solidarity, that people lived in close and extended families, were good neighbors, and felt a sense of duty toward one another and to society at large, that there was social stability, less crime, more respect for authority, and a powerful sense of belonging. Of course, this assumption by the communitarians has been challenged. For example, an anonymous writer of a piece on communitarianism in *The Economist* of London pointed out that the past, as seen by communitarians, is mostly nostalgia—a "past that never was." The anonymous writer noted (Dec. 24, 1995, p. 33) that communitarians think Western societies are "not just falling apart, but are falling apart at an accelerating rate; that is why the communitarian mission is so urgent." Perhaps the best criticism of the communitarian movement is a book (1993) by Stephen Holmes, a professor of political science and law at the University of Chicago. A main contention of Holmes in *The Anatomy of Antiliberalism* is that the communitarian antiliberals miss their target; they attack liberalism for its antisocial nature, where in truth such classical liberals (e.g., Locke, Hume, and Kant) never denied that man was a social creature. At any rate, the debate goes on; but it is safe to say that the restoration of community is the major plank in the communitarian platform.

British philosopher Isaiah Berlin, although not a self-styled communitarian, did believe (1969, p. 100) that "participation in common cultural forms and membership of communities that are . . . autonomous in their own affairs, are vital elements in human flourishing for the vast majority of the species." If people do not have their identities reflected in communities or institutions in their societies, he wrote (p. 101), "they will lack an essential element of human dignity." It may well be that the older citizens are the main hope of the communitarians to revitalize communities. Slater wrote that the younger a person is, the less likely he or she is to have any instinctive communal responses, but he said (1976, p. 128) that older people "still retain some vestigial ability to care what happens to a group or community, and this is a valuable resource for those seeking a more communal society."

Communitarians do not stand for any single political ideal, but they affirm tradition, authority, and especially "community," usually equated with a particular social unit. They have contempt for the idea of social units focused on individual rights and not on group welfare. Some of them favor an intellectual or philosophical elite that was, for Chicago philosopher Leo Strauss, the absolute requirement for a good social order. This, of course, is reminiscent of Plato's philosopher-king. What communitarians want is a community (or communities) to provide moral discipline and public sensitivity as well as enhanced communication ("conversations") in the public realm.

In the field of journalism, communitarians want to take the emphasis off of press rights (i.e., journalistic freedom) and put it on press responsibilities. When freedom of the press, for instance, is enthroned by journalists, there is almost complete neglect of the listener and the reader. Where is the community consciousness when such freedom is thought of as a press instrument to create a world to its own liking? What is needed is community participation in the press, where power is spread to the public in order to break out of a situation where power is only invested in the press itself. Just how this will be done in practice is still being debated among communitarians, but a recipe for much greater public involvement in journalism is in the offing. The growing corporate nature of the press (with its citizen-owners) and the increasing representation of voices of constituent groups in the media point to growing public power.

In most mass media the editors, news directors, and other decision-making elites treat the journalists who work for them in the same way that the media treat their audiences—as people to be directed. Communitarians (public journalists in this case) think that this situation needs to end. More democracy is needed in the newsrooms just as more is needed in society. One writer, Paul Weaver (1994, p. 111), referred to the priority and preeminence of the editor as an "editocracy" where the media publishes "whatever the boss thinks or says the story is, period." In order to lessen the importance and power of the press, Weaver gave some suggestions. For example, Pulitzer prizes and other awards should be eliminated. Journalism education should provide more political theory, ethics, and theology. Journalists should identify themselves as citizens, not professionals. Newspapers should use the *Wall Street Journal* as a model, reformatting front pages and downplaying pictures. Also, news media should use much more restraint in covering misdeeds, reporting crimes and trials, and cease invading privacy. Weaver even proposed (pp. 200–206) that emergencies, crises, and scandals should not be covered—or such coverage should be limited to brief items and put in a special section.

Certainly such suggestions reflect basic complaints of communitarians. Of course, the press has always come under attack. Even Thomas Jefferson, considered a defender of a free press, called journalists a "pack of liars" (Altshull, 1995, p. 10) who should be thrown into prison. In 1803 Jefferson wrote that "nothing in a newspaper is to be believed" and that the person who never looks at a newspaper is better informed than the person who reads them. No doubt Jefferson was exaggerating in these statements, but the spirit of such criticism has persisted throughout American history.

AN ANTILIBERAL MOVEMENT

Most communitarians, especially the political scientists and philosophers (e.g., Michael Sandel, Alasdair MacIntyre, and Charles Taylor) are anxious to confront classical liberalism. They argue that liberal ideas are to blame for the low state of Western society. Liberalism, they say, is wrong. What the human spirit desires, they argue, is not autonomy and self-determination, but a secure, settled, comfortable place in the world. Communitarians see the enthroning of the individual and the subordinating of society by liberals as breaking the ties that bind society, making the real needs of mankind impossible to fulfill.

One of the very first to presage such communitarian thought (along with Rousseau) was Joseph de Maistre (1743–1821), a French thinker who poured scorn on Enlightenment liberalism. He, perhaps more than anyone else, set the stage for today's communitarian thinking. A person needs authority, religion, and community, the Frenchman declared. Individualism, he said (Holmes, 1993, p. 24), is a lie. Maistre (Holmes, p. 25) felt that the antiliberal (today's communitarian) would rescue the world that was heading toward chaos.

According to Maistre (Holmes, p. 27), the classical liberals were very naïve, thinking that people are self-disciplined enough to form a good society individually, without the cooperation of community. Liberals, he said, expect peace, but this is naïve for "there is nothing but violence in the universe." Without a doubt, Maistre was an early leader in the revolt against Enlightenment liberalism. Berlin stated (Holmes, p. 35) that Maistre's arsenal of weapons against liberalism was the most effective ever assembled.

Maistre's ideas can be seen in modern communitarians like Alasdair MacIntyre, who criticized liberals as having no concept of community and who see the world "as a platform where naked egoisms haggle and brawl" (Holmes, 1993, pp. 91–92). Classical liberals, said MacIntyre, have no conception of the common good, and their atomistic individualism is largely responsible for the loneliness and anxiety of modern man. MacIntyre hated anarchy and disorder; authority, he said, can give people the certitude that they need. The Enlightenment concepts, he believed (p. 94), spread darkness everywhere, and these early attempts to rid the world of superstition and hierarchy destroyed the foundation of human civilization. He admired the ancient Greek *polis* that he described as the perfect human community, one that got the best from each member.

Christopher Lasch, another modern communitarian, cites Maistre and MacIntyre as his intellectual authorities. He, too, thinks modern society has taken a wrong turn and has fallen into cultural and moral disorder. Lasch especially is critical of mass media, the entertainment culture, the collapse of the traditional family, sexual permissiveness, irreligion, the drug culture, and the shirking of responsibility. In this he is typical of most communitarians, largely those on the right (e.g., Allan Bloom and Leo Strauss). He, being a firm advocate of "honest labor," is also against welfare programs, seeing them as shameful Enlightenment ideals. This separates him from other communitarians who have no liking for manly work. Lasch's aim is not only to rehabilitate community, but to enthrone the work ethic.

One of today's leading critics of Enlightenment ideas is free-lance journalist Daniel Lazare of New York City, who wrote (1996, pp. 4–5) that "latter-day Americans have got to take up arms against the eighteenth-century *philosophes* who wrote The Federalist Papers and created the Constitution and have been post-humously lording it over the United States ever since." And if we don't expurgate Enlightenment liberalism, then what? Lazare said the alternative "is continuing breakdown and decay." In his opinion (p. 5), the Founders of America "created a deliberately unresponsive system in order to narrow the governmental options and force us to seek alternative routes. . . . But America cannot expect to survive much longer with a government that is inefficient and none too democratic by design."

Quite often the communitarians, unlike Lazare above, resort to esoteric language, tinged with a mystical aura, reminding one of postmodern or New

Age rhetoric. Such rhetoric, philosopher Richard Rorty, a trumpeter of post-modernism, wrote (1995, p. 87), "exalts the intellectuals over the politicians, the academy over the legislature, large ideas over small, practical reforms." He continued, "It's the kind of thing that Europeans influenced by Nietzsche, such as the German philosopher Martin Heidegger, have been producing in quantity for most of this [the 20th] century." Rorty, according to Guroian (1998, pp. 18–19), believes that the Age of Reason is over and we have entered the Age of Sentiments (stressing feeling, not discussion) and that this accounts for much of the New Age language. Not all communitarians write New Age rhetoric, however. Nisbet and Etzioni, to name two sociologists, have been able to stay out of the stylistic clouds and write with great force and precision.

Hillary Rodham Clinton, who admits she is influenced greatly by communitarianism, illustrates some of its vague language. In 1993 she spoke of "a sleeping sickness of the soul" and called for a new "politics of meaning," and in another speech the same year, she said, "We lack meaning in our individual lives and meaning collectively. We lack a sense that our lives are part of some greater effort, that we are connected to one another." But that is clear prose compared to much academic rhetoric about communitarianism.

Other than its often esoteric style of "sentiment" instead of rationalism, there are other ways that communitarianism is opposed to Enlightenment liberalism. Let us consider a few, drawing largely on Glenn Tinder (1993, pp. 116–121). Communitarianism, in its antiliberalism, is often pessimistic in its view of human nature and history, and attacks liberalism for "naïve illusions concerning human goodness and the power of reason." It emphasizes "the social nature of human beings and construes liberalism as 'atomistic' — that is, as tending to regard each individual as a separate, self-contained universe." Antiliberalism stresses the absoluteness of values, "and sometimes asserts the reality of that supreme value God, and accordingly brings liberalism under judgment for its supposed moral relativism and its secularism."

Another antiliberal proclivity of the communitarians is a suspicion of the emphasis placed on rationalism by the Enlightenment thinkers. Reflecting postmodernism and existentialism, which we dealt with in the last chapter, the communitarians emphasize sentiment—feeling, instincts, neighborly love. They have seen that reason has not worked very well in the last 2 centuries and believe that communities are better constructed by sentiment than by rationalism. Even classical liberals (conservatives) such as Russell Kirk and T. S. Eliot identified a shift in our civilization from the Age of Discussion (Reason) to the an Age of Sentiments. Kirk admitted that this Age of Discussion was not all that it was made out to be. "It began," he said, "with such hardy thinkers as Addison and Steele, Pope and Dryden, Hume and Adam Smith, and Edmund Burke." Agreeing with the communitarians, he contended (Guroian, 1998, pp. 18–19) that this liberal emphasis on certainty and truth, predictability and rational discourse, has all but faded away. Today the emphasis is on sentiment, not reason. Today is a day when "I *feel*," not when "I *think*." It is a day when we argue emotionally and sentimentally, not when we discuss calmly and rationally, and, said Kirk, this Age of Sentiments has been with us for some time.

Frank Hughes, the *Chicago Tribune* author of the most devastating critique of the Hutchins Commission report of 1947, believed that this antirational, anti-Enlightenment trend in American journalism was ushered in by Hutchins and his associates. In a book published 3 years after the Hutchins report came out, Hughes contended (1950, p. 161) that the Commission had written "a complete new philosophy which, upon close examination, will disclose itself to be simply a restatement of German authoritarian thought." Hughes maintained that the Commission "turned aside from the true path of the liberal tradition of Locke, Montesquieu, Franklin, Jefferson, and Madison," and set out on a course previously followed by Immanuel Kant, Fichte, and Hegel.

DEPRECIATION OF INDIVIDUALISM AND FREEDOM

The 18th-century Enlightenment traits most often criticized by communitarians and by their cousins, public or civic journalists, are individualism and freedom. It is not so much the basic concepts behind these terms as it is the quantity of each: too much individualism today, and too much freedom. Some communitarians (e.g., Etzioni) are careful not to attack these Enlightenment values head on; rather they condemn the way they are used and the degree to which they are used. However, there is little doubt that communitarians of all kinds are dubious of the value of both individualism and freedom because they see them as contributing to the fragmentation, unpredictability, instability, and as they might say, the anomie of society.

John Locke, perhaps the leading figure of the Enlightenment, is often seen as the main instigator of this harmful individualism. According to Fukuyama (1992, p. 160), the kind of individual bred by Lockean liberalism is a "human being narrowly consumed with his own immediate self-preservation and material well-being, interested in the community around him only to the extent that it fosters or is a means of achieving his private good." According to Locke, there was no need for a man to be "public-spirited, patriotic, or concerned for the welfare of those around him; rather, as Kant suggested, a liberal society could be made up of devils, provided they were rational."

It is rather strange that individualism, given its asocial nature and the growing complexity and unruliness of societies, has clung on tenaciously in modern America. "Nonetheless," as Anderson wrote (1990, p. 8), "this strange and mechanical form of thought is the source of some of our firmest political convictions" and "liberals do believe that the individual is the ultimate immanent source of value."

Communitarians are trying to break this individualistic grip on society, and since 1990 when Anderson's book was published, individualism has lost considerable potency. An individual of course can retain freedom even if he or she enters a group and obeys common norms accepted by the community. Such a person can do this because these norms are seen as "just and right." Frohnmeyer maintained (1995, p. 10) that this person "has relinquished not the least bit of his freedom, for the will he responds to is still his own." Frohnmeyer wrote that it is because the "laws he is called upon to obey are just that he obeys them, and obeys from his own free will, and not because he is compelled to obey from fear, and without consideration of their justice" (1995, p. 10). This is exactly what the communitarian wants to see come about: voluntary order—order based on free association and cooperation—with the end being justice and social harmony.

In the field of journalism, which actually reflects the shifting values of society, one can see the need for a reduction of individualism and freedom. What has long been highly valued in American journalism—individualism and freedom—is largely what has brought on the press the public outcry of irresponsibility. Communitarians and public journalists point out that press autonomy has contributed to the development of social anarchy. This is evident in the deterioration of the content of the press generally and especially in the content of television programs for children, the increased pornography and violence, the invasion of privacy, and the growing carelessness with the truth. Outside journalism itself, the trend toward social disorder is evident in many places such as parks, plazas, and sidewalks, places people increasingly avoid, especially after dark. Gangs, drugs, random killings, broken families, carjackings, the use of private funds given to politicians for legislative favors, and a whole host of harmful social activities proclaim a tendency toward anarchy and social breakdown. Just how much journalism has contributed to this social breakdown is uncertain, but there is widespread belief that it is considerable.

Theologian Carl F. H. Henry noted (1996, pp. 7–8) a whole series of indications that America is becoming increasingly chaotic and that there is a need for less freedom and more order. Some of these indications are:

- One birth out of three out of wedlock.
- One out of two marriages end in divorce.
- One in three pregnancies ended by abortion.
- Three and a half million unmarrieds living together.
- Half the children born in largest cities have no father.
- Violent crime has increased fivefold in a single generation.

- More than 30 million Americans are victims to crime each year.
- Inner-city streets have become combat zones.
- Privately hired security guards now outnumber policemen.

Charles Colson, in *Against the Night: Living in the New Dark Age* (1989, p. 8), bemoaned America's "civil breakdown," and like Henry, wondered if democracy can withstand the strain. Supporting Colson and Henry's view that American society is in trouble have been such books as Christopher Lasch's *The Revolt of the Elites and the Betrayal of Democracy* (Norton, 1995), Jean Bethke Elshtain's *Democracy on Trial* (Basic Books, 1995), Daniel Lazare's *The Frozen Republic: How the Constitution is Paralyzing Democracy* (Harcourt Brace, 1996), Michael J. Sandel's, *Democracy's Discontent: America in Search of a Public Philosophy* (Harvard University Press, 1996), Philip Slater's *The Pursuit of Loneliness: American Culture at the Breaking Point* (Beacon Press, 1976), Stephen Carter's *The Culture of Disbelief* (HarperCollins, 1993), and Robert Bork's *Slouching Towards Gomorrah* (HarperCollins, 1997). Robert Kaplan's long cover story ("The Coming Anarchy") in *The Atlantic Monthly* (Feb. 1994, pp. 44–76) bolsters the view of the communitarians that nations are breaking up and something must be done.

Political philosopher Charles Taylor described the American political scene as dismal (Elshtain, 1995, p. 24), largely because the society has become ever more fragmented. "A political society is one whose members find it harder and harder to identify with their political society as a community," he says. According to Taylor, this leads to the entrenchment of atomism and, as Elshtain pointed out (p. 24), American politics can be characterized in three words: stalemate, gridlock, cynicism.

But what can be done? A good start, say the communitarians, is to restrain —presumably through collective social pressure—individualism and freedom, and, of course, at the same time encourage cooperation and loyalty to the community. According to communitarians, the collectivity, not the individual, is what is important. This concept has to a large degree taken hold in America. The trend began after World War II and developed slowly (with a brief interlude in the 1960s) toward a more group-oriented society, but it was in the 1990s, in the midst of accelerating social chaos, that the pendulum began swinging away from disorder to order. A basic question, posed by Etzioni, is this: Will curtailing individualism and reestablishing virtues cause a significant diminution of autonomy? Etzioni (Daviss, 1997, p. 73) saw this as "the core issue for the near-term future of American society, as it is for other societies in similar circumstances."

The desirability of the sublimation of the individual is nothing new. Plato was the first thinker to formulate a systematic view of a social order with collectivism as its culmination. He postulated that the real unit of reality and moral standard is the community as a whole, with each person wiping out his individuality and merging into the community. For Plato, the individual is simply a cell of the community organism. Similar to the communitarians, Plato saw the good life as one of renunciation and selflessness, with the individual negating his own selfish desires in the name of union with the group. This was somewhat different from Aristotle's view of man and a good life: a need for a rational pride in self and one's moral character, combined with personal self-fulfillment (Elshtain, 1995, p. 105; Peikoff, 1982, p. 27).

Since Plato's time, of course, there have been many thinkers who propagated the ideas of communitarianism as opposed to individualism. For example, Rousseau called for the individual being sublimated to the society, and Hegel saw the group as having primacy over the individual. There have been many right-wing dictators who followed Nietzsche (wrongly, we think) and touted a strong group-centered, communitarian nation-state. Also there have been many others—socialists with Marxist and non-Marxist inclinations—who have urged the renunciation of individual (egoistic) autonomy and the enthroning of collectivistic (altruistic) societies and communities. Individual autonomy and freedom have always been seen as detrimental to the smooth-running, orderly, cooperative, and harmonious community.

Because communitarians see the community as prior to the individual, this suggests that the individual should sacrifice much self-interest to the group solidarity. Although many would see signs of authoritarianism here and the potential to develop vicious and power-hungry people, there is no need that this should follow. Friedrich Hayek, the patron saint of modern conservatives, asked (1944) why it is not possible that the same sort of system (as the one that spawned a Hitler), in order to achieve important ends, be run by decent people for the good of the whole community? Hayek warned that the person who becomes part of a community must constantly consider morality and not assume that group membership shields him or her from immoral acts. Quoting Niebuhr, Hayek concurred (1944, p. 142) that there is "an increasing tendency among modern men to imagine themselves ethical because they have delegated their vices to larger and larger groups." Even in a small community, Hayek warned, stability and harmony are not easy to sustain and should not be taken for granted. In such a community, he said, "common views on the relative importance of the main tasks, agreed standards of value, will exist on a great many subjects." However, he continued (p. 222), these agreements will become fewer and fewer "the wider we throw the net; and, as there is less community of views, the necessity to rely on force and coercion increases." Because communitarians see their communities built on a moral foundation and nourished by consensus-norms, they have faith that force and coercion will not be necessary.

The press has too much freedom, the communitarians contend. Journalists tend to view press freedom as their freedom, not the people's freedom. But communitarians and others are increasingly challenging the press's elite and arbitrary use of freedom. Let us look a moment at five propositions or assumptions (Enlightenment-derived) that cause communitarians problems:

1. Freedom is good for the media system and a people.
2. Freedom is necessary for national or cultural development.
3. Freedom is needed for the best news coverage.
4. Freedom is needed for the discovery of truth.
5. Freedom is necessary for informational pluralism.

Libertarian journalists since the Enlightenment (at least in Europe and North America) have accepted these five basic tenets; they have largely remained convinced of their validity without giving them much careful attention. In reaction to these five tenets, the communitarian might very well suggest that we could substitute *supervision* for *freedom* in each of the five assumptions and question their validity. It is most likely that the substitution would make little rational difference in the context of the sentences, except in emotional connotations connected with "freedom" and "supervision."

THE "RAGE FOR ORDER"

Nisbet (1990, p. 26) said that today individualism is being destroyed by "the rage for order" and that is "the product of the devouring search for the conditions of security and moral certainty." People, he said, agreeing with Erich Fromm, want to "escape from freedom" and to "huddle into a safe, warm crowd." As to the plight of individualism, Nisbet added:

> I cannot help thinking that the concern for community, its values, properties, and means of access, is the major intellectual fact of the present age. Whatever evidence remains of the individualist conscience and the rationalist faith, it is hard to miss the fact that individualism and secularism are on the defensive. New imperatives are the order of the day. And these are not confined to the ranks of intellectuals.

Freedom, too, must be restrained, say the communitarians, for in a way it is part and parcel of individualism. Americans inherited their love of freedom from the Enlightenment philosophers and from a few in the 19th century, such as John Stuart Mill whose *On Liberty* is a classic work for libertarians, and until well into the 20th century, the concepts of libertarianism held forth in America. Today its great value is questioned. For example, Mensch wrote (Nisbet, 1990, p. 37) that societies need strict standards, and quotes Ortega y Gasset as saying that "barbarism is the absence of standards." Freedom, she said (p. 46), can cause social instability, and a structured society gives one "freedom from freedom." The appeal of authority is that it represents "an escape" from the responsibilities and trauma inherent in freedom.

Bellamy, in trying to establish a collectivist utopia in late 19th-century America, believed that it would be necessary to eradicate selfishness, a part of individualism, because it would destroy society. The individual, he thought (Lipow, 1982, p. 94), "must be welded into a bureaucratic machine that eliminated all possibility of conflict." What Bellamy (1967, p. 94) extolled was "planning in the place of anarchy, efficiency in the place of competitive selfishness, and suppression of conflict between the individual or group and society, in place of class and political conflict." Bellamy was expressing essentially the belief of all communitarians, past and present, that utopias are built on "solidarity" (a favorite word of public journalists) and there must be movement away from individualistic society toward a more ordered and organized society. To do this, the concept of freedom must be subordinated to authority.

Although John Stuart Mill handed down a legacy of freedom that today's communitarians oppose, his ideas were rejected even in his own day. His contemporary, James Fitzjames Stephen, whose *Liberty, Equality, Fraternity* is perhaps the best criticism of Mill's *On Liberty*, wrote (1993, pp. 11–12) that "the condition of human life is such that we must of necessity be restrained and compelled by circumstances in nearly every action of our lives. Why then, is liberty, defined as Mr. Mill defines it, to be regarded as so precious?"

Freedom, according to Stephen, is not just good; it can be either good or bad, depending on how it is used. He wrote further (p. 169) on the need for restraint of liberty: "[Mill] thinks otherwise than I of men and of human life in general. He appears to believe that if men are all freed from restraints and put, as far as possible, on an equal footing, they will naturally treat each other as brothers, and work together harmoniously for their common good. I believe that many men are bad, a vast majority of men indifferent . . . and that even good men may be and often are compelled to treat each other as enemies either by the existence of conflicting interests which bring them into collision, or by their different ways of conceiving goodness." Stephen, in stressing community and degrading individualism and freedom, stated (p. 86) that the metaphor that we are all members of a single body "is little more than the expression of a fact." He added, "A man would no more be a man if he was alone in the world than a hand would be a hand without the rest of the body."

One writer on journalism and public opinion, Benjamin Ginsberg, observed (1986, pp. 230–231) the shift away from freedom and individualism. He wrote that "at one time westerners were concerned with freedom and fearful of the state. But in the latter half of the twentieth century they have become so enamored of government that they have, for the most part, ceased even to perceive freedom and government as antipodes." He believes that people are increasingly acquiescing in their own control. "More and more the process of control," he wrote (p. 232), "is of the sort that Alexis de

Tocqueville foresaw two centuries ago—interludes in which citizens proudly and cheerfully wave their own chains."

Today's communitarians may not feel that people are so gladly giving up their own freedom as Ginsberg suggested, but they do believe that much personal freedom must be forfeited for the sake of a healthy community, and they believe that there must be a greater degree of authority, of order, and of cooperation if social stability is to prosper and any kind of meaningful social democracy is to survive. As we said earlier, not all communitarians speak with one voice, but there are definite commonalities in their messages.

In fact, we could probably include Karl Marx in our pantheon of communitarians, for as Altschull (1995, p. 195) wrote, "Communism is communitarian—a world without classes, each person contributing to the community to the best of his or her ability." However, later (p. 201), Altschull declared that Marxism does not equal communitarianism, but that "when blended with Leninism and institutionalized (as it was) in the Soviet Union," it has become the "most highly developed form of communitarianism yet to have been practiced." "Like all communitarians," Altschull wrote (p. 202), "Marx had contempt for the idea of a society focused on the rights of individuals and not the welfare of society." Of course, Marx saw the press as a collectivized social instrument for social cooperation and community building that must "recognize its own true nature; its goal must be no longer to interpret, to present an objective view of 'both sides,' but to work instead for change" (p. 206).

The "rage for order" that Nisbet mentioned includes the necessity for central planning within the communities, if they are political and not simply ideational. A German scholar much loved by many communitarians is Professor Hans Jonas. His emphasis is on individual responsibility in a communal setting, seeing a global plight that necessitates a new emphasis on planning, discipline, and order. In *The Imperative of Responsibility*, published in 1984 before the collapse of Soviet communism, Jonas noted (pp. 142–143) that Marxism was probably "the best chance for dominating nature and reshaping society." Central planning, he maintained (p. 175), could avoid much of the present waste and eccentric development. Although it is doubtful if communitarians would generally want communities as autocratic as Jonas seems to prefer, they obviously find solace in some of his suggestions. For example, he said that a threatening future demands order, that what is needed in society is "empathic moralism," that we must live "for the whole" not just for ourselves, that stability is better than instability, and security is better than insecurity.

In the remainder of this chapter, we present a few of the leading communitarians and summarize some of their main ideas. The reader will easily see that their main concepts are parallel to the views of public or civic journalism, a movement, that among other things, seeks to reconnect journalists to the communities they cover by giving ordinary citizens a voice in the news-gathering process. Public journalism is dealt with at length later in the book.

JOHN DEWEY: A FORERUNNER

In this community-based theory of society, one can see the clear hand of John Dewey, one who set the stage for the modern communitarians. He gave great emphasis to the "community" and popularized the idea of persons working together, harmonizing to accomplish practical things. What Dewey seemed to mean by *democracy*, Renita Coleman wrote in the *Journal of Communication Inquiry*, is quite different from Lincoln's definition (government of the people, by the people, and for the people); what Dewey saw as democracy "is the idea of community life itself" (1997, p. 61). Individual identity, said Dewey, is determined by group membership, and individuals are incomplete without a community, and they must pay their public debt by advancing the common good. According to Dewey (Peikoff, 1982, p. 127), there is no such thing as an autonomous individual, and a person's intelligence is conditioned by the collective thinking of others. The mind, Dewey insisted, is not a "private" phenomenon but a public one.

What America needs, according to Dewey, is less individualism, not more. He urged an "organized action in behalf of the social interest" and certainly he would agree with today's communitarians that journalism, for example, should be guided by the collective or social will, and that individual journalists must submerge their personal desires and act so as to benefit the group or community. Dewey (1963, pp. 65–67) did not reject individualism; rather he redefined it as a "new individualism" that places the person in a social context that harmonizes it with social action, prompted by the "social spirit."

The Enlightenment was wrong, according to Dewey. Men such as Locke and the Founding Fathers were wrong in their "doctrine of natural rights inherent in individuals independent of social organization." Today, said Dewey (pp. 4–5), we must "abandon the Enlightenment's peculiar idea of personal liberty; atomistic individualism, laissez-faire capitalism, the concern with private profit . . . all of it now must be discarded." Dewey would certainly have a different kind of press system, one related to a more involved citizenry through a more active and politically relevant press. There is little doubt that he would support today's public journalism and communitarianism in general. Such a people's journalism we are calling *neoauthoritarianism* (or public authoritarianism), where the authority is shifted to the people rather than remaining in the hands of profit-motivated elite journalists. Evidently the way these elite journalists would give up authority to the people would not be by force or law, but by voluntarily giving the public a greater voice in editorial decisions.

As for his affinity for Romanticism, Dewey saw his philosophy (Pragmatism) as accepting "fully the voluntarist irrationalism of the nineteenth-century romanticists" that openly dismissed reason in favor of feelings. But, as Peikoff noted (1982, p. 129), pragmatism goes one step further: it urges the same dismissal and calls it "a new view of reason." Certainly Dewey was a precursor of postmodernism in that he said that there were no absolutes, "no facts, no fixed laws of logic, no certainly, no objectivity" (Peikoff, 1982, p. 127). His voice contributed greatly to the 20th century's slow discarding of the basic ideas of the Enlightenment. His influence was great and widespread; his thinking even had an impact on many conservatives and neoconservatives, especially in respect to a repudiation of individualism and the importance of the community or the social network.

Communitarian themes are prominent in the writings of John Dewey during the first 2 decades of the 20th century. This, of course, was before the term *communitarian* was in vogue. Etzioni (1996, p. 19), probably the foremost communitarian today, paid tribute to Dewey, who, he said, dealt with many matters "in terms that today would be considered communitarian." Dewey early recognized what modern communitarians are now stressing: that there is a need to curtail excessive individualism and to encourage social cooperation. This, of course, often means restricting individual freedom, and it is this that bothers many journalists. Such an emphasis is seen by many as a foot in the door of authoritarianism, and indeed it may well be. As we have said, however, this new authority is spread horizontally among the people, not consolidated in a single authority.

ROBERT NISBET: CAUTIOUS ADVOCATE

In his classic book *The Quest for Community* [1990, p. xxii), Robert Nisbet noted that the present fascination with community is nothing new; it is timeless and universal and reflects a basic desire of people everywhere to have a sense of belonging, of participation and cooperation. For several hundred years prior to the 20th century, as we have seen, individualism had its brief moment on the world's stage, but by about 1950, it was clear that community—at least a *national* community—was very much a public desire. Nisbet, although extolling the human need for community, was careful to warn against the incipient totalitarianism that might come about from such a strong, centralized community. In short, he was not advocating nationalistic communities but rather "new forms" relevant to contemporary life—what he called "a new *laissez faire*, one within which groups, associations , and specialized communities would prosper and which would be . . . by their very vitality, effective barriers to further spread of unitary, centralized, political power."

So it should be noted that although Nisbet is usually mentioned as the modern father of communitarianism (even if he never used the term *communitarian*), his brand of communitarianism was definitely not statist or political; rather it emphasized church, family, neighborhood, professional, and other interest groups that would give individuals a sense of escaping the freedom of Enlightenment individualism and a respite from a feeling of isolation and anxiety. Nisbet believed deeply that the yearning for community is best fulfilled through a return of authority to intermediate associations— with emphasis on *the people,* individuals acting collectively, being the real authority.

Nisbet envisioned (p. 250) a State that seeks, without eliminating legitimate sovereignty stemming from the will of the people, "to maintain a pluralism of functions and loyalties in the lives of its people." It is a State that diversifies and decentralizes its administrative operations and relates them to the various spontaneous associations that rise to fill human needs. In short, he wanted a community-facilitating State. Finally, he maintained (p. 251) that "the claims of freedom and cultural autonomy will never have recognition until the great majority of individuals in society have a sense of cultural membership in the significant and meaningful relationships of kinship, religion, occupation, profession, and locality."

AMITAI ETZIONI:
RESPONSIVE COMMUNITARIANISM

A professor at George Washington University in the nation's capital and the author of more than a dozen books on social policy and ethics, Amitai Etzioni is the founding president of the Communitarian Network and the editor of the journal *The Responsive Community.* His influence has done much to move the public debate away from a preoccupation with rights over to at least equal consideration of responsibilities. Perhaps his most influential book is *The New Golden Rule* (1996) in which he urged his readers to respect and defend society's moral order as they would have society respect our freedom to live a full life. Certainly Etzioni can be called a moderate communitarian.

He preached a powerful sermon (1993, pp. 1–2): that law and order can be restored if we grant public authorities new powers, that the family can be saved, that schools can morally educate children without indoctrination, that people can live in communities without being hostile to one another, that people should accept more responsibility for their actions, and that public interest can reign in America.

More than other communitarians, Etzioni is a missionary for his new system. In one book, he actually called for membership (1993, p. 19), encouraging readers to "join the movement." A typical appeal is this: "Please do not just read this book. Please try to respond. We in the Communitarian movement are keen to hear from you, and we hope you will tell others about the Communitarian framework."

Etzioni, like other communitarians, is not sympathetic to liberals, either those of the Enlightenment or those of today. He said (1996, p. 94), "The fact that classical liberals, contemporary classical liberals, libertarians, and laissez-faire conservatives all make individuals their starting point is not accidental; in their paradigms, the individual carries the ultimate moral value." He, like all Counter-Enlightenment writers, thinks there is too much freedom in society. He says, for example, that in the West there is a general belief that more freedom is better than less. This notion, for Etzioni (1996, p. xv), ignores a principal sociological truth: "[M]ovement from a high level of social restriction to a greater measure of choice, and hence enhancement of individual liberties, at some point becomes onerous for the actors involved and undermines the social order upon which liberties are ultimately based." He believes that people hate an ethical vacuum, "one in which all choices have the same standing and are equally legitimate. . . . in short, the quest for ever greater liberty does not make for a good society."

Insisting that communitarianism must be "responsive" to individuals, Etzioni's brand of antiindividualism is as extreme as some others. He was concerned, as he pioneered the new orientation in 1990, that it would be confused with previous conservative or collectivistic communitarianism. His position (p. 5) relates to the balance between individual rights and social responsibilities, individuality and community, and autonomy and social order, but it is quite obvious that he tends toward social responsibility, community, and social order, seemingly sensing that moderate middle-of-the-roadism is not considered productive or progressive.

Moral order is what Etzioni stresses for the society and the community. It is, of course, distinct from other kinds of order in that it is self-imposed from inside the communities themselves, not by the leadership but by the people. It depends on shared values to which most members of the community are committed. Like all communitarians, Etzioni believed (pp. 93–94) that the community is antecedent to the individual. Such communities should, for Etzioni, have a strong "moral voice." Listen to him writing about this moral voice:

> The moral voice is the main way that individuals and groups in a good society encourage one another to adhere to behavior that reflects shared values and to avoid behavior that offends or violates them. . . . [I]t is informal, subtle, and highly incorporated into daily life. It often works through frowns, gentle snide comments (and some that are not so gentle), praise, censure, and approbation. (p. 124)

Critics of communitarianism often say that communities cannot be defined. Etzioni, in response, gave his definition: Community is defined (p. 127) by two characteristics: (a) "a web of affect-laden relationships among a group of individuals, relationships that reinforce one another," and (b) a "measure of commitment to a set of shared values, norms, and meanings, and a shared history and identity—in short, to a particular culture." The critics (and even some communitarians like Sandel) would still be unwilling to accept this definition, pointing out that antisocial "communities" (e.g., the Ku Klux Klan, Islamic terrorist organizations, et al.) manifest these characteristics. Presumably Etzioni's concept of a "moral voice" would diffuse such objections.

In short, Etzioni has made a notable contribution by stressing the need to regain personal "inner balance and normative course." He asked (p. xvi): Is not it time for the West, especially the United States, "to stress the shoring up of shared values and to set some new limits on autonomy?" He is not really presenting an extreme revolutionary idea, just an emphasis on responsive communitarianism (responsive to the individual), or what social conservatives might call responsive individualism (responsive to the community.)

ROBERT BELLAH: COMMUNITIES OF MEMORY

What Bellah wants is for Americans to reconnect to each other through *communities of memory,* where concern for one another rests on common sentiments emerging from common memories of shared events, troubles, and joys. For him, communities are cohesive groups pursuing common goals, preferably social democracy. In *The Good Society,* Bellah saw a participation in politics at the heart of the community and, unlike some other communitarians, did not place the family there. In fact, he believed (Frohnen, 1997, p. 21) that the traditional family structure with its concern for property rights is the wellspring of individualism.

Frohnen wrote (p. 23) that today we have no "good tradition to look to in combating the corruptions of individualism"; therefore instead of community, Americans seek individual satisfaction. What we need to do is to reestablish communities, believed Bellah, so as not to forget the past. These communities, he said, should be involved in retelling their stories, their narratives, in order to offer "examples of the men and women who have exemplified the meaning of the community." And, according to Bellah (p. 26), any community "short of the universal community is not the beloved community," and what is required is "turning away from preoccupation with the self and toward some larger identity."

In all his works, Bellah has seen religion's proper role as bringing about "sweeping cultural and institutional transformation," which only can result in community and spiritual fulfillment. Every religion, according to Bellah —from Zen Buddhism to New Ageism—shares hostility to America's economic individualism and seeks to create a sharing, brotherly community. For Bellah, wrote Frohnen (p. 26), democratic involvement in the group becomes the highest good because it makes one an active participant in communal creation. Without a doubt, Bellah is a social egalitarian, believing that political reform that redistributes the wealth more equitably is what is needed for America today. He tends to see religion mainly as civil religion that would support this reform, and believes, as did Rousseau and Marx, that the misery of the people is the result of political institutions supporting capitalistic economic structures. His hope is that this misery and anxiety can be eliminated by political reform that can bring about economic justice. Reminiscent of Rousseau and John Dewey, he sees the real genesis of this reform as resting with politically active communities.

Bellah's best known book is undoubtedly *Habits of the Heart,* written with four co-authors and published in 1986. The main feature of the world envisioned by Bellah et al. is one where a Rousseau-styled community of communities exists, participating actively in politics and having a deep fear of individualism, egoism, and economic inequality. Perhaps more than most other communitarians, Bellah blames economic inequality for America's problems. Poverty, for example, lowers self-esteem, causes individuals to reduce "social capital" by withdrawing from public life, blocks political participation, damages family life, and weakens the development of moral character.

For Bellah, religion—the church—is perhaps the most important community of memory, with the possible exception of the family. Such communities would also include a variety of cultural associations, schools, and universities. Through them, tradition and values are nourished and passed on. The communities of memory, about which Bellah is concerned (1986, p. 282), "in a variety of ways . . . give a qualitative meaning to the living of life, to time, and space, to persons and groups."

CLIFFORD CHRISTIANS: NORMATIVE SOLIDARITY

Of the four contemporary communitarians specifically dealt with here, Christians is the only journalism/mass communications scholar among them. His voice is powerful in the area of academic journalism. He is trained in theology and philosophy, and as director of the Institute of Communications Research and head of the doctoral program in communications at the University of Illinois–Urbana, he has written and lectured widely in the United States and abroad.

Christians believes that people have what he calls "inescapable claims on one another and these cannot be renounced except at the cost of their humanity." He and his co-authors of *Good News* [1993, p. 14) contended that such mutual claims must lead to universal solidarity that "is the normative core of the social and moral order." What contemporary media systems do (or should do), according to Christians, is to "engender a like-minded world view among a public still inclined toward individual autonomy." The communitarian press should devote itself to a "civic transformation" that will revitalize and liberate citizens, helping to engender in them what Christians calls "communal norms." These agreed-on norms will give the community cohesion and a sense of togetherness. This is what is meant, said Christians (p. 14) by having "normative solidarity."

What is lacking in the press, averred Christians, is any kind of accountability and a sense of responsibility to the community. He speaks of the "mutuality principle," which he believes revolutionizes the workplace. The concept of mutuality "insists that authority and decision making be allocated equitably," according to Christians. This would mean, Christians said (p. 15), that news media would be operated quite differently, with power disseminated horizontally throughout the operation, not coming from the top down, and, of course, this mutuality would extend beyond the press itself into the public, with the people having more input into what the press communicates.

Christians (p. 16) insisted that he would not want to do away with a pluralism of world views, but "to ensure that they contribute constructively to the master norm of universal solidarity." What he proposed are "responsible selves"—a community of persons accountable to one another. Such responsible selves must have guiding norms against which to test their responsibility, and Christians and other communitarians insist that there are such universal norms. For example, Christians (p. 56), drawing on communication ethicist Deni Elliott, pointed out that (a) news reports should be accurate, balanced, relevant, and complete; (b) reporting should avoid harm, and (c) reports should provide information the audience members need to know.

Furthermore, Christians referred (p. 57) to eight clusters of values that journalists share in the United States as found in studies by Columbia University sociologist Herbert Gans. Christians believed this list supports Elliott's contention that there are universal principles in journalism. In his *Deciding What's News,* published in 1998, Gans found these common values: altruistic democracy, ethnocentrism, individualism, moderation, national leadership, responsible capitalism, small-town pastoralism, and social order. Although Christians (p. 58) admitted that we must be careful of overgeneralization, he did think that the available evidence indicates that journalists "hold a litany of ethical principles and enduring values in common."

It is obvious, however, that Gans' common values are not universal when compared to values found in journalism in other parts of the world, and we are not even convinced that they are universal in the United States. Nevertheless, they are probably generally common—enough so that Christians can legitimately speak of "normative solidarity." What is needed, say the communitarians, is not simply to have these common norms, but to abide by them. And this is quite another matter.

At any rate, sharing common norms and acting on them is an important part of Christians' communitarian journalism. Certainly he feels that an emphasis on relativism is largely responsible for the uncertainty and varied views of ethics around the world today. Part of this, he seems to believe, is due to the education students are getting in school. He wrote (Cooper, 1989, p. 19), "I have insisted that the academy emancipate ethical theory from its parochial constraints by recovering the notion of normativity, and in the process developing an ethics of universal solidarity grounded in norms."

In all five of the persons named (from Dewey to Christians) who have commented on communitarianism, one can discern a common emphasis on acting responsibly in the society. Social responsibility, not personal freedom, is the goal. Now as we go into the next chapter, we see that this goal was stressed back in the 1940s by a group of intellectuals who studied the press and came away with the conviction that the American press was basically irresponsible and that it needed immediate attention or it would be in danger of losing its freedom. This group was the famous (or infamous) Commission on Freedom of the Press, chaired by Robert M. Hutchins of the University of Chicago. Certainly it was a 20th-century precursor of the communitarian and public journalism movements.

Although largely written off by journalists as naïve and dangerous to traditional press freedom, it made considerable impact in intellectual circles, and it is still being discussed. Lee Bollinger, president of the University of Michigan and a First Amendment scholar, wrote (1998, p. 63) that the commission's report (published in 1947) was an "articulate denunciation of the media's increasing pandering to the baser desires of the population" and a depiction of the "noble role" of the media in a democratic society. Therefore, said Bollinger, the report has the "potential to be an enduring document." In the next chapter, we look at the Hutchins Commission and its report more closely, and the reader can see that a modern foundation stone was laid for communitarianism and public journalism.

5

Anticipating Community

It (the press) must be accountable to society for meeting the public need and for maintaining the rights of citizens and the almost forgotten rights of speakers who have no press. It must know that its faults and errors have ceased to be private vagaries and have become public dangers. The voice of the press, so far as by a drift toward monopoly it tends to become exclusive in its wisdom and observation, deprives other voices of a hearing and the public of their contribution. Freedom of the press for the coming period can only continue as an accountable freedom.

—Commission on Freedom of the Press (1947)

It was soon after World War II. Into the journalistic wilderness, in the late 1940s, came a man out of Chicago warning the press it needed to shape up, to become more responsible, or its freedom might be diminished. The man was Robert M. Hutchins, and he was heading an unofficial group called the Commission on Freedom of the Press, inspired and funded in large part by Time publisher Henry Luce. The voice of Hutchins, then chancellor of the University of Chicago, and his group of intellectuals fell like a bomb on the press, infuriating it and prompting it to extreme reaction. At the same time, the commission's 1947 book, *A Free and Responsible Press,* generated support from many in the public and the academy who already were aware of the press's growing arrogance and irresponsibility. It was received with less enthusiasm from an enraged press that saw it as an attempt to curb its freedom.

The Hutchins Commission, as it generally was called, was an early harbinger of the rise of the so-called Social Responsibility Theory of the press that developed in the 1950s and 1960s and later the communitarian and public journalism movement.

CHALLENGING THE LIBERAL PARADIGM

Hutchins and Luce, classmates at Yale and lifelong friends, feared that newspapers and the so-called "pulp press" of mass culture and society were inching toward government intervention due to rapidly increasing concentration of media power in fewer and fewer hands, the failure of those few to provide adequate service, and the perception of irresponsible behavior by journalists and media owners. Luce, Hutchins and most members of the Commission (1947) also believed First Amendment freedoms were increasingly threatened by newly formed totalitarian regimes in key global positions. Scholar Theodore Peterson (1963) noted that a study panel was being assembled to assess journalism's 175-year-old foundation in Enlightenment principles of human rationality, personal freedom, trust in individuals, and development of individual moral character.

For midcentury advocates of social order and responsibility, this group of middlebrow technocrats certainly provided a welcomed affront to the libertarian paradigm of an "inalienable" and "natural" right of a free press. The order paradigm was emerging in a group of neoliberals beginning to push a formal agenda toward the neoauthoriarian philosophy of today's public and civic journalism movement. Margaret Blanchard (1977) wrote that "the secure world of *laissez faire* economic principles was giving way under the weight of the Depression. With public indignation against industry after industry becoming apparent, the question soon became whether the First Amendment could be interpreted in a way to hold back forces of rampant social and economic unrest" (p. 6).

Since release of its report, the Hutchins Commission has been a focal point in the ongoing debate over whether the press owns a franchise in editorial self-determination or whether it has an obligation, duty, or responsibility to share that function with others—readers, viewers, politicians, clergy—under the democratic assumption that when citizens are properly informed, they will make proper decisions. Today, the Commission often is mentioned, even in critiques of its shortcomings, as a catalyst for changes in policy, administration, and conventions as well as for its role in bringing credibility to media criticism. To proponents of accountability and responsibility, it offered a foundation for a new press theory. To proponents of laissez faire philosophy, it provided evidence that rules were being rewritten by likeminded, left-leaning New Dealers. As will be seen, the Commission's members as well as its work products built a foundation for the late-century communitarians.

HISTORY AND PURPOSE

The trouble for the free-wheeling libertarian press in America started early in Franklin Roosevelt's New Deal administration. Lee (1937, pp. 247–249) and Blanchard (1977, pp. 5–6) noted that the American Newspaper Publishers Association, representing the newspaper industry, submitted its plan to expand the workforce, lighten hourly workloads, increase wages, and control profits under requirements of the National Industrial Recovery Act in 1933. The publishers were concerned with NIRA provisions that would limit their use of school children as carriers, require collective bargaining, and, quite possibly, threaten the existence of smaller newspapers without the financial resources to meet the employment mandates. Most important, however, the publishers were seeing Star Chamber ghosts in a NIRA provision that would allow the president to license industries to stimulate recovery. After lengthy and bitter negotiations, Roosevelt backed down, but publishers felt the president had thrown down the gauntlet on the free-press clause in the First Amendment, signaling the first substantial fissure in institutionalized press freedoms. They subsequently joined forces with the National Association of Manufacturers and the U.S. Chamber of Commerce to fight for what they considered "free press" issues threatened by the Federal Securities Exchange Act, the Social Security Act, the Wagner Labor Relations Act, the Fair Labor Standards Act, the Wheeler–Lea Bill to regulate advertising, the Copeland Pure Food, Drug, and Cosmetics Bill, and a number of bills designed to reform child labor practices.

By 1937, the Supreme Court had entered the picture, ruling in *Associated Press v. National Labor Relations Board* that "a newspaper has no special immunity from the application of general laws," and ordered the wire service to recognize the American Newspaper Guild as a certified representative of its rank and file employees. On August 28, 1942, shortly before the Hutchins Commission began its deliberations, the U.S. Justice Department sued *The Associated Press,* charging that it had illegally restrained trade by acceding to *Chicago Tribune* publisher and New Deal opponent Robert McCormick's demands that the competing and pro-New Deal *Chicago Sun* be denied AP service. Three years later, the court sided against AP again, ruling that the wire service was a monopoly in restraint of trade. In 1945, Justice Hugo Black delineated expression from business practice, writing that the First Amendment "rests on the assumption that the widest possible dissemination of information from diverse and antagonistic sources is essential for the welfare of the public." In *Associated Press v. United States,* however, Black said the free press clause does not supersede the Constitution's commerce clause: "Freedom of the press from governmental interference under the First Amendment does not sanction repression of that freedom by private interests." At the same time, according to Blanchard (1977, p. 9), some press critics, alarmed by journalism as "big business" and motivated by postmodern neoliberalism, were shouting claims that newspapers specifically were exhibiting class bias and becoming less and less representative of the country. It was in this social, political, and philosophical context that Hutchins, having procured endowments of $200,000 from Luce and $15,000 from his University of Chicago-based *Encyclopædia Britannica,* announced in the *New York Times* on February 28, 1944, his intent "to discover where free expression is or is not limited, whether by governmental censorship, pressures from readers or advertisers or the unwisdom of its proprietors or the timidity of its management" ("Commission to Make," 1944, p. A11).

MEMBERSHIP

From the beginning, according to Hutchins scholar Jerilyn McIntyre (1979), some Commission members or staff wanted to conduct empirical research on "content, audiences, and effects," but Hutchins rejected all attempts, reminding his colleagues that the panel was selected more for its philosophical power than its sociological prowess. Toward that end, Hutchins had filled the Commission with educators, philosophers, and legal scholars whose collective worldview was as important to American journalism as their individual differences in how to position media as partners for the social good. In a collective biography, Blevens (1995) established a genteel tradition of collectivist thought among the Hutchins commissioners, most of whom devoted their lives to planning, order, and social harmony. According to Ashmore (1989, pp. 294–295) and McIntyre (1987, pp. 138–139), they took seriously their roles in social canon construction, which, despite Hutchins's claims that the Commission meant to focus on policy and not practice, was evident in the panel's exclusion of sex, race, and journalism experience as criteria for admission.

As Mayer (Mayer & Hicks, 1993, p. 257) and others noted, Hutchins and Luce were close friends, but Hutchins was not Luce's first choice to head the Commission. That distinction went to Learned Hand, a jurist whose philosophical approach most certainly would have differed from that established by Hutchins. Hand's reluctance to accept Luce's charge cleared the way for Hutchins, who set about inviting many of his friends in the academy, a group so closely knit that they often served together or in succession in government or university jobs and shared interests in most of the same issues (Blevens, 1995). They included Zechariah Chafee, Jr., a Harvard law professor who arguably was the leading scholar on the free speech clause of the Constitution in the first half of the century; John M. Clark, Columbia economics professor and former University of Chicago faculty member who was a consultant to the National Recovery Administration and other New Deal agencies; John Dickinson, a Pennsylvania law professor who also served as general counsel to the Pennsylvania Railroad and held top-level posts in the U.S. Department of Commerce and the U.S. Attorney General's office; William E. Hocking, a Harvard philosophy professor emeritus, the Commission's elder statesman, who had written extensively about metaphysics and the need to find a suitable replacement for what he considered America's supreme devotion to quaint but obsolete classical liberalism; Harold D. Lasswell, the Library of Congress' director of war communications research who later became professor of law at Yale and who penned the seminal "who says what in which channel to whom with what effect"; Archibald MacLeish, the Pulitzer Prize-winning Librarian of Congress who served the Roosevelt administration as Assistant Secretary of State; Charles E. Merriam, a Chicago political science professor and department chairman who was on the Public Works Administration's National Planning Board during Roosevelt's administration; Reinhold Niebuhr, a professor of ethics and philosophy of religion at Union Theological Seminary and perhaps the most influential theologian of the first half of the century; Robert Redfield, a Chicago anthropology professor whose field work in Mexico and Central America helped build the foundation for modern anthropological investigation; Beardsley Ruml, treasurer of the Macy's department store empire and the Federal Reserve chair best known for creating the payroll deduction for income taxes; Arthur M. Schlesinger, the Harvard professor who was one of the nation's most respected social historians; and George N. Shuster, the Hunter College president who was an education scholar, expert on Germany, and one of the leading Roman Catholic laymen of the first half of the century.

Appointed by Hutchins and Luce to direct the Commission was Robert D. Leigh, who received a Chicago faculty position as visiting professor of political science to lure him from his post with the Foreign Broadcast Intelligence Service of the Federal Communications Commission. International advisers were John Grierson, general manager of the Canadian Wartime Information Board; Hu Shih, former Chinese Ambassador to the United States; Jacques Maritain, president of the Free French School for Advanced Studies; and Kurt Rietzler, professor of philosophy at the New School for Social Research. Hu Shih did not participate in the commission's work after 1944 and Maritain resigned February 1945 to become French ambassador to the Vatican.

SHARED NEOLIBERAL CONSTRUCTS

Although some critics expressed concern and disappointment during and after the Commission's deliberations, few recognized the underlying collective worldview that signaled the start of a march toward neoliberal thinking about the press and the neoauthoritarian philosophy and practice in the final decade of the century. Three of the Hutchins Commission members, including the director, had extensive experience in propaganda research, technique, and practice. As partners in this bloc, MacLeish (1941, pp. 187–191) and Lasswell (1941, pp. 37–51; 1948, 37–38) believed the power of information was in its psychology and volume, the capacity to outwit and, if necessary, outshout any threat to the democratic process. Both men thought the press should be used for patriotic purposes during wartime and that the best way to keep the democracy informed was to promote the "right" information. As theoretician, Lasswell studied, formulated, and wrote toward that goal, proposing psychology and politics as necessary, if not sufficient, ingredients for the democratic assumption. As administrator, MacLeish attempted to harness the power of government information during World War II, hoping to promote and support the interventionist policies that had become popular on the Commission (Donaldson, 1992, pp. 1–8, 349–352). He wanted to solve the information gridlock created by obstinate military and executive offices, not for the sole purpose of freedom of information, but for a united front to rally the threatened democracy.

Their compelling arguments for an ordered and harmonious media structure were strikingly consistent with Commission members' abandonment of pacifist positions, a common theme brought on by Chafee's (1941) desire to avoid the mistakes of World War I; Niebuhr's (1946) and G. N. Shuster's (1929) emotional concern for Germany; Hutchins's need to make the University of Chicago solvent again through lucrative wartime grants (Mayer & Hicks, 1993, pp. 274–276); even Ruml's idea for an across-the-board income tax to pay for the guns and butter demands of the New Deal (Drury, 1943). As with most issues in this or any such complex group, common causes with uncommon motives are to be expected, but with key commissioners involved in such emotionally pitched personal and political dilemmas, their concerns were not in journalistic conventions inspired by the First Amendment but in their frustrations with an industry that, consciously or unconsciously, had made a habit of rejecting the regimentation and manipulation required of a propaganda machine dedicated to social and political stability.

These frustrations with the traditional libertarian press were most apparent in sensational polemics between several commissioners (especially Hutchins, MacLeish, and Chafee) and Robert McCormick, whose papers in Chicago, New York City, and Washington gave the legendary right-wing publisher a powerful pulpit from which to criticize, chide, and verbally abuse commissioners before, during, and after their service on the panel. In their writings and conversations about press freedoms, members of the Commission often expressed anger at McCormick, the cross-town *Tribune,* and his satellite publications (Blevens, 1995, p. 327).

Frustration with McCormick, however, was not the only proximate problem in Chicago. During the time in which Luce was making plans for the press study, Mayer (Mayer & Hicks, 1993, pp. 19–20) noted, Hutchins was actively involved in the Manhattan bomb project. A decorated ambulance driver in World War I, Hutchins had turned in his postwar pacifist badge, luring top physicists to his faculty, drawing a half billion dollars in war contracts, and giving over a handball court in the vacant Stagg Field stadium to create the first atomic reaction (Hutchins, 1942, 1945). Many of the commissioners involved themselves in some way with both world wars, contributing directly to the military effort, providing support services, serving in consultancies, or participating in the public discourse. Only anthropologist Redfield and the two commissioners specializing in political economy—Clark and Dickinson—avoided the fervor surrounding World War II.

At the same time, Hutchins was chartering a world congress of scholars to write a constitution that would make all nations part of a global government with enforcement powers designed to halt nuclear proliferation and head off a cold war. One of the constructs of such a document would have required media industries to join as partners in global order (The Committee to Frame a World Constitution, 1948).

Politically, these men were patriots, though with separate agendas and timetables in their support of American forces. Blevens (1995, pp. 124–320) conducted a collective biography of the commissioners, finding they were cultural heirs to the genteel tradition. Some, like Chafee, Dickinson, MacLeish, and Redfield, were born into the bourgeoisie, sharing in the spoils of wealth and privilege. A few—Schlesinger, Ruml, and Hutchins, for example—had some early struggles, but none was a bootstraps case. The average commissioner came from an upper middle-class household dominated by professionals—educators, ministers, merchants, physicians. Not surprisingly, then, one of those professions—education—was dominant among the commissioners. Nine of them devoted most of their careers to faculty appointments at prestigious universities. Three (Leigh, Hutchins, Shuster) were college presidents as well as professors. Ten were elected to Phi Beta Kappa and, although their undergraduate work was completed at 11 different schools, the commissioners attended some of the best in both public and private education: Ohio State, Iowa, Harvard, Brown, Amherst, Yale, Johns Hopkins, Notre Dame, and Dartmouth. Although some commissioners—Hutchins, Chafee, Dickinson, for example—fulfilled family traditions at the undergraduate level, their intellectual attraction to common ideals in higher education began at the graduate school level, where Columbia, Yale, and Harvard accounted for 6 of the 10 master's degrees. By the time the Hutchins Commissioners reached the terminal degree level, they had settled on a marked degree of institutional commonality. Of the 15 degrees, 10 were doctorates of philosophy and 5 were in law. Niebuhr was the only commissioner without a terminal degree, and two of the men in the study (Dickinson and Redfield) had earned both degrees. Overall, the Commission probably was one of history's most highly educated study groups. There were 38 degrees earned, and 26 came from Harvard, Columbia, Chicago, and Yale.

With such intellectual power, the commissioners earned faculty appointments at many of the same schools, where they often retired to the emeriti faculty in endowed chairs. The measure of their scholarly achievement, however, is in the number of books they produced as a group. Factoring out the works of MacLeish, a prolific poet, author, and playwright, 13 Commissioners produced at least 156 books as single authors and scores more as co-authors or editors. Their individual productivity ranged from Ruml with one book to Niebuhr with 30. Although Ruml and MacLeish primarily were involved in business and art, respectively, they came to the Commission on their acquired expertise in the upper echelons of civil service. Both had also been involved to lesser degrees in teaching and educational administration. In the genteel tradition and driven by such strong neoliberal underpinnings, all of the commissioners devoted significant energy to civic and philanthropic chores, serving as fellows or administrators of funds to be used for social science research.

A consistent criticism of the Commission involved its overrepresentation of liberals, and there is no argument on that point. Seven members were Democrats; four (Shuster, Lasswell, Leigh, and Hocking) were independents. Shuster, Lasswell, and Leigh, however, supported New Deal policies and worked with the Roosevelt administration. Hocking, whose Republican standing was swept away in the Boston mugwump movement in the late 19th century, also was a moderate. Even the two Republicans on the Commission (Merriam and Ruml) were politically cavalier, with Merriam supporting social and community research and Ruml joking that he voted Democrat just to "balance things." Niebuhr, a one-time Socialist party congressional candidate, was a member and officer in the New York Liberal party.

CRITICISMS, WARNINGS, AND RECOMMENDATIONS

The Commission began its formal deliberations in 1944, meeting 17 times over the next 2 years. The full Commission (1947, pp. v–vii) interviewed 58 witnesses, and the staff claimed to have spoken to 225 others. In addition, the Commission reviewed 176 documents prepared by members and staff. Commission members wanted to analyze both the philosophical underpinnings of a free press and the practical aspects of news conventions, monopoly, regulation, advertising, and outside influences. According to Blanchard (1977, pp. 15–16), however, two of its own procedural conventions—hearings and deliberations in secret and a new definition of the press that included radio, new media, and motion pictures—guaranteed a harsh critique by the print media when the study was complete. Newspaper publishers and editors could not understand closed meetings and could not tolerate being grouped with other media. A clear sign of impending controversy may have been the Commission's seeming inability to reach consensus. By the time of its release on March 26, 1947, the Hutchins panel's report had been revised nine times, mostly amid acrimonious debates over the degree to which government should be involved. The general report was divided into six sections, one each devoted to stating the problems, outlining the requirements, examining the communication revolution, assessing press performance, considering self-regulation, and making recommendations. In its statement of the problem, the Commission outlined three areas of concern: an increasing importance of the press with a corresponding decrease in public responsiveness; an inadequate level of service to the public; and a system of practice that often brought public condemnation. Those conditions, predicated on increasing concentration of economic and political power in a media elite, threatened to bring intervention. In its statement of problems, the Commission (1947) posited that because government probably could not solve the problem of media concentration, "great agencies of mass communication" must control themselves or "be controlled by government." It sternly warned that the media's failure to adhere to the principle of social order would bring dire results: "If they are controlled by government, we lose our chief safeguard against totalitarianism—and at the same time take a long step toward it" (p. 4). Some of the Commission's concern was centered on its naïve and historically inaccurate belief that the press was obligated to be all things to all people: "Our ancestors were justified in thinking that if they could prevent the government from interfering with the freedom of the press, that freedom would be effectively exercised. In their day, anybody with anything to say had comparatively little difficulty in getting it published. The only serious obstacle to free expression was government censorship" (p. 14). Most important, however, was the panel's expansion of responsibility from an implied negative freedom *from* "external compulsions." It said the press was not free from "pressures" necessary for robust public discourse and that, therefore, the First Amendment construed a positive freedom—*"for* making its contribution to the maintenance and development of a free society." The statement certainly foreshadowed an emerging communitarian philosophy, linking press freedom to a "moral right" conditioned on accountability: "Its legal right will stand unaltered as its moral duty is performed" (pp. 18–19).

Like the advocates of late-century communitarianism, the commissioners were admittedly patriarchal in their recommendations, placing the onus of distributive justice and social responsibility on the shoulders of press barons, reporters, and editors. The Commission said the press should provide "a truthful, comprehensive account of the day's events in a context which gives them meaning . . . a forum for the exchange of comment and criticism . . . a means of projecting the opinions and attitudes of the groups in a society to one another . . . (and) a way of reaching every member of the society by the currents of information, thought, and feeling which the press supplies (interpreted as access to a full day's intelligence)" (pp. 17–28).

The Hutchins findings harshly criticized journalism education, monopolistic press barons, and, most important and enduring, a lack of accountability on the part of American newspapers. The report said that serving the public needs required that newspapers redefine themselves as "common carriers of public discussion," a condition that, if patterned on the broadcast industry, would place publishers in the realm of regulatory purview. Even worse, though, was the Commission's condemnation of radio, which had given up control of its programming to advertisers, thus reducing its public affairs programming to less than 10%, and making it difficult for listeners to determine editorial material from advertising. No wonder critics from all sides came to the front in various states of hysteria, making serious claims and counterclaims on a number of points, including whether the Commission actually recommended government intervention and whether its members were "Reds" (Knutson, 1948; Lyons, 1947).

In its March 29, 1947, issue, *Editor & Publisher*, the trade publication of the newspaper industry, critiqued the report in an unprecedented series of six articles. Louis Lyons (1947), the Nieman Foundation curator who contributed to the Hutchins study, said the report did not go far enough in making sure that independent, outside criticism and evaluation of the press would be enforced. Some critics of the critics, however, applauded the work, primarily because it finally had made press criticism respectable, moving the theater of practice from an easily dismissed fringe into the core of power in the dominant social and cultural structure.

THE PROBLEM OF MONOPOLY

These were not surprising results or reactions, given the cultural, philosphical, and political backgrounds of the commissioners, but their individual reasonings were as varied as the arguments of antitrust theory. For Chafee (Smith, 1986, pp. 107–108), government intervention to spur competition in the print media was a "Pandora's box" full of potentially horrible surprises not worth the risk. For Dickinson (1944), a lone voice as a direct descendant from and purveyor of classical Enlightenment principles, the Commission's approach fit perfectly his hands-off record as a government antimonopoly agent who retreated from service when Roosevelt turned up the heat on the trusts. For Ruml (Drury, 1943) and for Clark (1926, p. 473), who extended his father's 19th-century version of nongovernmental social control and society's default to the individual, trust-busting media enterprises was inconsistent with their moderate capitalist values. Clark probably best represented this neoliberal approach when he said the insurmountable problem associated with the regulation of business was the seemingly impossible task of figuring out what government should control and what it should leave alone. In their deliberations, the commissioners never were able to reconcile the paradox of deeply held Enlightenment convictions and the nagging concern that the press somehow should be an equal social partner. This, like many issues facing the panel, required a genteel and orderly accommodation, even to the extent of the Commission (Blevens, 1995, p. 323) suggesting that government could keep its machinery of economic regulation away from the press in exchange for a competitive marketplace supplemented by "endowed" media units designed to raise standards for commercial outlets.

The capacity of this dilemma to frustrate even the most capable was evident in the Associated Press antitrust case that reversed the usual roles of business and journalism and put the case for public utility theory in the hands of Supreme Court justices. In that dispute, one of several unpleasant frays the commissioners experienced with Chicago publisher McCormick, industry attorneys claimed exclusive market contracts promoted competition, whereas government authorities said the wire service should be available to all, even at the risk of monopolizing the market and driving out wire competitors. More than 50 years later, Blevens (1995, p. 324) noted, the paradox proves a worthy opponent. On one hand, many media scholars and most communitarians advocate further accommodation of cross-media partnerships to expand pluralism and "reconnect" with the public. On the other, media owners argue their cases for market hegemony by using the Justice Department's own standards to prove that single-owner towns promote media efficiency and quality. Given the changing media landscape over the last half of the century, these approaches and philosophies are not inextricably tied, but the growth of monopolies generally since 1947 and specifically during the communitarian era has been exponential. Like the late-century public and civic journalism advocates, the commissioners agreed that although media enterprises are obliged—if not duty-bound—to be responsible and contribute significantly to social order and harmony, government should have no direct role in affecting change on journalism's problematic business side. The evidence in their writing and behavior, in fact, indicates that although they rejected the simplistic and arguably archaic Miltonian "self-righting" principle, they generally stood by the Enlightenment construct that freedom of the press, if not an inalienable right, was at least a sacred trust embedded in a constitutional mandate worthy of at least a middle-of-the-road default.

TECHNOCRATS AND MIDDLEBROWS

Baran and Davis (1995) described at least one ideological division that is useful in explaining once again how the Hutchins Commission could arrive at such a neoliberal focus on responsibility and social order. Under their formula, Lasswell would join political communication scholars in a group that believed "information gathering and transmission had to be placed under the control of wise persons—technocrats who could be trusted to act in the public interest . . . that media content would serve socially valuable purposes, for example, stopping the spread of totalitarianism" (p. 77). Those Baran and Davis define in their other category are what might be called cultural guardians or middlebrows, those people, like Hutchins, who see their cultural mission as one designed to bring the Arnoldian "best" into every living room in America. They see the media as democratic adult education tools, very much like today's communitarians in their emphasis on a media structure whose primary responsibility is to repair a social fabric ripped by the irresponsible excesses of Enlightenment-based journalism. But just as the Hutchins Commission shied from third-party intervention and the thorny issue of media concentration, late-century proponents of community have forged a movement that advocates more voices and more public power, while competitive media markets vanish from the landscape.

Using the technocrat/cultural guardian model, we see strong similarities among the commissioners and the proponents of public and civic journalism. Joining Lasswell in the technocrat group was MacLeish, the Commission's practicing artist who strangely showed no concern for cultural degradation as he pursued control of the wartime information machine. The group also includes Schlesinger (1963, pp. 3–14), who helped MacLeish establish the Nieman Fellows program designed to elevate the practice of journalism; Ruml, who promoted the idea of an ongoing press council (Blevens, 1995, p. 330); Leigh, whose government service revolved around intelligence and information monitoring; Clark, who saw nongovernmental social control as necessary in business; Chafee, who thought of communication as a public utility (Smith, 1986, p. 97); Hocking (1942), who believed legal rights were built on moral rights; and Merriam (1939, pp. 150–155), who championed Great Community approaches that saw the press as an important supporting actor in society. Chairman Hutchins, with his campus war machine and Great Books movement to democratize culture, had the unique distinction of falling into both categories. The cultural guardians included Redfield (Leslie, 1976), who termed communication a compromise of form and content, and the theologians: Niebuhr (1960), whose neo-orthodoxy rejuvenated America's recognition of original sin; and Shuster (1929), who saw censorship as a form of training and believed beauty outweighed message in art. John Dickinson, a proponent of the free, unfettered market, was neither because he never expressed a need for press controls (Blevens, 1995, pp. 328–332).

IMPACT ON JOURNALISM

Eventually, the Commission's recommendations percolated through the porous stone of reigning libertarianism, when Peterson (1963, pp. 73–103) used them as the underpinnings of a normative social responsibility theory of the press. Peterson said the Enlightenment-based theory of libertarianism had been displaced by technology, the industrial revolution, criticism of press conventions, a "new intellectual climate" that looked critically on "built-in correctives," and the emergence of educated and sophisticated press barons following a growing sense of responsibility in almost all areas of American business and industry. Peterson wrote that "the belief that each entrepreneur would automatically serve the common good as he selfishly pursued his own interests gave way to the belief that American business and industry must assume certain obligations to the community." In other words, Peterson said, "the public be damned" had been displaced by "the consumer is king" (pp. 82–83). Such obligation on the business side made "moral duties" explicit. Because the Commission's philosophy required of citizens the moral duty that they be informed, the press had the moral duty to provide the information necessary for citizens to carry out their duty. Peterson could not have constructed a better frame for the communitarians of the 1990s. Press freedom, he said, is a moral right conditioned on media operators making certain that "all significant viewpoints of the citizenry are represented . . ." (p. 101). Peterson's theory posited that the public shared with editors and media owners the task of deciding what ideas were worthy of public airing. That mandate, reflected in "public" and "civic" media movements, recognizes the shift from the classical liberal theory that freedom of the press is a natural right to one of neoliberal construct of social right with conditions. Scholar Jay Jensen (1962) marked Peterson's theory as the death knell for libertarian press rights and the establishment of the neoliberal theory of social responsibility.

Since its inculcation into journalism education and practice, Hutchins-based social responsibility has been the subject of intense debate. The furor ebbs and flows with the rapidly evolving media environment and, remarkably, changes little from the key points made by scholars and media professionals in 1947. Beyond dispute, however, is the influence of the Commission on the news industry. McIntyre (1987) wrote that the Commission's shifting emphasis to a positive freedom is most important in its concept of accountability that serves "as a practical proposal to deal with specific social conditions" (p. 137).

Indeed, imprints of Hutchins conventions can be found in newspaper master plans, mid-career programs, textbooks, and ethics manuals, leaving little doubt that the Commission's proclivities and theory are shared, consciously or otherwise, by journalism's editorial and educational institutions. Since the Commission's report, newspapers have devoted more space to opposing editorial opinions, created new positions (ombudspersons and reader representatives) to field and write about complaints, and opened their editorial boards to outsiders (Lambeth, 1992, pp. 104–119). During the past decade, newspapers have devised new and controversial coverage philosophies that adopt many of the communitarian goals that position the collective press as a partner with government and citizens to solve the social ills brought on by classical, Enlightenment-based liberalism (Lambeth, 1992; Shepard, 1994). Since the establishment of the Neiman program during the Commission's deliberations, dozens of private foundations have stepped forward to fund training programs for journalists at all levels of career development. Examples include the Poynter Institute for Media Studies in Florida, the Newspaper Management Center at Northwestern University, and New Directions for News at the University of Missouri.

One social instrument of Hutchins-based philosophy already has become an artifact. The National News Council, an idea proposed by Ruml and strongly suggested by the commissioners as a means for providing independent monitoring and systematic evaluation of press performance, was founded in 1973 with the financial support of the Twentieth Century Fund and lasted just 11 years. The council was composed of 18 citizens, 8 of whom were from the communication industry. It heard cases mostly of national import, but complaining parties had to sign a waiver of future legal action in exchange for a council hearing on their grievances. University of Missouri professor Edmund Lambeth (1992, pp. 110–111) noted that the council, a victim of inadequate support and a dearth of coverage of its decisions from the media, closed its doors in 1984.

Ben Bagdikian (1992), in an assessment of the raucous merger decade of the 1980s, found that the nation lost eight major newspaper markets to monopoly. During the 1990s, four more fell to a pattern of limited antitrust enforcement set by Ronald Reagan and David Stockman in a "trickle down" formula that equates corporate capitalism with public and social good. At the same time, Blevens (1995, p. 25) noted, two newspaper chains, Gannett and Knight-Ridder, rolled out what appeared to be revolutionary plans to reform the ritual of American journalism, its practices and approaches to news. This strategy, motivated in part by the perpetual concern over luring young readers into the newspapers, met with limited success, but it has attached itself to a philosophy that news needs to get back to some Hutchins basics. Essentially, the core of the new civic and public journalism demands that the press speaks to all people, lets them speak back in a dialogue that makes all parties partners, then delivers a full news report "in a context that gives it meaning." In addition, the press has a mandate to find the "truth behind the truth," and make itself "accountable" to the public.

So, much of what has been formulated in cutting-edge news strategy has its roots in Hutchins; indeed, the Gannett map shows all five Hutchins recommendations in News 2000, the corporate manual designed to guide the chain's news processes well into the next century. News 2000's components —as well as those at other chains and independently owned papers—are varied and controversial, but their collective philosophy is one that seeks to reconnect news operations to their publics and that commits to a more egalitarian and inclusive presentation of news. At Gannett and Knight-Ridder, news executives are taking a hard look at job candidates to make sure they fit the philosophy, and they are making it clear to employees that they must follow the strict game plan for gaining back the public favor. Freedom Forum, Gannett's private foundation for funding news and news institution research, was so enthralled by Hutchins that it rewrote the five recommendations to fit the commitment of the organization to its proposed "Newseum," which opened in Arlington, Virginia, on the 50th anniversary of the Hutchins Commission in 1997.

One of the leaders (others are featured later) in the academic charge for civic journalism is Lambeth, whose second edition of *Committed Journalism* (1992, pp. 48–51) framed a whole philosophical and ethical method on the Hutchins recommendations. Lambeth proposed an elaborate and reasoned plan for a journalism based on trust, justice, stewardship, and truth-telling. Over the Commission's findings, he layered the communitarian thinking of Alasdair MacIntyre, whose constructs of "internal goods" (virtues such as Lambeth's) and "external goods" (profit, fame, and glory) allowed Lambeth to draw a middle-of-the-road ethical approach, attempting to do justice to Hutchins while preserving autonomy. Without saying so, Lambeth endorsed Machiavelli's concept of *virtu* and *fortuna* and the Florentine theory that too much of the particular (individual) leads to a corrupting of the universal (society and culture).

Lambeth used what he calls a *neo-Aristotelian* approach to build a concept of civic journalism in which all parties—reporters, editors, readers/viewers, cross-media partners, and, to some extent, advertisers—are involved in a news package that seeks to bond all in momentum to improve society and participatory democracy. In 1994, the Association for Education in Journalism and Mass Communication recognized Lambeth's movement by granting it a separate designation as an interest group within the organization. The civic journalism group even conducts its own scholarly paper competition with juried works earning their way onto the umbrella organization's agenda at its annual national convention. As a founder of this scholarly group, Lambeth's leadership position, bolstered by the warm reception afforded his academic fusion of Hutchins-based social responsibility and MacIntyrean communitarianism, has been instrumental in positioning civic or public journalism as what some in the news industry believe to be their responsibility to develop and promote participatory democracy.

6

Rise of Public Journalism

What I call "public journalism" and some call "civic journalism" is . . . an attempt to build a conversational space that has not emerged from professional training on the one hand, social science research on the other, or the culture of academic critique on a third. . . . So, what exactly is public journalism? It's at least three things. First, it's argument about the proper task of the press. Second, it's a set of practices that are slowly spreading through American journalism. Third, it's a movement of people and institutions.

—Jay Rosen

We have just seen that, in spite of much press opposition to its findings, the Hutchins Commission (Commission on Freedom of the Press) had a significant impact on journalistic thinking and prepared the soil of social consciousness so that an emphasis on press responsibility could take root. The Commission's report, released as a book soon after World War II, especially influenced vast numbers of journalism students who had to study it in journalism and communication schools. It even made inroads in journalism education in other countries. Without a doubt the Hutchins criticism and recommendations influenced the rise of public or civic journalism that made its debut in the early 1990s. Edmund Lambeth noted (1998a, p. 15) that the Hutchins Commission provided reformers a "philosophical counterbalance to classic, laissez-faire liberalism."

This important influence, coupled with the Counter-Enlightenment movement discussed earlier, and fueled by growing public criticism of the media and the ideas of the communitarians, led mainly by American sociologists, opened the door for the public journalist advocates, and they have stepped in and set up shop. Professor Jay Rosen, director of the Project on Public Life and the Press at New York University, was one of the pioneers— perhaps the main one—in the movement. He realized that the academic community, as well as the general public, was estranged from journalism. For Rosen, it was largely the fault of the press. Many practicing journalists, even editors, were aware of the problem and eager to participate in a new community-oriented journalism. To the chagrin of public journalists, many others were not.

Public (a.k.a. civic) journalism grew out of a sense that citizens are shunning public life, and the implications for democracy are serious because democracy depends on citizens participating and taking government seriously. Public journalists are trying to provide ways for citizens to grapple with community problems in a meaningful way. "In a word," wrote Rosen, "public journalists want public life to work, and in order to make it work they are willing to declare an end to their neutrality on certain questions—for example: whether people participate, whether a genuine debate takes place when needed, whether a community comes to grips with its problems" (Hoyt, 1995, p. 28).

Rosen believed (Corrigan, 1999, p. 9) we should be talking more about journalism and democracy and about "vision and judgment" and not get sidetracked into debates about such things as "objectivity." The New York University professor called for the press to be active in "strengthening citizenship, improving political debate and reviving public life." He added (p. 9) that journalists must dare to try something different. They must, he says, reinvigorate public spaces and public dialogue, because "when the life of the community no longer matters, neither does journalism."

"COMMUNITY" IS THE MANTRA

Following the path of the communitarians, the public journalists look to John Dewey as their pioneering ideological guru. His suspicion of Enlightenment liberalism and great concern for community has been passed down to the public journalists as a basic philosophical foundation. According to Dewey, we need a community for meaningful discussion, and public opinion can only be "made active in community life" (J. W. Carey, 1989, p. 81). According to Carey, the purpose of news is to tell a story and activate inquiry and action. But, he said (p. 82), the press, "seeing its role only as informing the public, abandons its role as an agency for carrying on the conversation of our culture." This emphasis the public journalists and many cultural critics get almost directly from John Dewey. Dewey saw a democratic community as one of equals who try to advance their shared purpose through discussion and openness where everyone could talk. He would have us restore public life that has been virtually destroyed by "a new breed of professional experts" within the mass media (J. W. Carey, p. 88).

The central ideas of the public journalists are simply slight variations on these Deweyite themes. Shepard, writing in the *American Journalism Review,* said that public journalism's goal is to reconnect citizens with their newspapers, their communities, and the political process, "with newspapers playing a role not unlike that of a community organizer" (1994, p. 29). According to "the gospel of public journalism," she continued (p. 29), "detachment is out, participation is in, press passivity is disdained, and activism is encouraged. And experts are no longer the quote-machines of choice; readers' voices must be heard." Day (1997), wrote in a recent book on media ethics that the news media serving as *agents of change* form "the animating principle of the public journalism." He noted (1997, p. 193) that "public journalism includes the audience members in news decisions as partners with the community in confronting social problems."

The early and basic blueprints for public journalism were provided largely by Jay Rosen and another pioneer, Davis ("Buzz") Merritt, Jr., former editor of the *Witchita Eagle* in Kansas. It was not long before other academics and journalists joined the movement, conferences and workshops were convened, newspapers began projects that would involve the public in editorial decisions, courses were added to university curricula, books began to be published discussing public journalism, and a controversial new emphasis in journalism was underway.

Institutional support was early given to the movement by the Knight Foundation, the Pew Charitable Trusts, the Kettering Foundation, and the Poynter Institute for Media Studies. The Washington-based Pew Center for Civic Journalism, created in 1993, has been the chief supporter of public journalism. It is an arm of the foundation set up from the estate of Joseph Pew, oil man and staunch conservative, and is a self-styled "funding catalyst" of projects involving public journalism (Diamond, 1997, p. 11).

One of the chief objectives of public journalism has been public-spirited reform, attempting to return journalism to its mission of public service. Most of the devotees of public journalism thus far have been professionals within the press, plus a smaller number from the academic world. Rosen said (1995, p. 36) that "public journalism tries to provoke discussion within the profession, spread the lessons of practice, and put like-minded people in touch with one another." At present most of the public journalists are from small to medium-sized dailies in cities like Charlotte, NC, Norfolk, VA, and Wilmington, DE, but there are some larger dailies (e.g., the *St. Louis Post-Dispatch*) that are experimenting with public journalism.

VOICES OF DISSENT

The movement, as one would expect, has met with some resistance—usually from journalists (e.g., Michael Gartner, editor of the Ames, IA, *Tribune* and one-time head of NBC News; William Woo, former editor of the *Post-Dispatch;* and Leonard Downie, editor of the *Washington Post*) and academics (e.g., Don Corrigan of Webster University, Ralph Barney of Brigham Young University, and Everette Dennis of Fordham, former executive director of the Freedom Forum Media Studies at Columbia University) who feel that journalists should not be involved in the public sphere—in community boosterism— and should not be actors but observers and recorders of the passing scene.

Barney, while admitting the strong appeal of communitarianism and public journalism, warned (1997, p. 73) especially against their tendency toward collectivism and depreciation of individualism. He declared communitarianism "a threat" because, he said, "changes toward communitarianism, unlike those toward individualism, tend to be irreversible, or reversible only at great social cost." He elaborated, "Communitarianism at its most effective is intolerant of individualism and controlling of information." As he sees it, on the other hand, individualism must tolerate both "communitarian and pluralistic information."

Barney maintained that public journalists envision participants in society sharing values and making decisions with community interests in mind. But, he said (p. 85) that "the basic information system installed by those with shared values will be inadequate to inform the discussions," and that "ultimately decisions by these groups will be flawed by the ignorance resulting from restrictions on information."

Everette Dennis of Fordham University believed (1995b) that public journalists are overly concerned about the state of American society and American journalism. He compared these journalists to Chicken Little, waiting for the sky to fall. He did not think that America is in deep trouble and public life is decaying. Nor did he believe that the press overall is doing the terrible job that the public journalists believe it is. Dennis also wrote (1995a, p. 48) that seldom is there a forum about public journalism where the pros and cons are considered. Rarely, he added, is there an opportunity to discuss the topic candidly and openly, where opponents as well as cheerleaders of public journalism can have their say. If there were such an opportunity, Dennis (1995a, p. 48) contended, many questions would be asked.

Dennis proceeded to provide some 20 of these questions, such as:

1. How does a public journalist differ from a community organizer?
2. Who are public journalism's main advocates and detractors and what are their motivations—and who pays for public journalism and why?
3. Does public journalism create better journalism that is more responsive to defining and demonstrating the public interest?

These questions asked by Dennis are not just rhetorical; they are questions loaded against the public journalists who are, in his view, mainly faddists and alarmists.

Many critics of public journalism are also concerned about foundations like the Pew Charitable Trusts getting into the newsrooms. For example,

Gartner said, "I don't like the role of the Pew Center in projects—would newspapers who take Pew money be willing to take money or put in their newsrooms 'coordinators' paid by General Electric, say, or the United States Information Agency? What's the difference? Why is Pew money somehow not tainted?" (Lambeth, Meyer, & Thorson, 1998, p. 231). This is an ethical problem that is assuming increasing emphasis: newspapers taking grants and awards from private—even nonjournalistic—sources like Pew for practicing a certain kind of journalism (Abel & Woodward, 1999, p. 33).

Since the introduction of public journalism in the early 1990s, the *Wall Street Journal,* the Boston *Globe,* and the Philadelphia *Inquirer* have questioned the ethics of newspapers receiving private funding. G. Bruce Knecht (1996) wrote in the *Wall Street Journal* that major dailies that took great pride in their independence "are suddenly lining up for cash from this powerful outsider." Knecht claimed that what the Pew journalism grants often do "is use tax-free money to subsidize big private businesses—large chain-owned newspapers —that use the cash to run puffy stories that don't challenge the power structure." Just what the influence on newspapers receiving Pew money and awards has been is really unknown inasmuch as recipient media have been reluctant to discuss the subject.

William Woo, former editor of the *St. Louis Post-Dispatch,* a staunch opponent of public journalism, offered this critique: "When the lion lies down with the lamb, when the editor and the real estate broker and the banker and the elected official form a team, whose ethics, whose culture prevails?" He also expressed concern (Woo, 1995, p. 12) about where news and editorial discussions are formulated. "Are they made in the newsroom or at the town hall meetings, within the deliberations of the editorial board or in the place where the editor sups with the civic coalition?"

Another strong critic of public journalism is Ed Bishop, editor of the *St. Louis Journalism Review,* who has been in the forefront of those who see public journalism as cult-like and overly sensitive to opposition. He pointed out (1999) that public journalism experiments have backfired on newspapers in New Jersey, Iowa, Indiana, Illinois, Missouri and elsewhere, but these failures have largely been unreported.

The best critique of public journalism so far, believes Bishop, is Corrigan's *The Public Journalism Movement in America: Evangelists in the Newsroom* (1999). Corrigan, a journalism professor at Webster University in St. Louis and a weekly newspaper editor, believed that media credibility will suffer under public journalism. He called public journalists "evangelists" because supporters are eager to convert other reporters to their kind of journalism. Some of these evangelists (in the media or media foundations) listed by Corrigan are Jan Schaffer, Chuck Stone, Bob Steele, George Killenberg, David Mathews, Hodding Carter III, Chris Gates, Davis Merritt, Arthur Charity, James Fallows, Ed Fouhy, E. J. Dionne, Cole Campbell, and David Broder.

For their part, these public journalism advocates and their supporters discount criticism that comes from Corrigan and other traditionalists, saying that it is simply an attempt to discredit anyone or any group that tries to change the elitist and profit-motivated press-centered system. What the public journalists say they want is to reestablish communities in which the people have a say in journalism and politics and where the trend toward disorder is halted and a spirit of cooperation is fostered. Public journalists draw on the same impressive array of philosophical and sociological sources as do the communitarians, people like John Dewey, John Rawls, Robert Putnam, Juergen Habermas, Michael Sandel, Herbert Gans, Gerald Dworkin, and also social conservatives such as Russell Kirk, Michael Oakeshott, and Gertrude Himmelfarb. These persons to varying degrees, like the public journalists, realize that society is basically disorderly and they desire to establish communities in which order and responsibility are stressed. Public journalism also gains support from a significant number of prominent academics, more specifically associated with journalism, such as James Carey of Columbia, Theodore Glasser of Stanford, Dan Schiller of San Diego State, David Craig of Oklahoma, Edmund Lambeth and Lee Wilkins of Missouri, Philip Meyer of North Carolina, David Rubin of Syracuse, and Clifford Christians of the University of Illinois.

COMMUNITY: NEWSROOM AND OUTSIDE

Public journalism's concern for community begins at home, right in the newsrooms. Cooperation and mutual respect in the newsroom (the concept of a team) is a tenet of public journalism. In fact, it may well be the starting point of the public journalist's concern. Community, you might say, begins at home. Christians, who directs the doctoral program in the University of Illinois' College of Communications, wrote about the editor as first among equals:

> The editor who orders reporters into danger and grief without respecting their on-site judgment thwarts growth toward mutuality. Likewise, the editor who gives no direction or seems constantly preoccupied has surrendered the possibility of the strong mutuality that makes a newsroom more than the sum of its parts. The editor in dialogue with trusted colleagues can build a news team united on goals of justice, empowerment, and care for the voiceless. This model is rare, but its congruence with the human condition—personhood-in-community—makes it a model with normative obligations. (Christians et al., 1993, p. 145)

In a chapter titled "Public journalism and newsroom structure" in a 1998 book, Scott Johnson proposed that newspapers do away with the traditional vertical (hierarchical) structure. He would have the newsroom restructured as an organization using teams or "circles" that would replace the old "command-and-control system." This new structure, he said, would be based on what he called *participatory management* (Lambeth et al., 1998, p. 126). Johnson contended that under this new structure, meetings would be open and input from all staff members would be expected on all aspects of the news operation. He believed that public journalism would broaden the definition of news, eliminate the conventional "beat" system, knock down walls separating departments and staffs, establish clear lines of accountability, and allow for brainstorming groups that cut across department lines (Lambeth et al., 1998, pp. 128–129).

Some have called it "democracy in the newsroom," and as Noack wrote in *Editor & Publisher* (1999, p. 26), such a notion brings "a swift, deep growl to the still legions of hierarchy-minded editors at papers across the country." According to Noack, this staff participation in decision making is spreading rapidly. In 1998 the *Arizona Republic,* for example, began having open meetings—out of the conference room and into the newsroom. Often the sessions are informal free-for-alls. They do adhere to an agenda, with the main focus on critiquing and planning coverage. At another newspaper, *The Morning Journal* of Lorain, Ohio, editor John Cole said that the chief purpose of such meetings is "to communicate and share information" (Noack, 1999, p. 7). Added Cole, "I think it's important that they [staffers] know the meetings are open . . . that there are no hidden agendas, and there's no editor who is trying to run a particular story for a particular reason that it's his own personal gripe."

Social philosopher Peter Drucker (October 1999, p. 57) would surely agree with Cole. He saw good reason for involving "knowledge workers" (including journalists) in the knowledge-based institutions. Drucker saw a future where news media would have to satisfy the values of their workers "by giving them social recognition and social power." This would have to be done, said Drucker, "by turning them from subordinates into fellow executives, and from employees, however well paid, into partners" (p. 57).

Public journalists believe it is not enough to democratize their newsrooms; they should also involve the public in their business. Newspapers are beginning to invite members of the outside community into the newsroom conferences. *The Sacramento Bee,* for example, gets a number of readers to commit to coming to afternoon meetings for a week. They have a chance to say which stories they would play on the front page for the next morning. The editors find this procedure very helpful to them. There have been more than 400 such citizen participants in these sessions over a period of 8 years. Another California paper, *The San Jose Mercury News,* does much the same thing, and its editor says that there is no "better way to dispel questions about our motives than opening up the meeting and letting readers see just how we think" (Noack, 1999, p. 30).

Whether with the staff of the newspaper or with the citizens in the wider community, public journalists want to develop more harmonious relationships and better understanding. One of the important aspects of a community is the idea of interaction, of conversation. James Carey (1987, p. 13), for one, emphasized a "journalism of conversation" and differentiates it from a "journalism of information." He preferred the former and said that the news media have elevated "objectivity and facticity into cardinal principles . . . [abandoning] conversation or discussion as a primary goal." If participation in the political sphere is to increase, said Carey (p. 14), the news media must help bring about a shift in their de-emphasis from a "journalism of information" to a "journalism of conversation." Such a concept is reminiscent of John Dewey and Juergen Habermas and is an important part of the public journalists' reshaping of the journalistic paradigm.

Traditional journalists have thought that the press's duty was to provide information to citizens who could then use it to participate in government. In other words, journalism was necessary to democracy in that it automatically motivated people to use press-supplied information for democratic participation. Public journalists and others have questioned this. For instance, Columbia University sociologist Herbert Gans said (1998, p. 7) that this is the "underlying shortcoming" of the traditional libertarian theory of democracy. Gans believed that this theory continues to assume that democracy "can be preserved as long as journalists do their best to keep citizens informed." But, said Gans (p. 7), journalists actually report little political material except about "powerful officials making decisions and engaging in partisan squabbling," a situation that gives citizens the impression "that politicians are not very interested in their problems and that there is little reason to become informed."

Journalists need to get away from the idea that supplying information to the public will lead to democracy, believed Gans. What is needed, Gans contended (p. 10), are more "topic-centered features"—even heated controversial topics—that stimulate debate and public conversation. The day is past when a meaningful journalism can produce "daily event-centered reportage that confronts the news audience with a continually repeated potpourri of unrelated stories." Dialogue among the citizens of a community is what is needed, and opinions and information must move laterally across the audience and not be poured into it from an "omniscient" press. Audiences must participate, not just read and listen; that is the essence of Gans' new democratic theory. Although at present rather vague, such a theory is developing rapidly as public journalists are busy thinking of ways to help the press stimulate public dialogue.

Most people today simply cannot participate in such public dialogue, believed noted educational philosopher Paulo Freire of Brazil. Either because of illiteracy, poverty, unconcern, or because they are excluded from public communication potential, contended Freire (1989, p. 13) the majority of the world's people "are kept submerged in a situation in which critical awareness and response are practically impossible." Freire, like Gans, believed that citizens must break out of a "culture of silence" and become capable of looking critically at the world "in a dialogical encounter with others." Sounding much like Habermas, Freire wrote that conversation is the key to democratic progress, and he said that citizens must discourse, converse, and argue—all of which brings the individual persons to a kind of equality.

Journalism, according to Freire's thinking (p. 58), should not be bestowed by those who are the press elite—by those "who consider themselves knowledgeable" and who look at the public as those who "know nothing." Freire called this the "ideology of oppression." He agreed with public journalists that the citizens themselves should be made to feel they can stand on equal footing with journalists in the determination of worthy media messages. Freire (p. 144) offered a warning, however: Those journalists who push for populist decision-making power must be careful. It is natural that "by means of manipulation, the dominant elites (publishers and other media executives) will try to conform the masses to their objectives." He continued, "The greater the political immaturity of these people (rural or urban) the more easily they can be manipulated by those who do not wish to lose their power."

Public journalists, spurred on by the Pew Charitable Trust and a core of dedicated academics, are doing their best to push public journalism around the globe. Corrigan (1999, p. 157) noted that as early as 1996, Ed Fouhy, former executive director of the Pew Center for Civic Journalism, was announcing to journalism educators at their national convention that civic journalism (his preferred term) had gone international. Fouhy told the professors that civic journalism was becoming popular globally and mentioned that the Pew Center was carrying the message that year to Fulbright scholars from more than 50 countries. In addition, he said (p. 157), foreign journalists in growing numbers were visiting the Pew Center to learn about civic journalism, and Pew-sponsored seminars and conferences were touting public journalism in Latin America and even Eastern Europe.

SHIFT IN JOURNALISTIC FOCUS

In America, with its competitive and commercial base, it is natural that journalism's focus has been on two main objectives: preserving its freedom and autonomous status in society, and making a profit for its owners. Both of these, according to traditional libertarian press theory, are needed for a third objective: providing news, entertainment, and advertising. Through its freedom, journalism is able to better serve the public, and only if it serves the public will it make money. At least, this is libertarian theory, and, in fact, the status quo defenders of the press say that the press has, for the most part, served the public well. On the other hand, the critics of the press say that it really has not, that it is too concerned with profits, leading it to deal mainly in sensation, gossip, crime, sex, and other titillating material not helpful in popular sovereignty.

So the public journalists are taking issue with this libertarian model. They want a press that is altruistic, not egocentric; they want a press that is community oriented, not institution oriented; they want a press that places more emphasis on its responsibility than on its freedom; they want a press that increases the citizens' political participation; they want a press that encourages public conversation about serious matters; they want a press that brings people together; they want a harmonious and noncontentious press that fosters community stability; they want a press that not only informs the public but engages it. In short, they want the focus shifted to the community and taken off of the press itself.

Journalist James Fallows, in a book contending that the American media undermine democracy, was sympathetic with the views of the public journalists. There can, and must, be a change of focus. He said that today's journalists can choose to continue entertaining the public, as they have been doing for the last generation, or they can engage it. What they have been doing, he wrote (1996, p. 267), is "concentrating on conflict and spectacle, building up celebrities and tearing them down, presenting a crisis of issue with the volume turned all the way up, only to drop that issue and turn to the next emergency." However, he continued, if journalists choose to engage the public, "they will begin a long series of experiments and decisions to see how journalism might better serve its fundamental purpose, that of making democratic self-government possible."

The American press has been deficient in giving enough different perspectives of the events and issues of society, say the critics of liberal journalism. The principal perspective is big business combined with support of the basic ideology of the government. Sociologist Herbert Gans of Columbia University advocated another emphasis—what he calls "multiperspectival news," believing that such a concept can give a boost to democracy. Perspectives can be multiplied by journalism including "more people into the ranks of the decision makers," and he saw public journalism as an attempt to do just that. This should provide, he said, "relevant information to those who have not been able to make much use of the type of information that the news media now provide" (Newman, 1989, p. 127).

Gans was touching on a central factor of public journalism: involving the people—not only in government, but also in journalism. He seemed to be saying that the interest of diverse groups (communities) are really more important than the needs of nations or society in general. Communities should have their special voices in society, and people in the communities also should be able to participate in their group dialogue. A word of caution is provided here by philosopher Jay Newman (1989, p. 128) who wrote that multiperspectivism of this kind gives the public "only a random barrage of images, and though it may give a certain type of participatory power" to the community members, "it threatens to leave them without an orderly pattern of images around which to organize their activity."

The objective of the public journalists, however, is clear. They want a true pluralism of citizen views provided by the press. They feel it is time for a definite change of emphasis, this one on the people rather than on the press and its freedom and power. Such a shift in focus is a big order, and the public journalists know it. Profit-making and journalistic autonomy are deeply ingrained in the American press. So is the desire to furnish entertainment instead of useful information. Public criticism and philosophical appeals have helped to dissipate these traditional press tenets somewhat, but there is still a way to go. After all, the press is a business and a highly competitive one. Naturally, then, the focus is on profits and freedom. The public is necessary, of course, but as consumers having little or nothing to say about how the press is run. This fact is at the heart of much of the public journalists' criticism.

The objective is to bring the public into the press's decision making, to literally revolutionize journalism so that it will become a people's press in a meaningful sense of the term. How will this be done? Many factors, not all of them developed at present, enter into this question's answer. At present, focus groups and outreach experts are used to involve the community in the determining, collecting, and processing of news. One thing public journalists want to do is to democratize journalism and stimulate public discourse about the media and their problems. Another is to get the public involved in conferences, workshops, and round-table discussions with journalists so that helpful conversations will develop.

Public journalists talk about building *civic capital,* by which they mean developing community spirit, a feeling of being positively engaged with one another. Writing about public journalism, Charity (1995, p. 47) endorsed a belief of David Matthews': "If there is no sense of community, it stands to reason that it will be difficult to solve common problems." Charity continued in his own words, "A purely instrumental, problem-solving politics isn't adequate by itself. People in a community have to have public spirit and a sense of relationship . . . to be positively engaged, not just entangled with one another."

PARTICIPATION IN THE PUBLIC SPHERE

Public journalists also want the focus to be put on what they call *public discourse,* and taken off of straight information and objectivity. These new journalists are much impressed with the German theorist Juergen Habermas. Lambeth (Charity, 1995, p. 21) would name him as public journalism's "philosophical patron saint." We would nominate somebody else—John Dewey, probably. At any rate, among contemporary thinkers, Habermas (with the possible exception of James Carey of Columbia University) seems to have had the most influence on the development of a theory of public journalism.

Habermas stressed an impartial public discourse patterned on the ideal speech situation. This seems to us quite unrealistic in journalism because it would limit communication mainly to the face-to-face situation. According to Lambeth, Habermas accepted as valid only "those norms affirmed through the rational, consensual and impartial agents affected by the norm who are equally well-equipped to articulate their interests" (Charity, 1995, p. 22). We wonder how many rational and impartial agents affected by the norm can be found. They may well be difficult to locate—especially when they must be equally well-equipped to articulate their interests. The "public sphere," believed Habermas, is critical for community building, and he proposed that journalists enter it and take part in it. For Habermas, the public sphere is the space between civil society and the state. Habermas went on to say:

> This space allows citizens to address the state but demands that they leave their individual interests behind when they do so. The citizen must frame all arguments in the public sphere according to two complementary rules: personal negation and universal supervision. Negation means that the citizen must hide personal interests behind a veil, as it were-something similar to the concept of the veil of ignorance that John Rawls discussed. Universal supervision means that we must assume that everyone in a society (actually or virtually) observes every action in the public sphere. (Nerone, 1995, pp. 154–155)

A basic concept is "shared understanding," in Habermas' thinking, people discussing in the public sphere, or people interacting with media, so as to reach a kind of consensus about the directions of the community. From such public discourse will come a shared understanding about the norms and purposes of the collectivity. Out of such democratic, participatory community within the public sphere, believed Habermas, will come not only the most pragmatically correct answers, but also the most ethically correct answers (Habermas, 1996, pp. 202–204). For the press, the essence of the new focus is this: Let the journalism sphere and the public sphere overlap. Let there be conversation in the public sphere, not simple one-way communication. Let there be a real symbiosis between journalists and the people. Let people power increase and press power decrease.

At least it can be said that public journalism is critical of traditional libertarian insistence on editorial self-determination or journalistic autonomy. What the public journalists want is a more monolithic press, at least in an ethical sense, one that they believe will be more predictable and responsible. But they want it to develop through much wider public participation in discourse that will lead to a sense of empathic sensitivity. Unlike the older tendency to one-way communication—from the elite to the nonelite majority—this new Habermasian discourse theory would give equal respect for the personal dignity of each participating citizen. Decisions, values, and social practices would be transformed into truly democratic ones. The people and not an elite would be the community authority.

This is why, in this book, we are suggesting that public journalism is a kind of neoauthoritarianism. Please note that *authoritarianism* is not per se a negative term. Nerone wrote (1995, p. 38) that "authoritarian practices need not be negative in form," and that such practices occur when there is a "concentration of power." Wise and public-centered authoritarianism (what we are calling neoauthoritarianism) can be positive and can lead to social order, and away from what the public journalists see as libertarian media chaos.

Actually we can make a case that all press systems are "authoritarian." Instead of the common four theories (Siebert, Peterson, & Schramm, 1963), we could propose only one theory: the authoritarian. For every press system, there must be an authority that controls the press. What we are calling neoauthoritarianism in this book is a system where the people serve as the authority. Of course, there are other systems based on where the authority lies: (a) state authoritarianism—what we normally consider authoritarianism, (b) press authoritarianism—what we usually think of as libertarianism, (c) religious or theocratic authoritarianism—e.g., what obtains in Iran, (d) royal authoritarianism—e.g., what obtains in Saudi Arabia, (e) party authoritarianism—what we see in China or in Vietnam, and (f) populist or people's authoritarianism—what the public journalists seem to be enthroning. Other loci of authority can be imagined, for example, corporate, ideological, and foundation–philanthropic. All press systems are authoritarian, however, having some authority or combination of authorities that in some way guides the direction of journalism.

What public journalists want is a "people's authoritarianism." They want to solidify the community through journalism, to move forward toward a "people's journalism" in keeping with the democratization principle. Let there be more interaction and concerted action. Let there be more participation by the public in the vital decisions of journalism. Such are the admonitions of the public journalists. What the public journalists are saying, in effect, is that the public can determine good journalism (more reflective of community values) just as well, if not better, than journalists. At least, many public journalists feel that much more help is needed from the public in ushering in a better, more socially responsible media system.

Out of this people-centered journalism will come a responsive, therefore a more responsible, press. This is seen as a step toward order and social harmony, and it is being taken without throwing out, at least for the time being, many of the vestiges (at least the terminology) of libertarianism. Public journalists, like the communitarians, find the basis of such community-oriented journalism in the belief that the community is prior to the individual and is more important. Contradicting this increasingly popular belief are writers who play down the importance of groups and stress the importance of the individual.

Hayek, for example, contended (1944, p. 144) that if the community is prior to the individual, it would have "ends of its own, independent of and superior to those of the individuals." Therefore, said Hayek, "only those individuals who work for the same ends can be regarded as members of the community." Hayek further stated (p. 144) that under such a collectivist view it follows that a person "is respected only as a member of the group, that is, only if and in so far as he works for the recognized common ends, and that he derives his whole dignity only from the membership and not merely from being man." Public journalists respond that writers like Hayek overstate their case, that individuals in a group can be respected for their ideas and personal qualities and not simply for their group membership, and one should derive dignity from contributing to the common good and not from simply being a person.

NEGATING THE NEGATIVE

Public journalists have a long list of preferences and objectives, among them being the establishing of community, cooperation, and group solidarity and loyalty. They also espouse social stability and harmony, public discussion, egalitarianism, democratization, and audience participation. Along with these, they have a list of dislikes such as sensational news coverage, competition, press arrogance, journalistic autonomy, atomistic individualism, objective journalism, autocratic press management, and negativism in the news. Let us look briefly at that last one—negativism.

Too much negative news is in the press, the public journalists say. Such negative emphasis, hand in hand with sensational elements of the news, gives the public a skewed and erroneous view of the reality around them. There is negativism in reality, they admit, but proportionately far less than is reflected in the news media. What the new public journalism must do, they insist, is to negate the negative. The natural angst prevalent in mass society is only exacerbated by a negative array of news that flashes before the citizen every day. The world is made to seem far worse than it is, and the press therefore injects a sense of hopelessness and helplessness into public consciousness.

The libertarian or traditional journalists retort that much of the news *is* negative. It is not possible to have completely objective journalism, they respond. We never have had it; we never will have it. Contemporary media critic Ben Bagdikian (1992, p. 179) agreed, saying that "every step of the journalistic process involves a value-laden decision." For another thing, the traditional libertarian journalists say, biasing the news positively (as the public journalists would do) is no more objective than biasing the news negatively. Objectivity or no objectivity: that is not the question, say the public journalists. What we need is helpful, responsible journalism that solidifies the community and emphasizes morality, and if it is biased, so be it.

DE-OBJECTIFYING JOURNALISM

According to Merritt, public journalists are "not rejecting objectivity." He said that journalistic objectivity, "taken to mean being clear-eyed about the facts, honest with ourselves and others about them, fair-minded, balanced, etc., is an absolute necessity." He added, "Being detached is not." What Merritt wants to see "is a move away from detachment, which is not the same as becoming inappropriately attached." It's a continuum, he believes, and "journalism has moved in recent decades too far to the pole of detachment, to the great detriment of ourselves and our communities" (Letter to John Merrill from Merritt, Nov. 18, 1998).

Merritt has said that reporters must go beyond "merely providing and interpreting information" and must abandon their "detachment." A leading critic of public journalism, Michael Gartner (1997) of Ames, IA, was quick to respond to Merritt. "Well," he said in a speech at the University of Kentucky, "if you're not detached, you're attached, and the attached journalist is the dangerous journalist. . . . Detachment in reporting is a great asset, something to be sought, not something to be abandoned. If you abandon detachment, you abandon credibility—and credibility is the greatest asset of a reporter or a newspaper." What Gartner was saying seems consistent with the views of a majority of American journalists; they connect the concept of detachment with the concept of journalistic objectivity. Dennis (1995a), commenting that public journalists do, indeed, have an aversion to objectivity, asked, "Does public journalism contribute anything original to a long-standing critique of objectivity that goes back at least three decades?" At least some public journalists (e.g., "Buzz" Merritt) seem to believe that a journalist can be attached without losing objectivity.

This belief is rather strange. When one loses detachment, he or she also loses even the pretense of objectivity; at least it seems so to us. It seems to us that it is much easier to be detached than to be objective in the philosophical sense, and it is really this sense of neutrality (or detachment) that the average journalist means by "objectivity." One wonders why most people seem to think that the press *should* be objective or detached. Not all journalists believe this, but it is a widespread belief. A belief in objectivity is relatively recent; it certainly did not exist in early America where newspapers were very partisan, and it was not really until the late 19th century, with the development of the Associated Press and its writing style, that the idea of objective (neutralist, detached) journalism caught on (Schudson, 1978, pp. 4–6).

Being detached—or objective—appears to the public journalists as a kind of cowardice in the face of social responsibility, a pretense at neutrality when social participation is called for. The press, say the public journalists, must be involved in social change and make an impact. Newfield (1974, p. 56) wrote that the "men and women who control the technological giants of the mass media are not neutral, unbiased computers. They have a mindset. They have definite life styles and political values, which are concealed under a rhetoric of objectivity." For the public journalists, these life styles and political values should be brought out of this veil of objectivity and put into action in the communities.

ENTHRONING RESPONSIBILITY

By the frequent indictments of the press as being irresponsible, the institutional press freedom is being eaten away. What is being enthroned in freedom's place is press responsibility. Such a notion is, of course, a noble aspiration, thrown dramatically into the journalistic maelstrom by the Hutchins Commission in the 1940s. We all want a responsible press but, in the process of somebody defining what such a press would be, press freedom is compromised, and this is increasingly what is happening. The public journalists, for instance, think they know what the press's role in society is, and they have developed their new theory of "community-building." As the concern for press responsibility grows—and it will—the old libertarian concept of journalistic autonomy will disappear.

Of course, what many would like is both a free *and* responsible press, but this might well present a difficult paradox: If the press is really free, then it (or portions of it) will be considered irresponsible to somebody. David Gordon, a communications scholar at the University of Wisconsin–Eau Claire, saw freedom of expression as basically contradictory to the concept of responsibility. He admitted that the "ideal situation . . . would be to have *both* freedom and the responsible exercise of that freedom. However, human nature being what it is, there will always be people who abuse protected freedoms of expression. . . . Any efforts to legislate or otherwise require ethics at the expense of the First Amendment will aim for a cure that is worse than the disease" (Gordon & Kittross, 1999, p. 27).

Libertarians, of course, are skeptical of the concept of press responsibility. They see its advocates as incipient controllers using the virtue-term *responsi-*

bility as a rationale to increase restrictions on the press. Public journalists, however, believe that responsible journalism has a rather precise meaning and that most people know it. That aside, they say, the emphasis put on responsibility is preferable to putting it on freedom if for no other reason than that insistence on responsible journalism, regardless of its precise meaning, evidences an ethical motivation, rather than the egocentric one of the freedom lovers.

If the press is to be responsible, say the public journalists reflecting the views of the Hutchins Commission, it must perform a public service of a specific responsible kind, negating its own selfish ends and promoting news and views that benefit the people. The Hutchins Commission in its 1947 report limited press freedom to a responsibility to report facts accurately in a meaningful context. Debunking such ideas and the Hutchins Commission generally in a very spirited and systematic way is Hughes' *Prejudice and the Press* (1950), probably the best critique of the Hutchins report. Important reading also is a long section ("The Hutchins Report—a Twenty-Year View," 1967, pp. 8–20) in *Columbia Journalism Review*. Social responsibility advocates insist that any freedom the press has is only justified by its responsible use. What other rationale would there be for this one profit-making institution to have so great a freedom? It seems only natural that at this point in history, after having given a free press ample opportunity to show that it can be responsible, the American people are ready to propose some significant change in press theory. What seems clear also is that such a change is not one toward a stronger and more restrictive government, but rather one that places press functions in the hands of the people. As we said earlier, this would be a kind of democratization of journalism, whereby the press would represent and serve a new authority—the people. Maybe, then, when the elite and autonomous press has lost its tremendous power, the people-journalists will be more responsible to themselves, even if it is for collectively selfish reasons only. It is only then, and by some such democratic journalistic revolution, that journalism can ever be considered responsible to the society.

WHAT ABOUT ADVERTISING?

All one has to do today is listen to comments about the press to realize that advertising is perhaps the most viciously attacked aspect of modern journalism. Critics blame advertising for being too obtrusive, for being too demanding and repetitive, for creating economies that lead to media concentration, for encouraging waste and greed, for determining in large measure the news and other media content, for simply taking up too much space and time in the media, and for capturing the attention of unwilling audience members.

Advertising is thus seen by many critics as being irresponsible for encouraging the media to be irresponsible.

Does not advertising embrace and defend the libertarian press theory? Of course, say the public journalists, because the advertiser wants as much freedom as possible and is able to find it in a free press. Just what does responsibility mean to an advertising person? Perhaps it is not too cynical to suggest that it means selling the product and stimulating the economy. Advertisers would not deny this, but would go on to say that advertising makes the news media possible by largely financing it, thereby keeping the press free from government control, and they will pay lip service to truth. However, they say little or nothing about objectivity, or balance, or fairness. *Effectiveness* is the key word, and to be effective, advertising must snare the audience member's attention and cause him or her to desire the product and ultimately to purchase it.

Kim B. Rotzoll, professor of communication at the University of Illinois, told us (Nerone, 1995, p. 115) that advertisers may think they are responsible, because they are within the market system, even though they are "pursuing clearly self-interested ends." However, Rotzoll noted that the very nature of advertising is biased communication, and therefore he wondered if such messages constitute "responsible market information" (p. 117).

Publisher of the *Toronto Globe and Mail* Roy Megary offered this strong statement about advertising's place in journalism: "[P]ublishers of mass circulation daily newspapers will finally stop kidding themselves that they are in the newspaper business and admit that they are primarily in the business of carrying advertising messages" (Bagdikian, 1992b, p. 195). This may well be more a criticism of publishers than of advertisers, and we think it is, but it plays up the contrast between journalism and advertising, which may account for the fact that many educators think advertising courses should be in the business school rather than in journalism.

Is advertising responsible or irresponsible? That depends, of course, on who is judging it and whether or not that judge agrees or disagrees with the intent of the advertiser or the worthiness of what is advertised. For example, birth control advertising may well be responsible to many people (and governments), but not to Roman Catholics. What we believe to be a valid generalization, however, is that most serious Americans think there is too much advertising, that it distracts from editorial material, and that it affects the nature of media coverage. Rotzoll (Nerone, 1995, p. 119) posed this question: "When was the last time that you saw a serious investigative piece on the activities of used car dealers in your community?" The question suggests that advertisers do compromise forthright and serious reporting.

It might well be, if public journalists would not pull their rhetorical punches, that they would even go so far as to advocate the abolition of advertising. To replace advertising's sponsorship of the press, the public journalists might suggest subsidies from community-minded donors or foundations that would give no-strings-attached money to the cause. If advertising would be curtailed or eliminated, the newspapers, for instance, could be much smaller and therefore sell for a fraction of their prices today. Fewer pages would mean fewer rolls of newsprint used, and this would mean fewer trees cut down. The journalists, not having to worry about alienating advertisers, could presumably write with more integrity. Along with the demise of advertising, the public would be increasingly involved in the actual production of journalism, therefore changing the press from a money-oriented enterprise to a people-oriented enterprise. This would be a big step in the direction of true democracy. Besides, say many critics of the modern press, in the next few decades newspapers will not be too important, as they are slowly being replaced by the journalism of cyberspace where the people will be a part of journalism.

EVERYBODY A JOURNALIST

It should be quite clear by now that public journalism is a new kind of journalism that puts its main emphasis on the people's participation in journalism and government. For the public journalists, "the people" are at the center of their program. They are interested in opening the press to the people, motivating the people for community service, stimulating a civic conversation for the people, further democratizing the people, encouraging them to set their news agenda, facilitating message outlets for the people, and creating a public sphere in which the people can talk and act.

In the face of stubborn institutional resistance, public journalists seem determined to fracture the once-solid jar of elite media freedom and let the contents spill out into the hands of the public. The press would thus become little more than a conduit for the people's communication. Naturally this would cut into press's autonomy and take away much of its power. With its former freedom now allocated to the public—the new agenda setter—journalism would tend to be truly of the people, by the people, and for the people.

Just how this long-term objective will be reached is something that the public journalists have not specified as yet. Herbert Schiller of the University of California, San Diego, wrote about the problems facing public journalists and others who try to change the system:

> [It is] important to imagine other possibilities, alternatives to the existing arrangements [in mass communication]. This would be a formidable assignment. The debris of obsolete and self-serving rationales blocks the way. Anything that suggests a different course is labeled either unrealistic or dangerous to what once may have been unassailable, bedrock principles (Mazzocco, 1994, p. ix).

A good place to start in breaking down these "bedrock principles" might be for the press to listen to actual and potential audience members, and at present the focus of public journalists is indeed on listening more to the people's voices and trying to provide more public-desired news. Also, efforts are being made to bring representatives from the public into news-planning sessions, and to set up various kinds of focus groups to discuss media problems.

The next few years should see the discovery of many other techniques for bringing the public under journalism's rubric. Just how far this people's journalism will extend is at present anybody's guess, but there is little doubt that it will extend well into the future. In fact, the old concept of press freedom, and maybe even the press itself, will likely have disappeared by the end of the 21st century. Journalists in that far-off day will, in a sense, be everyone, and the press (the news media) will be the totality of technology used to disseminate information.

7

Talking Public Journalism

While the (First) Amendment was written to empower people rather than any institution, it has become, for the organized "press," a license to self-define unique among American institutions. Neither clergy nor bar nor medicine nor academe can claim, and have validated by the courts, more latitude in action and deed. That enormous latitude is a mixed blessing.

—Davis "Buzz" Merritt

Re-creating the news media into a social instrument responsive to the will of the people is an alluring idea to those championing the growth of public journalism. To fulfill the potential of journalism, the press needs to be more responsible, placing more value on consensus building, problem solving, and community. For some, public journalism represents a philosophic journey, for others, an exercise in adhering theory to practice. Many journalists who have embraced the idea see it as a practical response to the shortcomings and greed of an increasingly commercial press. Proponents of the movement see the media as implicated for the decay of public life in the late 20th century and are serious about the need for fundamental change in the triad relationship of press, politics, and public.

The ideas of those who have shaped public journalism are summarized in this chapter. These people—editors, scholars, philanthropists, consultants, and news executives—see themselves as activists in the role of placing the press back in touch with its democratic roots. They envision a journalism that gives the public a sense of community cohesion and togetherness, a journalism that activates public-spirited reform. They see public journalism as a mechanism for hope, a way for people to imagine a better life, and a means to create that life. With no less significance, they believe that by making the media more public, the public will make the media more successful. This success is realized in two ways: the institution of the press becomes more democratic, and the public become more active consumers of the media.

128

JAY ROSEN

More than any other scholar, Rosen, a professor at New York University and former reporter in Buffalo, NY, has advanced the cause of public journalism from the academy into the newsroom. Rosen's interest in advocating a new type of journalism was largely shaped by his doctoral studies and by political events of the late 1980s.

Rosen wrote that his study of democratic theory and the press led him back to the 1920s debate between Walter Lippmann and John Dewey (Merritt & Rosen, 1998). Lippmann (1922) proposed that the world had become too complex and complicated to expect individual citizens to be informed and interested in all the questions and challenges facing a democracy. Citizens, having their own lives to live, had neither the time nor inclination to engage themselves. The role for the press was to rely on the relatively few experts to guide the debate in a way that informed citizens and deflated popular stereotypes. The press also served by shining the "light of publicity" on officials and institutions that had betrayed the public trust. Dewey (1927) took a much more populist view, arguing that a role of the press was to help give shape to an unformed—inchoate—public. For democracy to work, the press must provide a public space where common problems could be discussed and understood. The press, along with politics, culture, and education, played a key role in helping form the public in a way that allowed the potential for democracy to be fulfilled.

During the 1988 presidential campaign, Rosen wrote, he became convinced that Dewey's press views were much closer to correct than Lippmann's, who, Rosen suggested, "declared the whole thing unworkable" (Merritt & Rosen, 1998, p. 50). The news coverage of that campaign—focusing on polls, the "horse race" mentality of who's ahead, and the strategy of image makers, political handlers, and media-created events—distanced the public from the political process. Journalists, too, were aware of and confused by these developments but, compelled to accept their roles as objective professionals working in a commercial media, they reacted generally by doing nothing, leaving the public to fend for itself. Rosen perceived a growing disconnect between the media and the public, which encouraged him to make his ideas for media reform more public.

In 1991, Rosen met Davis Merritt, then the editor of the *Wichita Eagle,* at a Kettering Institute-sponsored seminar for journalists, and the two men—one academic, one practitioner—recognized the similarity of their ideas (Shepard, 1994). They began to lecture together on the need for press reform and wrote some of the fledgling movement's seminal works, including the 1994 co-authored work, *Public Journalism: Theory and Practice,* which Rosen refers to as a "joint manifesto" (Merritt & Rosen, 1998, p. 55). A year earlier, Rosen secured a half-million-dollar Knight Foundation grant to create the Project on Public Life and the Press at New York University. Also in 1993, the Pew Center for Civic Journalism was created by a $4 million, 3-year grant from the Pew Charitable Trusts (Hoyt, 1995; Shepard, 1994).

From the beginning, Rosen has anchored the need for reform in his belief that the news media have failed the public. The goal for public journalism is to create a more active media that is less detached (or objective) and more rooted in nudging communities toward confronting and solving their problems. Journalism's contribution to citizen apathy and alienation is the rationale for changing the way journalism is practiced. Journalists need to reinvigorate public life, and this can by done by providing a means for the public to participate more in journalism.

Most of the initial experiments in public journalism were confined to newspapers. Relying on focus groups, polls, and community meetings often sponsored by the newspapers doing the reporting, some public journalism projects drew praise for their efforts at listening to "real people" (members of the public not in positions of making policy) and attempting to make the public's agenda more visible in newspaper content. These same projects also created targets for skeptics, who claimed public journalism was too involved in making news, a threat to press credibility, and little more than community boosterism (Frankel, 1995; Hoyt, 1995; Shepard, 1994).

Rosen responded by pointing out projects at newspapers that he thought were good examples of the public journalism he envisioned—the *Wichita Eagle, Virginian Pilot* in Norfolk, and *Charlotte Observer,* to name a few. He also asked critics for time to let public journalism develop. Rosen (1994a) conceded at an American Press Institute seminar that "we're still inventing it. And because we're still inventing it, we don't really know what 'it' is." The inability to define public journalism, or what it should be, became a focal point for critics. In subsequent writings, Rosen (1996) acknowledged the vagueness of the movement and expended considerable effort trying to articulate a set of parameters about what public journalism is and isn't, all the while being sensitive not to create a specific formula or recipe.

In *Getting the Connections Right: Public Journalism and the Troubles in the Press,* Rosen (1996) wrote that the culture of the American press is conservative, not in a political sense but in its ability to experiment and accept new ways of doing things. This conservativism is driven by conflicting pressures: those of the audiences, media owners, political figures, sources, and daily deadlines. Rosen saw journalism stymied by these pressures because of the "relatively thin credentials of the journalist as a maker of professional judgments" (p. 8). Unlike other professions, such as medicine and law, journalists are not required to have advanced training or licensing; there is no obscure vocabulary, no particular expertise on subjects in the news, no scientific methods, and no peer review. The result is a press that hangs onto its "objectivity" and "detachment" as practical methods to deflect public criticism and maintain the sacred tenet of credibility. This mentality, he suggested, creates an insular media culture in which journalists turn to one another for cues on how to act and what to value. Rosen (1999) called this approach *fortress journalism,* adding:

> In fortress journalism, the press is criticized by all, in conversation with none. Journalists rely on their professional culture—a peer culture—for approval and status. Liberty of the press, that ringing phrase, offers insulation more than inspiration. Journalism is what journalists do, not what democracy may need done. (p. 27)

Rosen (1996) envisioned public journalism in stark contrast with fortress journalism. He did not see the movement as a "thirst" for engagement or action but rather as a form of "proactive neutrality" (p. 13). When the aggressive reporting and angry editorials that characterize traditional journalism leave a community's problems unresolved, Rosen suggested the choices of editors are narrowed to remaining within the conventions of the craft and accepting the "impotence of journalism," or rethinking what journalism can be in hopes of stimulating useful engagement. He asked, "When articles and editorials are not enough, does not the responsibility of the press extend to other forms of prodding?" (p 60).

The controversial nature of public journalism, Rosens wrote, is not that it demands journalists get involved as players in public affairs, but that public journalism "lifts their involvement into public view, acknowledging what everyone already knows: the press is a player" (p. 69). Once the press is ready to place itself as a player in public life, then it is much easier to accept and support certain public values: civic participation, deliberative dialogue, political problem solving, and "the cultivation of democratic dispositions" (p. 69).

Rosen acknowledged that with or without the help of a civic-minded press, U.S. citizens are likely to find ways to solve their problems, but, he wrote, "people in the press need some sense of what they are working toward, what it all adds up to. This sense, earlier characterized as 'spiritual,' cannot be found within journalism itself. The mission of good journalism is not, I think, to do good journalism" (p. 82).

Rosen (1999) saw public journalism as an "idea that happened," "a concept with a career," and "an abstraction that became an adventure" in the U.S. press (p. 21). He characterized it as an argument, experiment, and movement. He wrote that the world's shortest definition of public journalism is "what Dewey meant," and then expanded that to include the thinking of several contemporary scholars: James Carey, who called the public the "god term" of journalism; Clifford Christians, John P. Ferré, and P. Mark Flackler, who advocated a journalism ethic grounded in the common good; Theodore Glasser, who called communication the "cultivation of citizenship"; and Edmund B. Lambeth, who called for "committed journalism" (p. 24).

Rosen also believed that public journalism is a journalism of hope (Merritt & Rosen, 1998). As a counter to the irresponsible, negative, detached world of journalism, he posed the question, "In what sense is the reporter responsible for the scene that unfolds in front of him?" He contended that if journalists felt they were as responsible for everything they saw as they were for everything they did, then they would understand how he and Merritt arrived at the ideals of public journalism. "I think we both wanted to observe a scene that would give us some reason to hope. Public journalism has been the result. You must decide what you think of it, but when you do decide, ask yourself a simple question: Where do I want to place myself, and from where can I find some reason to hope?" (p. 56).

DAVIS "BUZZ" MERRITT

For Merritt, too, the 1988 presidential campaign was a turning point. Disgusted by the "armies of handlers, consultants, and theorists who for decades had been relentlessly distorting campaigns into empty contests," Merritt, then the editor of the *Wichita Eagle*, "decided that something had to be done to change the triangle of politics, public and press that defines modern election campaigns" (Merritt & Rosen, 1998, p. 37). Convinced that politics would not change, he wrote, "It was equally clear to me that the public couldn't change on its own, being merely a victim of the incestuous partnership of politics and the political press" (p. 37). This left only the press that could change, and Merritt set out to change it.

In the 1990 Kansas gubernatorial election, the *Eagle* conducted a "modest election project" called *Your Vote Counts*. Merritt wrote that the project drew some national attention because:

> . . . it was an unabashed and activist effort to restore some role for citizens in the election process. Doing so meant, for the *Eagle* and its staff, stepping over 'The Line,' that quasi-mystical rubicon separating 'Good Journalism' done by 'Real Journalists' in a mind-set of determined detachment from, well, something else. That something else, intimidating for traditionalists to contemplate, was a mind-set of caring whether our constitutional democracy could work well enough to fulfill its promise. (p. 37)

The *Your Vote Counts* project was the *Eagle*'s first foray into public journalism, and possibly the first U.S. experiment in the idea of public journalism, although the term had not yet been created. Merritt wrote that the project produced some "tantalizing signs of hope," including higher voter turn-out rates than other parts of the state and voters who felt they understood the issues better than voters outside the *Eagle*'s circulation area. He continued, "But, most satisfyingly for me, an acquaintance whose intellect I respect commented during our Voter Project, 'You're trying to save democracy, aren't you?' I modestly agreed" (p. 38).

Merritt (1997) established the rationale for public journalism as a press response to two 1990s dilemmas: (a) an American public increasingly withdrawn from public life, cynical about their leaders' ability or interest in doing the right things, while at the same time increasingly discouraged about their ability to affect the woeful situation, and (b) *the fact* that journalism is rapidly reaching the last supply of its credibility and authority with citizens (emphasis added). In other works he referred (1998) to the 1994 Times Mirror poll that found that 71% of the respondents agreed that "the news media gets [sic] in the way of society solving its problems," whereas only 25% agreed that the news media help society solve its problems (p. 5).

Merritt (1996, 1998) believed that to understand public journalism—that is, to go beyond the "Sturm und Drang of debate and angry dismissiveness" —requires a philosophical journey grounded in some base assumptions:

- The viability of public life and the value of journalism are inextricably linked.
- Public life cannot regain its vitality if the news media provide a diet of information. There is too much information for citizens to digest. Journalists who view their jobs as simply telling the news in a detached way are not helpful to public life or their profession.
- The objective of journalism must be to reengage citizens in public life.

If these assumptions are accepted, then the next step for journalists is to recognize that "journalism's integral role in public life imposes an obligation on us . . . to do our journalism in ways that are calculated to help public life go well *by reengaging people in it*" (Merritt's emphasis; 1996, p. 30). This step, Merritt acknowledged, is a point of journalistic departure that requires moving away from traditional detachment and calls for a declared intent.

Merritt, an editor with 4 decades of newspaper experience including about 20 years at the helm of the *Wichita Eagle*, is critical of journalists and how the institution of journalism has come to define press freedom. Bemoaning the lack of professional mandates, he wrote (1998) that "journalism's conventions are only tangentially governed by the laws of man. This absence of external control means that journalism's culture has evolved into what journalists have chosen it to be" (p. 17). He continued that the authors of the First Amendment, by choosing to frame press freedom in a negative context with the famous words "Congress shall make no law . . ." invariably ensured that American journalism was "born in a defensive crouch" (p. 17). Merritt wrote that this First Amendment proclamation of freedom constituted "so potent a prohibition . . . consistently buttressed by court decisions (that it) could hardly have resulted in anything else but a subculture of special privilege; the vacuum was too great, the opportunity too unfettered" (p. 18).

Journalistic instincts and routines—questionable reflexes driven by questionable values—are also reasons why the press needs to become more accountable, Merritt believed. Among the reflexes that need reconditioning is journalists' perceived need for objectivity and detachment. Objectivity, he wrote, serves the economic needs of publishers who want to appeal to mass audiences and advertisers by not offending either with opinionated, highly politicized content. However, this tenet does not serve journalists well because it requires them to separate their minds from their souls. Merritt contended objectivity nurtures a transience in journalists because "when caring about a place or circumstance is considered a negative, roots cannot be comfortably put down or useful relations established" (p. 25). Merritt also asserted that "determined detachment" leads to a blindness or trained incapacity to understand people and the environment, which also ensures that more will be reported on what is going wrong than what is going right. Reporters avoid reporting positive news because they lack the faith that what is going right will continue to progress well. Merritt wrote, "The deeply held belief that detachment insures our credibility creates yet another disconnection with non-journalists, who simply don't see it that way" (p. 25).

The disconnect is further solidified by journalists who see balanced reporting as seeking out extreme, polarized positions on issues. This approach means that conflict becomes the central narrative to reporting. "Conflict," Merritt wrote, "real or contrived, is the highest coin in the journalistic realm. Journalists love it" (p. 27). The emphasis on conflict drowns out ideas that can lead to resolving problems. It also creates a false frame for most issues, a frame in which most people do not find their ideas illustrated. This framing of stories around conflict results in an increasingly larger percentage of the public feeling left out of the public debate and disenchanted with journalism. "The quoted sources (and the journalist who presents them) become participants in a closed, detached cycle" (p. 27).

Merritt's critique of the press extended to the "watchdog" role. Although this role served journalism and democracy well in relation to the government, he contended that this ideal has cultivated a general adversarial mentality among journalists that evolved from journalism's "defensive crouch" borne of the First Amendment. "Unfortunately, journalism's determined adversarial relationship with government is not confined to that; it reaches into and damages our relationship with all authority, and even beyond to our dealings with regular citizens. This has proven to be less than helpful" (p. 29).

Merritt believed that journalists can maintain their independence and participate in public life. He likened the role of the public journalist to that of a "fair-minded participant," who functions in a similar fashion as an umpire or referee facilitating the outcome of a sports competition. This role requires a knowledge of the rules and a commitment to see the game is played within those rules. Merritt, like Rosen, conceded that public life can, and does, go on without journalists playing their appropriate role. However, the resolution of issues, if it occurs at all, is decided on the same risky basis as the playground pick-up game. Merritt wrote that journalists' responsibility when critical issues arise is to make sure something more substantial than playground rules governs the issue-resolving process. "That's where the journalistic fair-minded participant becomes important. We act out of the value that 'public life should go well'" (p. 97).

In an era of stagnant newspaper circulation and fragmenting audiences for all mass media, Merritt believed that journalism also has an economic interest in seeing public life work well. "When issues are resolved, when hopelessness and cynicism are replaced by hope and optimism, people are encouraged to become engaged in attacking the next issue. People engaged in public life, many studies have shown, are avid consumers of the journalistic product" (p. 103).

Merritt's conviction that journalism was contributing more to the problems of public life than encouraging possible cures led him to initiate the *Wichita Eagle*'s *Your Vote Counts* project in 1990. The effort included surveys and focus groups to find out what the public thought were important issues and then directed the coverage of candidates to those issues. Beyond this, Merritt said, "We did a number of things and in effect changed the campaign. We abandoned neutrality in whether people should vote. We actively were getting people to register and urging them to vote" (Shepard, 1994, p. 31). Consistent with the public journalism philosophy of "entering the fray . . . as facilitators and referees" (p. 31), the nudging was done on news pages.

Charity (1995) wrote that Merritt was taking full advantage of the "drama" of public judgment when he wrote a front-page editorial kicking off the *Eagle*'s 1992 public journalism initiative called *The People Project*. Merritt wrote:

> We have it within our reach to powerfully affect our surroundings and to rejuvenate the idea of collective problem-solving. That, in turn, can rebuild communities at all levels. But we must solve it ourselves. *Government can't do it . . .* [italics added] At the end of (this project) we'll know an important thing about ourselves: whether we have the will, given the opportunity, to take responsibility for our lives and our community. (Charity, 1995, pp. 85–86)

Merritt's belief that journalism must seek guidance from the public as an antidote to ineffective government was shown when he proclaimed proudly that "there were hundreds of voices in The People Project (as it ran in the paper) and not a single expert or politician" (Shepard, 1994, p. 31).

In several venues, Merritt expressed his frustration that the controversial nature of public journalism has encouraged a superficial debate that has not allowed a thorough examination of the philosophy that underlies the practice. He wrote (1998), "The tragic fact is that the way most journalists have treated the idea is a telling catalogue of what ails my profession" (p. 114). In short, he, along with Rosen, laments that public journalism has had journalism done to it. They believe journalists have treated the idea with too much emphasis on conflict and adversarialism, while refusing to see it in a broader context of events and issues. Both men, who have worked together creating, building, and expanding the ideals of public journalism, see it as a philosophy with a future and a practice that should transcend "project journalism." Merritt (1996) wrote, "Its useful future lies in our learning to do daily and weekly journalism in ways that reengage people with public life, including politics. 'Learning' is an important word here, because no one really knows how to do that yet; it's an unfulfilled intellectual and occupational challenge" (pp. 30–31). For Merritt, public journalism's call to learn will require journalists to embrace broader responsibilities that actually transcend journalism. The goal of public journalism, he wrote, "is not to better connect journalists with their communities, but to better connect the people in communities with one another. So public journalism is as much or more about public life than it is about journalism, a fact universally overlooked" (p. 30).

JAN SCHAFFER

The irony of Schaffer's job is readily apparent to her. Formerly the business editor of the *Philadelphia Inquirer,* Schaffer oversaw an investigative series on the abuses of the nonprofit sector that referred to the sector as the "Shadow Economy." A Pulitzer finalist, the series was later turned into the book *Warehouses of Wealth.* At that time, she probably never envisioned herself becoming an executive in that warehouse. However, Schaffer, executive director of the Pew Center for Civic Journalism, wrote she is "indebted to the philanthropic community for having the opportunity to encourage innovation and risk-taking in journalism" (1999b, paragraph 3).

A subsidiary of the Pew Charitable Trusts, the Pew Center for Civic Journalism was founded in 1993 to fund projects in civic (or public) journalism. The center had its funding renewed for a third 3-year period in 1999 with a $4.65 million grant, pushing to more than $10 million Pew's commitment to civic journalism. The center's quarterly newsletter, *Civic Catalyst,* boasts that the renewed commitment allows the center to continue sponsoring civic journalism projects and educational seminars, expanding the base of more than 1,700 journalists who have attended Pew civic journalism workshops through 1999. In its first 6 years of advancing civic journalism, Pew has given money to 148 news organizations involved with 77 initiatives ("Pew Center is Renewed," 1999). Pew supplements the Center for Civic Journalism with two corollary interests: the Pew Research Center, a polling institute, and the Project for Excellence in Journalism (Schaffer, 1997a).

Schaffer (1999b) wrote that when the Pew Charitable Trusts decided to get involved in journalism, the interest was not so much in journalism as civic engagement. "They feared that democracy was broken—that citizens were not voting, volunteeering or participating actively in public life" (paragraph 6). The fear extended to journalism because the trusts questioned whether journalism was part of the problem. Schaffer (1997a) wrote:

> The idea for the center is this: Maybe some of the ways journalism is being practiced these days are partly—not totally—responsible for the U.S. turning into a nation of civic couch potatoes. For the cynicism. For a declining can-do spirit. For a sort of learned helplessness.
>
> The theory behind this grand experiment—and it is a grand experiment—is: If journalists did their jobs differently, would citizens do their jobs differently? (paragraphs 7–8)

The Pew Center for Civic Journalism provides seed money to news media that are willing to take risks to reinvigorate civic engagement. Schaffer wrote that the center is a "venture capital fund" that is serious about supporting journalism and related research projects and then educating the rest of the profession. "We'll have some hits and outs. But that's the nice thing about being a non-profit. We don't have to worry about being profitable. We can afford to take risks," she wrote (1996b, paragraph 43).

Schaffer believes civic journalism is about addressing the impotence of journalism. The experiments that Pew funds are about new practices that enable journalism to better reflect the reality of readers. These experiments are based on two premises that combine economics and civics: (a) fewer people are reading newspapers or watching television news, which, she wrote, "tells us that our journalism is ineffective at engaging the people we mean to serve," and (b) "something is eating at the foundations of American democracy" (1998, paragraphs 13–14).

Schaffer asserted that by focusing so much on conflict, scandal, celebrities, bad news, and crime, journalists have lost their self-respect. To regain it, journalists need to worry more about their responsibilities. "A conscious sense of our responsibilties to readers and the community at large is the core of civic journalism," she wrote (1998, paragraph 27). She saw civic journalism as a "broad label put on efforts by editors and news directors to try to do their jobs in ways that help overcome people's sense of powerless [sic] and alienation" (1999b, paragraph 14). This is done by creating a "neutral zone of empowerment, arming citizens" (paragraph 17). She asserted that civic journalism employs all the tools of good journalism, but "it's not afraid to get more involved with the community—in listening, in being a catalyst for activity, in helping the community build its own capacity. And it's not afraid to say: If the old journalism is not working, let's reinvent it" (paragraph 19).

Schaffer juxtaposed some of the what she considers problems with journalistic practices with potential solutions offered by civic journalism. Traditional journalism focuses on "elites," whereas civic journalism focuses more on "everyman." A shift toward the everyman approach, she wrote, "often comes at the expense of coverage of elected officials, community leaders and so-called experts . . . After all, citizens can be very smart about their own lives and civic journalists are not afraid to dignify the ideas of ordinary people" (1996a, paragraphs 16–17). She also urged journalists to move away from the interview model of journalism to a conversational model. This latter model requires journalists to embrace the notion that the media should not "talk at" people (simply provide them with information) but instead strive to "talk with" them. Journalists refocus their information gathering by "listening for patterns and common threads that link stakeholders" (1996a, paragraph 24), and they do this by bringing citizens together into civic spaces, such as focus groups, town hall meetings, and living-room conversations. The conversational model enables journalism to become more interactive, creating a two-way conversation between media and the public. The conversation is facilitated by technology, such as voice mail, e-mail, audio text, and the Internet. Schaffer called civic journalists "active pioneers" in using technology to make their stories more interactive. Whereas traditional journalists use these electronic communication forms for feedback after a story, "civic journalists are using them as starting points in the reporting process" (1996a, paragraph 32).

Civic journalists also sacrifice the control exerted by most journalists over their work for a greater "connectedness." Schaffer contended that traditional journalists are empowered by "gotcha stories" that give them a sense of one-upsmanship over their peers. The thought of giving ordinary people a voice in journalism is a departure from the conventional way of doing business that requires journalists to relinquish some control. She wrote, "It may even mean journalists have to give up some of their voice to give citizens some space" (1996a, paragraph 39). For example, citizens have more of an appetite for repetition than journalists, who expect readers to remember that the paper (or media outlet) has already reported on a specific subject. Control is perceived by many citizens as a form of media arrogance, and Schaffer sees civic journalists trading in their "arrogance" for "accessibility." Accessibility means giving citizens a place in journalism to publicly state their views in a way that makes them feel their efforts are worthwhile. Accessibility can also give the public more than a voice; she wrote, "It shows them some roles they can play. For instance, can they volunteer to do something, join a task force, belong to a roundtable discussion, come up with a solution, respond to a questionnaire" (1996a, paragraph 48).

Schaffer believes that giving the public more access allows the media to expect the public to be more accountable. Traditional journalism tends to rely on "feel good" or "feel bad" models; however, Schaffer called for civic journalists to aspire to a "feel accountable" model, with accountability shared between the media and public. She wrote, "Part of civic journalism is holding citizens just as accountable as we hold public officials" (1997a, paragraph 16). By giving citizens a voice in the media to make public their ideas, criticisms, and solutions, then the public, as well as journalists, become accountable for media content. This concept of using accessibility as a means to accountability should be a goal of journalism. Schaffer explained, "If (the public) can buy into the problem in some way, feel some ownership of it, they are much more likely to get involved in finding a solution" (1996a, paragraph 54). Schaffer believes the public is yearning for more interaction and accessibility, whereas many journalists, mired in their reflexes, are afraid of change. "Citizens have a tremendous appetite for this kind of engagement and new ways of getting information. Unfortunately, they have a bigger appetite for it than some journalists" (1997a, paragraph 39).

Civic journalists conceive of their jobs in fundamentally different ways than traditional journalists, and Schaffer posed a series of "What would happen if" scenarios that ponder a journalism future based on civic journalism ideals. She wondered what if journalists would redefine news to include more coverage of consensus and collaboration. She suggested, for example, that journalists covering meetings don't know what to report if "people are talking and working on solutions" (1997a, paragraph 19). Conventional journalism does not have a story model that includes this type of reporting. She mused about what would happen if journalists redefined balance so it was not defined by extremes, but the middle. Using the abortion issue for an example, she writes that the great majority of people are not really for or against abortion, but see merits to both sides of the argument. The ability to write about ambivalance without making it boring is a skill mastered by novelists and something journalists should aspire to as well.

Schaffer also asked what if the news media expanded the watchdog role to include a "guide dog" role. As guide dog, the media would show citizens how they can get involved and make a difference in public life. "Papers," she wrote, "are helping to create all kinds of civic spaces where people can actually do something. And editors are stunned by the response. They know they are helping their communities help themselves" (1997a, paragraph 35). Schaffer cited the *Seattle Times* as an example. The paper offered to pay for pizza for anyone willing to host a house party where citizens could discuss growth in the region. There were 230 parties, after which 100 citizens were invited to become "part of a mock jury that heard prosecutors and defense attorneys questioning expert witnesses on growth. They found the government and themselves overwhelmingly guilty for failing to plan adequately"

(1997a, paragraph 37). The participants were then "sentenced" to come back the next week to develop and discuss ideas.

It is these types of activities that are yielding some positive results, Schaffer believes. Models of public engagement spurred by civic journalism projects can be used as examples for other communities to follow. The *Argus Leader*, in South Dakota, Schaffer wrote, "engaged the entire town of Tyndall in confronting community problems. And then sent a corps of ambassadors to help other small towns replicate Tyndall's successes" (1998, paragraph 33). Another example comes from Binghamton, NY, where the *Press & Sun-Bulletin* helped citizens form 10 groups called action teams to address issues caused by corporate downsizing in a project called "Facing Our Future." The action teams developed scores of ideas, many of which have been implemented with the blessing of the local Chamber of Commerce, which was initially hostile to the project. The benefits of civic journalism can also be measured by how projects have influenced some people to have more positive perceptions of the media, Schaffer wrote. "We have seen people running for office in Peoria, Portland, Bradenton—people who never aspired to elected office until they got involved in a civic journalism initiative" (1999b, paragraph 72).

To continue the momentum of civic journalism, Schaffer asserted that journalism needs to change. She contended that journalists who do not embrace civic journalism have become so embedded in their current practices that they have forgotten or lost their journalistic mission. "I've come to learn that change freaks journalists out—even change that seeks to get them back to their core values" (1997b, paragraph 14). Schaffer urged media managers to focus on hiring new people who can fill three needs:

1. the need for entrepreneurs and risks takers who will find new groups of news consumers and develop products to meet consumers' needs. These are people "who will break out of the box and enter joint ventures with local magnet schools or religious groups who may fulfill a journalistic function— if we guide and train them";

2. the need to "let go of our words" by hiring fewer wordsmiths wedded to long narrative stories. The goal should be to include more "information purveyors," skilled at "quick charts and grids," and writers who can develop "some new writing styles that will better synthesize complex webs of concerns";

3. the need for new leaders, people who are not going to look over their shoulders and wonder what their peers think, but those who have "the courage of their convictions to carry on" (1997b, paragraphs 22–24).

Schaffer believed "civic journalism is working at creating the journalism of the future . . . it has initiated a stepped-up conversation and a lot of introspection in the profession over the role of journalists and the way we practice our craft, our credibility" (1997a, paragraphs 48–49). She added these conversations are being formally conducted by the Freedom Forum, the American Society of Newspaper Editors, and the Pew Charitable Trusts.

ARTHUR CHARITY

As the civic (or public) journalism movement was gaining momentum in the mid-1990s, Charity (1995) wrote that Rosen hired him to compile a list of sources and resources that editors and reporters could use to get ideas for public journalism projects and network with each other. That effort, funded by the Knight Foundation, focused on the why and how of public journalism, and became the foundation of Charity's book, *Doing Public Journalism*, published by the Kettering Foundation.

The book instructs journalists in the goals of public journalism and provides suggestions about how to implement new public journalism practices. These suggestions are grouped throughout the text under the running head *Pushing the Envelope*. The book is organized around the principles that Rosen and Merritt defined in some of the movement's early writings, and it is grounded in democratic theory and communitarianism, including works by Daniel Yankelovich, Robert Putnam, Amitai Etzioni, Robert Bellah, Frances Moore Lappé, and Paul Martin DuBois. There are sections instructing journalists in public listening, helping citizens work toward public judgment, reframing news coverage, building civic capital, and helping citizens act.

Charity contrasted the ideals of public journalists with those of conventional journalists, writing that public journalists believe "something basic has to change because journalism isn't working now"; old habits, however sacred, need revision; journalists need to lower the hurdles that prevent people from participating in public life; and "citizens deserve a bigger place in the newspaper itself," in part because "public life should work, and journalism has a role in making it work" (p. 10). Conventional journalists, on the other hand, believe the practice of journalism might need to improve, but the traditions are fine; the media and political life provide the public an opportunity to participate and if people do not become engaged, it is their choice; the media is a profession in which journalists, not readers, write newspapers; and it is beyond the role of the media to make public life work and dangerous for the media to think this is their role (p. 10).

In public journalism, the media need to improve at helping the public set a news agenda. Charity, borrowing from Yankelovich, wrote that the public is frustrated by the media's news agenda, and the media (he refers specifically to newspapers) can continue trying to persuade people that unpopular issues warrant attention, but citizens would be more engaged if the media learn to focus news coverage around those issues and priorities that citizens set for themselves. Regarding agenda setting, he wrote, "Newspapers have to learn not to dominate the process; they must figure out how to follow the public's own lead" (p. 5). Developing new ways of public listening is key to learning this process. Newspapers practicing public journalism are sponsoring community conversations, helping create citizens' panels, running clip-out ballots in the paper, and experimenting with polls and focus groups. The *Des Moines Register* required all its full-time news staff to conduct at least four face-to-face interviews with residents of the metropolitan area "just to find out what was on their minds" (p. 34). In Fort Wayne, IN, the *News Sentinel* had the temerity to take public journalism to its logical extreme. The paper asked representatives of city neighborhoods to simply tell the paper what it could do to make their local efforts more effective. The *News Sentinel* set up no guidelines or constraints (except on requesting financial assistance), thus offering "a complete tabula rasa" (p. 34). In a *Pushing the Envelope* section, Charity suggested that journalists at news-budget meetings should begin asking themselves, "How can we rachet up public journalism in this story?" (p. 46). He also urged journalists at daily postpublication reviews of the newspaper to ask themselves whether the page-one stories start from citizen viewpoints. Newspapers should even consider appointing an internal ombudsman whose job would be to read through the entire paper each day "just to look for the public journalism quotient . . . He or she could then circulate memos to make staff aware of successes and failures" (p. 46).

Once the media has figured out the issues the public wants to address, the challenge becomes creating a public conversation with the eventual goal of moving the people toward public judgment. Charity wrote, "The initiative for convening these conversations ought perhaps to rest with politicians or private citizens rather than the news media, but—even if you feel this way— the facts are that politicians and private citizens are doing an inadequate job of it" (pp. 101–102). Helping citizens work through problems requires a degree of expertise that most journalists find strange within the confines of their journalistic conventions. Successful public journalists become experts in public life. Using the example of a police reporter, Charity wrote:

> (A "public" police reporter) aims to bring the police, their official overseers, the victims of crime, even the criminals, and the residents of various neighborhoods in a city into constructive dialogue with one another about crime. The center has shifted from the police blotter to the public agenda. This calls upon the reporter to be part diplomat, part interpreter, and to be an expert of a very different, subtler, and more creative sort: an expert in what each and every segment of the community wants, thinks, and worries about when it comes to crime. (p. 11)

Charity wrote that this approach to journalism challenges all citizens to do what needs to be done if public life is to succeed. Newspapers experimenting in public journalism are expending an "unprecedented effort on helping citizens buy onto the decision-making process" (p. 51). Public journalists work from the conviction that citizens will see journalism as more essential to their lives. Citizens will continue to read and pay for the newspaper, Charity wrote, "even if they balk now and then when their own complacency, bigotry, or wishful thinking is put on the spot. Public journalists, in short, are the clear-eyed pragmatists that conventional journalists only pretend to be" (p. 51).

Once the public has worked through an issue and reached a judgment, the media should become active in "prodding action on the public's choice." Charity wrote, "The press ought to champion (the choice) as vigorously as it champions any other fundamental part of democracy, like free speech or the right to vote" (p. 8). Charity saw this work tied to the origins of public journalism and having many potential benefits:

> The first public journalists reasoned that if they could create ways of doing their work that buttress this process of "coming to public judgment," they could make the public happier with the news profession, make the newspaper more essential to citizens, help solve some of our perennial national and local problems, and get more job satisfaction in the process. (p. 9)

If done well, the media's helping people reach public judgment should achieve the additional benefit of creating *civic capital*. Whereas economists view capital as a physical or human resource that improves worker productivity, democratic theorists see civic capital as a resource that improves community productivity and makes better communities. Civic capital improves a community's ability to confront and solve problems and allows a community to live happily. Beyond giving citizens what they need to work through issues, Charity wrote, "public journalists have to look for ways to strengthen their community's goodwill, cooperative habits, insights into where other social groups are coming from, shorthand ways of talking, and so on — the groundwork factors of democracy" (p. 12). Newspapers help their communities build civic capital by creating a public space for citizens to socialize. Charity continued, "not just as we'd socialize at a bake sale, but as we'd socialize in the Athenian agora, as fellow citizens sharing ideas" (p. 47).

Given these expanded media goals of helping people toward public judgment and the creation of civic capital, public journalists must redefine what is newsworthy. Charity insisted that for public journalists the question of news value comes to center on two questions: (a) Does a piece of reporting help build civic capital? (b) Does the reporting help move the public toward meaningful public judgment and action? These questions set a "benchmark of realism," he wrote, "which means the final word on a public journalist's news choices can never come from the publisher, colleagues, or the Pulitzer Prize committee, but only from what happens or doesn't happen in the community as a whole" (p. 50). Journalists trying to help their communities build civic capital go beyond solving particular problems and see the bigger, "more compelling master narrative," asking, "Will this community work? Is this community succeeding? Can we make a good life with one another?" (p. 88).

Charity likened public journalists to activists in the communitarian movement who are trying to nurture community-mindedness and grassroot cooperation as a way of local problem solving. He suggested that Lappé and DuBois's (1994) "arts of democracy" are excellent skills that, if practiced by public journalists, will help diminish the "lack of community" problem. Among these skills are listening actively with empathy, agreeing to disagree while searching for common ground, seeking mediation that helps discover common interests, imagining a world as we wish it to be, engaging in public dialogue, taking time to celebrate and appreciate what one learns, and mentoring that helps people to guide one another in the lessons of public life. Charity wrote, "A newspaper can give its readers a benchmark of the community's health by taking any hard-news beat it already covers—politics, city hall, crime, or business—and asking when, where and how much citizens are practicing certain basic skills. A newspaper can *foster* the community's health by creatively trying to embed those skills in its reporting" (Charity's emphasis, pp. 89–90).

Public journalism's ability to reengage people in democracy and public life gives it added value that should make economic sense to media companies. Charity asserted this added value comes at a time when "everyone agrees that journalism as a business is in trouble" (p. 155). As news media have responded to fragmenting audiences with sensationalism, shorter stories, and slicker packaging, public journalism's added value provides "a strong persuasive argument about *why* it should work in the long run" (Charity's emphasis; p. 155). This argument is supported by numerous success stories, including higher reader-approval ratings, the extent of public participation in newspaper-sponsored events, citizens submitting pledges to act in specific ways, increased community volunteering, increased networking of formerly unaffiliated organizations, and, "most impressively, as a direct result of public journalism coverage citizens have organized entirely new grassroots groups . . . many of which are now major forces for policy making and public action" (p. 157).

EDITORS TALKING PUBLIC JOURNALISM

Rosen and Merritt remain the "fathers" of the public journalism movement and continue to be its most prolific and ubiquitous leaders. Following principles they articulated, media outlets across the country—often with the assistance of foundations such as the Pew Center for Civic Journalism—are exploring ways to make journalism more public. Many of the ideas for putting the principles into action have come from Charity's book, which remains the foremost instructional manual on "doing public journalism." What follows are some samples of what those editors most experienced in public journalism are saying about it.

Rick Thames, editor, *Wichita Eagle,* and former government editor, *Charlotte Observer:* "We used to heighten conflict. We'd say to people, you go fight, we'll hold your coats and go write about it afterwards. But we've learned that doesn't serve our readers very well. They are tired of conflict. They want to see solutions" (Fouhy & Schaffer, 1995, p. 18).

Thames (1998) wrote that public journalism is rooted in a basic belief: "Our nation is only as strong as its civic life, and journalists have a responsibility to inform in ways that allow citizens to get involved in solving society's problems. Somehow, many journalists have drifted away from this vital role" (p. 113). He continued, "After all, we've spent decades alienating the public with our traditional approaches. We've got a lot of mending to do. I think it's safe to say that we're at least heading in the right direction. . . . Some still fret that we are treading on a slippery slope. They are right. But the same can be said for almost any form of journalism we practice. Think of what would happen to an investigative reporter who decided that anything goes. For that matter, imagine the outcome for any reporter who strayed from basic principles on even the most routine daily story. Our slope is a bit slicker at the moment because we're still learning. That makes many of us uneasy, as well it should" (p. 122).

Kate Parry (1999), senior editor, Politics and Special Reports, *St. Paul Pioneer Press:* "Our parent company, Knight-Ridder Inc., has enthusiastically supported civic journalism for many years with grants to individual newspapers on a project-by-project basis. This year, our corporate leaders asked those of us on the frontlines to consider ways it could be mainstreamed into daily reporting beats. We all feel it is time to take civic journalism techniques that have been sequestered in large projects and spread them into grass-roots journalism. But it's still unclear how we will do this. Although some reporters who have had the opportunity to work on the projects have embraced civic journalism, the movement remains largely an editor-driven endeavor. How do we drive it more deeply into newsrooms?" (p. 12).

Dave Iverson, executive producer, Wisconsin Public Television: "Maintaining a citizen focus, doing citizen-based journalism, is enlightening. It is illuminating and insightful. It can be maddening, but not nearly as maddening as dealing with the candidates" ("Elections '96," 1996, p. 9).

Lou Heldman, executive editor, *Tallahassee Democrat:* Public journalism "is really about changing the way people think and act. If those now calling themselves 'residents' or 'taxpayers' begin thinking of themselves as 'citizens,' and acting in intelligent and empowered ways, it follows that public officials will begin to think differently about citizens and their own responsibilities" (Charity, 1995, pp. 133, 135).

Richard Harwood (1996), of the Harwood Group, a consulting and research business, and a former editor at the *Washington Post:* Civic journalism "is a work in progress. No one is entirely sure what it is or ought to be. But it has attracted the interest and financial support of Pew Charitable Trusts, the 20th Century Fund, the Knight-Ridder newspaper chain and a number of individual newspapers and televisions. In some of the experimental efforts so far, newspapers have undertaken extensive surveys of their readers to find out what 'the people' want from politicians and government. Conferences and 'town meetings' have been organized. Political debates have been sponsored. Whether initiatves of this kind will achieve their purpose—a much broader base of civic and political involvement and better 'outcomes'—is uncertain. It may turn out that 'civic journalism' is more appropriate and doable in smaller communities than large metropolitan areas" (p. A21).

Frank Denton (1998), editor, Madison *Wisconsin State Journal,* writing with Esther Thorson, associate dean, University of Missouri School of Journalism: "What is arguably new about public journalism is the active *involvement* of the public. Even increased public awareness of an issue, a traditional measurement of mass communication effects, is not enough. The mass of people can be quite aware of community or national affairs and still be so alienated or simply uninterested that they neither engage in public discourse nor express their will, even by voting. Democracy is no more served by informed but uninvolved citizens than it is by ignorant uninvolved citizens. Public journalism . . . means to place responsibility for public affairs squarely on the public, by informing, involving and empowering them with information. Its champions likely would admit to the idealism, even utopianism" (Denton's emphasis; pp. 146–147).

Jennie Buckner, executive editor, *Charlotte Observer:* "Our experience has been the opposite of boosterism. We have told the community hard truths about itself. We have asked the people of Charlotte and the neighborhoods to look at some of the most damaging pathologies in cities today. They have looked at them, owned up to them and decided to do something about them. We have not skirted around issues, we have taken them on. We have entered into a dialogue with the community about how we came to have these difficulties, but we have also talked to the community about solutions and committed to change" (Fouhy & Schaffer, 1995, p. 18).

Ken Doctor, managing editor, *St. Paul Pioneer Press:* "Public journalism is a means, not an end. It looks like a noun, but it's actually a verb. It's about trying different approaches and seeing what works for our readers. Public journalism is about closeness and distance. We've got the distance part of it down clearly . . . but the closeness, sometimes the intimacy of our contacts, is far more important" ("Civic Journalism," 1996, p. 9).

Matthew Storin (1996), editor, *The Boston Globe:* "The one caution flag that I would raise is that I think editors should think long and hard before they undertake a project where it might be argued they are replacing the function of their duly elected public leaders. I do think it is more than advisable for newspapers to bring citizens together and listen to what they have to say. We sponsor debates of office seekers, so why not sponsor discussions by voters? Whether a paper wants to commit to following the consensus, should there be one from these meetings, is an option we might not all embrace. But I think getting folks out from in front of the TV one night and getting them to talk about the problems and dreams of their community is a terrific thing" (p. 11).

Cole Campbell (1999), editor, *St. Louis Post-Dispatch:* "We journalists have some beliefs that need reconsideration if we want to help our communities work through problems confronting them. We believe, in a phrase of Alabama-born journalist William Bradford Huie, that we are in 'the truth business.' We believe that our product is information, offered up with a dash of entertainment. And we believe . . . that journalism has nothing to do with philosophy" (p. xiv). Campbell wrote that after 20 years of listening to citizens talk about their lives and their newspapers, he has come to three different beliefs: journalism is in the problem-solving business, not the truth business; journalism's product is a contribution to understanding, which means that journalism is as much about models for understanding as it is about information; and journalism is philosophical construct about what is worth paying attention to and how to best do it.

Campbell suggested two ways that journalism can refocus its attention that could radically transform the philosophy and practice. He wrote, "What if we reoriented our journalism away from the sources of news and toward the recipients of news? Instead of building our beats around institutions and agencies, what if we built them around the troubles and joys in people's lives? Instead of having a City Hall beat, we might have a political participation beat that tracks what's happening at City Hall in a way that helps citizens directly influence it. Instead of covering doctors and medical breakthroughs using patients as illustrations of what health care professionals can accomplish, suppose we covered patients and used doctors and medical breakthroughs as illustrations of problem solving. What if we thought of institutions and agencies not as *sources of news* but as *resources for problem solving* that citizens could tap and work with?" (Campbell's emphasis; pp. xxv–xxvi). Campbell continued by suggesting, "What if we reoriented our journalism away from a description of the present and toward an imagination of a better alternative?" (p. xxvi). He perceived imagination as a means through which people can assemble a coherent world; imagination contributes to making empathy possible and permits the understanding of alternative realities.

The leaders of the public (civic) journalism movement, although not in complete agreement, can be seen as greatly influenced by the same thinkers, and, to a large extent, each other. Finding their intellectual base in communitarian theory, the ideas of Dewey, Carey, Habermas, Yankelovich, Putnam, Etzioni, and Christians appear throughout the thinking of the movement's leaders discussed in this chapter. As the philosophy and practice of public journalism evolves, those people at the forefront of the movement are committed to several base concepts:

• The condition of the American republic is unhealthy and the implications for the future are ominous. The media are partially to blame for the failings of government and citizenship.

• Public journalism is a response to this condition that expands the news media's responsibility into that of organizer and promoter of democracy. The media are seen as largely responsible for the quality of public life.

• To meet this responsibility, the media need to redefine, and to a large extent eradicate, their canons of detachment, objectivity, and agenda setting, while striving to enthrone the issues and concerns of the public.

• The media's obligation extends to increasing civic involvement, sponsoring and initiating dialogue that leads to an increased sense of community, helping communities work through issues, and striving for consensus and solving social problems.

• Journalism, then, under the public journalism model, becomes a means to a desirable social end. This is accomplished by the media learning how to listen better to the public, giving the public more latitude to set the media's agenda, and redefining news in a manner that focuses less on conflict and negative news and more on building civic capital, reporting ambivalence, and educating the public about the tools of democratic decision making.

8

Practicing Public Journalism

Public journalism does not begin with information as the imperative. It does not begin with the day's events. It begins with an act of imagination. Every day of the year public journalism is looking out at a community and imagining the following kinds of changes: the missing-but-needed connections. The conversations that are not occurring because they are not embracing enough of the community to make a difference. The shrunken horizon. The community's growing inability to recognize what it is becoming as it changes. The unavoidable but scheduled crisis. Finally, of course, the dwindling resource of hope. In public journalism, a community is well reported when these things are visible. This is the lens it offers to the world.

—Jay Rosen (Charity, 1995, p. 159)

In the previous chapter we profiled the rationale, concepts, and goals of public journalism as explained by the people defining the movement. This chapter examines how these ideals are put into journalistic practice. The shadow that public journalism casts across the news media extends far and wide, and continues to grow. Although newspapers have been the primary practitioners, many of the most ambitious experiments have teamed newspapers, television, and radio in an attempt to broaden the exposure and appeal of public journalism to citizens. The goal of cross-media projects has also been to produce a type of synergy, which researchers hypothesize increases impact or media effects. What follows is a sampling of projects, beginning with the early attempts at the *Wichita Eagle* and *Charlotte Observer* that became exemplars for the development of public journalism practice. It is worth noting that from the start public journalism was seen as a fundamentally different practice that extended the recommendations of the Hutchins Commission from social responsibility into activism. Much of the controversy about public journalism has focused on those practices that use the media's resources to stimulate activity aimed at producing a desirable social end. Bare (1992), in a case study of two seminal projects titled, *Wichita and Charlotte: The leap of a passive press to activism,* saw newspapers combining public journalism practices with emerging electronic media to create a new role for the press. He wrote:

> By allowing readers to decide which issues newspapers cover and giving read-ers opportunities to interact with their local newspaper through citizen pan-els, phone banks and electronic bulletin boards, editors of the *Eagle* and the *Observer* are working to elevate newspapers to new media status. By rejecting the role of the passive observer and leaping into community problem-solving efforts, newspapers have an opportunity to move beyond the role of town crier and toward the role of town healer. (p. 158)

WICHITA EAGLE

After the 1988 presidential election, editor Davis Merritt used the paper's editorial page to bemoan the state of political campaigns and the media's coverage of them. He feared the same type of coverage—focusing on the "horse race," political strategies, and little discussion of issues important to the public—was being repeated in early stages of the 1990 Kansas guberna-torial campaign. In August 1990, Merritt (1998) sought to change the focus of the state's campaign away from what he wrote was "carefully managed sim-plemindedness" into a reporting effort more centered on issues that citizens wanted candidates to address. In an editorial in early September, Merritt (1990) announced "the *Eagle* has a strong bias. The bias is that we believe the voters are entitled to have the candidates talk about the issues in depth" (p. 13A). This early public journalism effort experimented with ways of al-tering coverage by taking the focus off the candidates and putting it on the public. The idea was that if the media covered issues the public thought were important, then more people might feel involved in the political process, thus reversing a trend of low voter turn-out. The *Eagle*'s owner, Knight-Ridder, provided resources to survey public opinion and conduct postelec-tion research. The *Eagle* also got ABC television affiliate KAKE to join the project, hoping to increase the visibility of the effort. At the *Eagle,* the plan became informally known as "the voter project," and it was promoted in the paper under the heading *Your Vote Counts.* Merritt (1998) wrote, "The thrust of the plan was a straightfoward, unabashed campaign to revive voter inter-est backed by a total focus on the issues voters were concerned about as reflected in survey results" (p. 85).

The *Eagle* and KAKE directed campaign coverage on the issues identified in the survey, whether the candidates were interested in talking about them or not. An integral part of the *Eagle*'s coverage was an "issues box" that ran every Sunday. The two-thirds-of-a-page graphic detailed the candidates' stances on the public's issues. When a candidate chose not to articulate a clear position, the *Eagle* quoted the "rambling abstruseness," causing the angry candidate to issue a translation (p. 86). Merritt wrote that even though the candidate who was more clear on the issues lost the election, the coverage was related to some desirable results: voter turnout increased and voter awareness of the issues was higher in the *Eagle*'s circulation area. He continued:

> Something intriguing and promising had happened . . . We had, in effect, left the press box and gotten down on the field, not as a contestant but as a fair-minded participant with an open and expressed interest in the process going well. It had involved risk, but it had paid off. It was also a liberating moment, for me and the journalists at the *Eagle*. We no longer had to be victims, along with the public, of a politics gone sour. We had a new purposefulness: revitalizing a moribund public process." (p. 87)

Buoyed by the results of this first project and the national exposure it had gathered, Merritt decided the *Eagle* should continue providing citizens with "mobilizing information" and working to connect with the community (Dykers, 1998, p. 71). The second project, called *The People Project*, was kicked off in 1992 with a front-page essay urging the public to rejuvenate the idea of collective problem solving and community building because government was incapable of these tasks. To guide the effort, the paper had conducted in-depth interviews with about 200 Kansans about the issues that troubled people. These interviews became the basis for a series of stories about political life in Wichita that were prominently played from June to August of that election year. The topics were traditional issues (education, crime, families, government gridlock), but the stories featured ordinary citizens discussing the issues and quoted no political candidates. At regular intervals, the paper published special packages exploring each issue. Each package publicized community meetings where citizens could go discuss the issues with other citizens, experts, and reporters. A clip-out questionnaire asked readers to express themselves on each issue. The paper also encouraged citizens to get involved with the issues, providing the names, phone numbers, and addresses of volunteer and advocacy groups under the heading "Places to Start." The newspaper once again partnered with local media, and both radio and television outlets held on-air forums on the same issues on which the paper was reporting. Charity (1995) wrote that the editors knew that, beyond this type of reporting, the public needed inspiration to get involved. The result was the newspaper printed some success stories about people who had made a difference or programs that worked. The *Eagle* also ran photos of people participating at the community meetings and reported as news their discussions and experiences of exchanging ideas and coordinating action. On one issue, the paper printed the names of every citizen that participated.

Merritt wrote a front-page column in June 1992 announcing the series and its rationale, labeling the 1990s as a period of frustration when people were losing faith in their ability to address their problems. He lamented that people were committing an act "of sure civic suicide" by abandoning community and retreating into "determined individualism." The series was aimed at resurrecting the idea of community in order to face the realization that people must act together if they are to solve common problems. He wrote, "The People Project . . . is a collaborative effort to give shape and momentum to your voices and ideas, with the goal of reasserting personal power and responsibility for what goes on around us. It breaks new ground in the relationship between a newspaper and its readers and community" (Dykers, 1998, p. 73).

In 1994, the *Eagle* took the next step, trying to broaden public journalism beyond specific projects into everyday practice. Using consultant Richard Harwood, the paper set out to "map" places in Wichita where public discussions initiate. Charity (1995) wrote that after Harwood consultants pumped the *Eagle* reporters for all they knew about specific neighborhoods, the reseach team "went into Wichita periodically to walk the streets, hold focus groups, and just hang out" (p. 37). When the only large grocery store in a poor section of the city announced its impending closure, Harwood associates claimed their map helped *Eagle* reporters identify four levels of places where public discussion "bubbles up," two of which were untapped by reporters.

The *Eagle* also extended public journalism into the Kansas legislature's 1994 capital punishment debate. Under a story headlined, *Facing a decision: Weighing all sides of the death penalty debate,* the paper ran five "quick-read sections" not more than two paragraphs long that summarized death penalty arguments pro and con, as well as suggesting books to read and films to watch. Three Wichita citizens were quoted prominently as examples of diverse opinions under the headings: Should Society Kill? Should Society Punish or Rehabilitate? How Should Democracy Work? The paper also asked readers about their values on capital punishment, and challenged them to identify areas in which they were willing to compromise. The paper urged people to study the issue, contact their state representatives, and reported, "You may want to contact groups pro and con that will provide you with information and enlist you in their causes" (Charity, 1995, p. 98).

CHARLOTTE OBSERVER

The *Observer* saw an opportunity in 1991 to change the nature of campaign reporting in North Carolina when the Poynter Institute for Media Studies was looking for volunteers to experiment with new approaches to election coverage. Aware of the *Wichita Eagle*'s experiment in 1990, and dissatisfied with its own coverage of the 1990 Senate race between incumbent Jesse

Helms and civil rights leader Harvey Gantt, the *Observer* teamed with Charlotte's ABC affiliate, WSOC-TV, and began a 1992 election project that former editor Rich Oppel said was "driven not by the candidates, but by the voters" (Thames, 1998, p. 112). Oppel appointed Rick Thames, former government editor at the *Observer,* to lead the effort. Thames, reflecting later that the term public journalism had not yet been invented, designed all the paper's political coverage around four components that were to become integral to public journalism: polling citizens to find out what issues were important to them, focusing news coverage on the issues citizens identified, involving citizens in planning and executing news coverage, and holding candidates (or public officials) responsible to address citizens' concerns.

Editors and reporters at the *Observer* wrote a questionnaire to explore which issues the voters deemed newsworthy, and a research firm was hired to conduct about 1,000 telephone interviews in a 14-county area that included the newspaper's and television station's audience. The poll identified a set of issues—the economy, taxes, health care, crime, education, the environment and values—the paper called the "Citizens' Agenda" and began to direct its reporting toward citizens' questions related to these issues. To keep citizens actively involved, the researchers asked the 1,000 respondents if they would continue "advising" the two media throughout the campaign and nearly 500 people agreed, creating a "Citizens' Panel." Thames (1998) wrote that this panel gave the newspaper a data base of citizens that it could turn to as easily as political candidates. Aware that many of the members of the Citizens' Panel were not registered to vote, the editors reasoned that new approaches to reporting would mean little if those people shaping the coverage, and the public in general, did not bother to vote. The *Observer* encouraged the public to get involved in the political process in some traditional ways, with stories about how to register to vote, registration deadlines, and how to read the ballot. The encouragement became less conventional when the *Observer* and WSOC set up voter registration booths in the their lobbies, and the paper ran a joint letter on its news pages written by editor Rich Oppel and the county elections supervisor urging people to register.

The *Observer* used the issues identified in the poll results as a basis for a 6-week series that tackled one issue at a time. The packages ran on consecutive Sundays with a front-page lead story and graphic packages on candidates and issues on the front of the Perspective section. The paper decided not to let its political reporters write the issue stories; these were written by reporters from other departments who might have more expertise on the issue (e.g., the medical reporter writing about health care, or the features reporter writing about family values). Thames suggested this approach had an additional benefit: the reporters, having little journalistic expertise in politics, were political outsiders and their reporting offered a perspective closer to that of ordinary citizens. Thames (1998) wrote, "Our deeper understanding of the public's actual information needs demanded that we rethink our news values" (p. 116). Daily coverage of the campaign was also impacted. *Observer* editors decided that "much of the clatter of the campaign was irrelevant" (p. 116), relegating it to an inside page while keeping the front page open for the public's issues.

The paper assumed responsibility for keeping candidates focused on the public's issues. More than 300 candidates, from school board to the presidency, were informed that the paper's news coverage would require candidates to address issues identified in the paper's polling. For offices of less importance, this accountability amounted to candidates filling out questionnaires; for prominent offices, candidates were interviewed and their responses edited to 25 to 30 words by *Observer* journalists to fit a predetermined space in the issues graphic that ran on Sundays. When candidates balked that they did not want to address an issue or their stance could not be summarized in a couple of sentences, the *Observer* ran "white space" in the graphic as an indication the candidate would not address the issue. The paper also began using a different approach to asking questions at press conferences, having reporters ask the candidates questions supplied by citizens. An example might be: "Mrs. Sally Jones of Pineville would like to know. . . ." This approach prompted *Wichita Eagle* editor Davis Merritt (1998) to take notice, writing, "Candidates could not dismiss (the citizen's) question as readily they might a reporter's, so they responded with care" (p. 87). Thames acknowledges that reporters at the *Observer,* at first skeptical, began to feel empowered by this mandate of the people.

Evaluating the outcome of this first project yielded mixed results. Thames (1998) wrote that the *Observer* received a 20% increase in phone calls from readers asking for more information, and, although voting was up across the state, voter turn-out in Mecklenburg County (where Charlotte is located) surpassed an all-time high. Furthermore, the research found readers reported: (a) increased political interest during the campaign, (b) feeling more positive about the newspaper's helpfulness in making them feel part of the political process, and (c) feeling a greater connection between the coverage and issues that affected them personally. These positive findings were contrasted with two negative results: *Observer* readers sensed more bias in political stories than in other stories in the newspaper, and readers' perceived understanding of state and local issues actually went down. Thames speculated the perceived lower understanding of state and local issues might have been a result of the *Observer*'s heightened coverage of the presidential race (p. 121).

By 1994, *public journalism* had been born as a proper noun and the *Observer*'s coverage of the previous presidential election had become a "must study" for interested media outlets. The paper in 1994 embarked on a more ambitious project that moved its public journalism outside of campaign reporting and into "a more direct and activist role" (Lambeth, 1998a, p. 19).

Concerned by Charlotte's high crime rate, the paper identified 10 high-crime neighborhoods and surveyed 401 citizens in these neighborhoods, asking respondents to suggest methods to combat the crime problem. Among the responses: "add police, improve courts"; "curb drug abuse"; and "get neighbors involved" (Charity, 1995, p. 65). The paper, using foundation funds, hired a former television reporter as the project's community coordinator. The coordinator's role in the project, which the paper promoted as *Taking back our neighborhoods,* was to organize neighborhood meetings at which residents would identify community needs and have solution-oriented discussions. These discussions were reported as news in the paper. The community coordinator's office was in the *Observer* building. Reporters and editors also met with a citizens' advisory panel of leaders from the various neighborhoods to help steer coverage.

The project's reporting effort lasted more than a year, with each of the 10 high-crime areas the focus of 6 weeks of coverage. Charity (1995) wrote that the real test was when the paper, teamed with radio and television outlets, introduced audiences to Seversville in a day-long media blitz that focused on that area's crime-related problems and struggles. This report spurred positive results: the YMCA put 41 children into free day camp, a local sign company donated signs to mark neighborhood pride, citizens volunteered to renovate housing and tutor, and a bank put up $50,000 to build a new recreation center. The newspaper-sponsored meetings also began to draw politicians, who, whether looking for positive news coverage or not, began asking citizens what they could do to help. Summing up the effort, Charity wrote:

> The fact is, citizens probably get the bulk of their motivation from working in common enterprise. They need to see things are happening, that their own contributions are adding on to those of others. They like to be swept up in the tide of a great cause. And this is precisely what the *Observer* gave them. (p. 136)

Not all of Charlotte's neighborhoods were swept up in the coverage. Grier Heights, which ranked 11th in violent crime of the city's 73 neighborhoods, had a community organization whose leader flatly refused to cooperate with the *Observer*'s efforts. He claimed his neighborhood did not need to be "taken back." Because of his resistance, Grier Heights was not included in the coverage, prompting the project community coordinator to say, "I didn't look at Grier Heights as a major flaw in what we were doing. I just felt bad they didn't take advantage of an opportunity that could have been helpful" (Lambeth, 1998b, p. 247).

The 1996 election year saw the *Observer* team with 14 media outlets across North Carolina in a concerted effort to put the citizen's issues before the candidates and focus statewide reporting on these issues. The project, *Your voice, your vote,* used similar tools as in past public journalism election projects: polling to identify the people's issues, reporting efforts that focused on those issues, citizen involvement in shaping the questions and coverage, and the media's assurance they would hold the candidates responsible for addressing the issues the people had identified as important. What was different was the scope of collaboration among media. The consortium of media included most of the large outlets in the state, with six newspapers (*Charlotte Observer, The* (Raleigh) *News and Observer,* Greensboro *News & Record, Fayetteville Observer-Times, Asheville Citizen-Times,* and Wilmington *Morning Star*), six television stations (WBYV, Charlotte; WTVD, Raleigh-Durham-Chapel Hill; WGHP, Greensboro-High Point; WLOS, Asheville; WWAY, Wilmington; and the University of North Carolina Center for Public Television [PBS], and three radio stations (WFAE-FM, Charlotte; WUNC-FM, Chapel Hill; and WFDD-FM, Winston-Salem).

Polls were conducted in January (for the primary season) and July (for the general election). *Observer* editor Jennie Buckner (1996), former Knight-Ridder vice president of news who replaced Oppel in 1993, wrote that the poll results were not surprising, identifying crime and drugs, taxes and spending, affordable health care, financial security, families and values, and education as the people's most important issues. The media partners then developed questions on those issues and invited the 13 candidates for senator and governor to make themselves available for 3-hour interviews before both the primaries and general election. The only candidate who refused was Senator Jesse Helms. The interviews became the basis for in-depth stories on each issue that ran on successive Sundays, packaged with full-page grids explaining the candidates' positions on three questions related to each issue (Buckner & Gartner, 1998). The consortium shared 12 issue stories, with each outlet running basically the same story each Sunday. Each newspaper produced some of its own coverage, which was also shared among the participating papers. Buckner believes the approach had several benefits: it was unlikely that candidates would have made themselves available for 3 hours to numerous media outlets, the reporting was focused on issues chosen by the public, and the partnership was designed to complement the coverage each outlet produced on its own.

Your voice, your vote drew critical acclaim. Merritt (1998) wrote that the media made an important distinction between the campaign and the election, moving focus away from the campaign (dominated by candidates and their handlers) and toward the election (the process of citizens making a choice). The Pew Center for Civic Journalism, which helped fund the project, distributed press releases announcing that its follow-up research to the "unprecedented statewide effort by 15 news organizations" found that about one in four North Carolina voters were aware of the project. Of those who said they recognized the effort, 38% said they thought there was more discussion of issues in the campaign and 34% said they felt better informed (*New Voter Education Project,* 1996).

The project also drew criticism, both for its research methodology and collaborative coverage. Michael Kelly (1996) noted that the list of issue choices for those polled in January was limited to issues the consortium had preselected. He pointed out that the public never got a chance to choose the "public" issues, but were limited to a list of issues created by journalists. The primary poll, which identified eight issues, was then narrowed to four issues after the general election poll: crime and drugs, taxes and spending, affordable health care, and education. On the taxes and spending issue, 78% of respondents in the second poll indicated the issue was "very important," while 79% had responded that families and values were "very important." However, families and values did not make the general election list of issues. Kelly wrote that the consortium's decision to focus on taxes and spending instead of families and values had important repercussions, especially in the Helms–Gantt senatorial race, as there were many clear-cut differences between Helms and Gantt on value-related issues such as abortion, prayer in public schools, Affirmative Action, and the government's response to AIDS. Thames, the *Observer*'s public editor, called the decision to exclude families and values and include taxes and spending "pretty much a coin toss" (p. 48). Kelly concluded that the *Your voice, your vote* effort, despite its good intentions and some excellent reporting, had two detrimental effects: reporters spent less time covering the campaign and candidates' speeches because the newsworthy issues had been determined through polling, and, by not declaring "values" a consortium issue, the senatorial candidates, especially Gantt (Helms had snubbed the consortium) felt compelled to address these issues through advertising, and both candidates engaged in a series of mudslinging ads. The irony of the second effect, Kelly wrote, is that the media coverage encouraged the type of behavior it was hoping to avoid—a repeat of the negative, misleading political ads from the 1990 campaign.

Criticism of the project was not limited to the senatorial candidates. William E. Jackson Jr., an unsuccessful House of Representatives candidate and former political science professor at Davidson College, in a letter to the editor of the *New York Times* published during the campaign, wrote that after entering the race in February, he was not asked for an interview, but instead was asked to fill out a candidates' questionnaire on the public's issues. He asserted that by focusing coverage on poll-discovered issues, the media failed to realize that candidates are discouraged from trying to raise issues the public had not thought much about or even taking controversial stands. He questioned why candidates would develop their own agenda when they are being asked "feel-good banalities" such as "What should government do to keep children out of trouble?" Jackson (1996) wrote:

> Sorry, but I am skeptical about this high-minded venture conducted in the name of "the people" . . . I quickly discovered that it didn't matter what a House candidate did or said. . . . The major newspapers decided to concen-

trate on issues that did well in their surveys: crime and drugs, taxes and spending, health care and education. The coordination among the papers is so tight that they are running virtually identical articles Sunday after Sunday—raising the spector of statewide group think. (p. A17)

Buckner responded to the criticism by saying political coverage should not be purely poll-driven, and the consortium coverage accounted for only an estimated 20% of the total election coverage in the *Observer.* She believes the most powerful lesson of the *Your voice, your vote* project was that journalists can learn to do better political journalism. Buckner wrote, "We know many readers in North Carolina got much broader and deeper information because of the partnership. And we know we focused the candidates, and ourselves, on issues that really mattered to the people" (Buckner & Gartner, 1998, p. 226).

NORFOLK VIRGINIAN-PILOT

Public journalism at this seaside locale that includes five cities in its circulation area was introduced as part of a broader effort to reorganize the newsroom, news coverage, and news values. In 1992, civic-minded newspapers were still experimenting with altering political coverage by focusing their efforts on citizens' interests during campaigns. At the *Virginian-Pilot,* editor Cole Campbell, borrowing management techniques that had been adopted in other manufacturing industries, was initiating a reorganization plan that had a much loftier goal of changing the culture of the newspaper. The beat structure and five cities in the coverage zone had created feifdoms that Campbell saw as barriers to citizen-focused and readership-oriented reporting. The newsroom was reorganized into coverage teams of five reporters and an editor; each team's goal was to create collegial groups that take responsibility for planning coverage and connecting it to readers' lives. A key to success was abandoning the idea of stories being rooted in institutional settings and defined by a specific geographic area. The teams assumed names: Public Life; Public Safety (that renamed itself 911 Jump); Women, Family and Children; Education; Criminal Justice; and Real Life (e.g., traffic, home life, consumer technology; Rosen, 1994b). Conte (1996) wrote that the *Virginian-Pilot* took a less flashy approach than other newspapers initiating public journalism, "quietly building into much of its daily reporting what Campbell describes as a 'strong citizen orientation' that 'engages people as political players, not consumers'" (p. 822). A staple in the citizen orientation was the convening of "community conversations," which were sometimes organized around a specific issue and other times created to get people together to talk with reporters about issues important to them or their dreams for the region's future. The idea was not only to get more citizen voices in the paper but to bring people together to deliberate on issues (Charity, 1995).

A test of the paper's commitment to citizen-based reporting occurred when a group that wanted to build a church sought to have the property, which had been a farm market, rezoned. The congregation was planning to create a televised ministry, and support or opposition to the rezoning developed generally along racial lines. The *Virginian-Pilot* assembled eight citizens, four for rezoning and four against, to meet and discuss the issue. The meeting was taped and excerpts were published verbatim in the newspaper. The paper's willingness to give the citizens a portion of the "newshole" to deliberate on issues and attempt to solve problems fits well with the public journalism philosophy. The paper's sense of responsibility to make public life work is perhaps best illustrated by the Public Life team, which drafted this mission statement:

> We will revitalize a democracy that has grown sick with disenchantment. We will lead the community to discover itself and act on what it has learned. We will show how the community works or could work, whether that means exposing corruption, telling citizens how to make their voices heard, holding up a fresh perspective or spotlighting people who do their jobs well. We will portray democracy in the fullest sense of the word, whether in a council chamber or cul-de-sac. We do this knowing that a lively, informed and most of all, engaged public is essential to a healthy community and to the health of these newspapers. (Charity, 1995, p. 151)

Getting reporters to rethink their news values became a critical part of the *Virginian-Pilot*'s reorganization. The paper hired consultant Richard Harwood to conduct seminars in "public listening" for the Public Life team. Harwood teaches reporters how to look for ambivalence, underlying values, connections between issues, and to pay attention to areas of agreement. Campbell also invited public journalism leader Jay Rosen to train a larger group of journalists (Conte, 1996). The paper adopted an exercise that required reporters to write two versions of the same story, a "public" version, which ran in the paper, and a traditional version. Campbell said of the paper's reorganization, "Now that we have radically altered the way reporters and editors work, we want to change the way they think" (Charity, 1995, p. 97).

By the time Campbell left the *Virginian-Pilot* in 1996 to become editor of the *St. Louis Post-Dispatch*, the paper had institutionalized its public-minded approach. Lambeth (1998b) wrote that the paper comes closest to operationalizing into journalism practice some of the key ideas in Daniel Yankelovich's 1994 book, *Coming to Public Judgment*. Before the reporting process begins, team members are encouraged to identify stakeholders in issues or events, identify the nature of their stakes, and create coverage that is proportionate to the needs of the stakeholders. Reporters are schooled in how the public works through issues, and they understand how stories can address public literacy, utility, and mastery. This hierarchical process suggests that literacy stories give readers the knowledge to converse and pursue information on a topic; utility stories help citizens form opinions and connect with others who have a similar stake; mastery stories allow citizens to understand their opinions and those of others. It is this mastery phase that allows citizens to reflect and reach judgment on public issues.

In practice, this translates into the paper's reporters promising to cover state government and elections "as an exercise in civic problem solving," and its editors considering two factors in their news judgment: "the paper's community stewardship," and a search for stories that "reflect the news organization's 'emotional bond' with the community" (Schaffer, 1999b, paragraph 76). These ideas are addressed in part by the paper running three pages per week on public life, public safety, and education that contain status reports and score cards with public input that address such questions as: How well are our leaders doing? Am I safe? Are my kids getting a good education? Schaffer (1998) wrote that civic journalism pioneer Dennis Hartig, a *Virginian-Pilot* editor, says he has redefined his job description so that he sees his job as an editor as simply to "create citizens" (paragraph 28).

TALLAHASSEE DEMOCRAT

Few civic (or public) journalism experiments have been as ambitious and well-publicized as the *Democrat*'s *The public agenda*. The Pew Center for Civic Journalism and The Poynter Institute for Media Studies, financial cosponsors, promoted the project as one of the most complex exercises in civic journalism, combining research, reporting, community outreach, and public dialogue. The newspaper teamed with Tallahassee television station WCTV6 and the city's two universities, Florida State and Florida A & M, to coordinate its reporting and community outreach. The project also employed the Harwood Group to conduct "living room conversations" with small groups, which then became the basis for a larger survey of residents and community leaders. The Pew Center for Civic Journalism awarded $450,000 in 1994 for a 3-year project; the money paid some administrative and outreach expenses and the salaries of four nonjournalists hired to coordinate and promote the effort. According to a joint report by the Pew Center and Poynter Institute, the goal behind *The public agenda* was "to change the way people deal with all elections or issues that affect their lives and their community" (*The public agenda*, 1995, paragraph 7).

The initial research identified areas of citizen concern, and the *Democrat* ran a four-part, front-page series that introduced readers to the project and issues. The series reported the results of the research; the top four citizens' issues were crime, traffic, juvenile crime, and growth. To create the report, citizens who participated in the initial survey were contacted for in-depth conversations on the issues they had identified. The writing relied on the pronoun "we" to explain the survey results to the public: "We remain many small communities within a community"; "With all the growth going on around us, we're frustrated we don't have more of a say"; "We say we'd devote more time to help solve community problems if someone would tell us how to get involved." The series attempted to weave the issues into a "biographical sketch of the city" and then posed the question: "What choices do we make from here?" (Charity, 1995, p. 26).

The public was then invited to get involved with a high-profile event in the chamber of the Florida House of Representatives. To publicize and attract people to the "community dialogue," the newspaper published maps showing where people could park, provided child care and transportation, served refreshments, and placed signs at all the Capitol entrances marking the way to the House chamber. Event organizers had hoped to attract 150 to 200 people; when 300 attended they ran out of information packets. The turnout so pleased the newspaper and its partners that plans were immediately made to hold another community dialogue 2 weeks later at a local church. The report by Pew and Poynter wrote of the chamber event, "In the end, what was said during the two-hour session didn't matter nearly as much as the fact that so many people came" (*The public agenda,* 1995, paragraph 1). The meeting was videotaped and turned into a WCTV6 television special, and the *Democrat* reported the news with a page-one package the next day that included a wide-angle photo to capture the size of the crowd under the headline "Full House establishes a dialogue" (paragraph 43).

The Sunday after the chamber meeting, the *Democrat* began what became a staple of the project, a monthly feature called *A public agenda page.* The page included reports of issues that people were talking about in their community forums, publishing lengthy citizen viewpoints, as well as updates on public agenda projects, lists of groups and meetings, and information on how to get involved. Executive editor Lou Heldman wrote on the initial public agenda page:

> What's new is the structure the Public Agenda provides for seeking active citizen involvement that goes beyond voting or writing letters to the editor. That structure includes small discussions groups, in addition to this page, news stories and the larger community dialogues. If you are interested in setting up a group of your own, we will help and train a discussion leader. (Charity, 1995, p. 145)

In the first year of the project, about a half-dozen groups formed and were meeting regularly. Two *Democrat* reporters were assigned to report on the project, and two community coordinators helped schedule and mediate small group meetings. Some of the original groups split into smaller groups to address various aspects of issues. The Community and Race Relations group split into four subgroups, and each was assigned the exercise of agreeing on five things that would benefit the Tallahassee area. The four groups then reconvened and forced themselves to come to common agreement on the five ideas, which ultimately were: personal responsibility, integration, symbolism, affirmative action, and the media. These five ideas for community improvement then became the group's agenda. One member of this group said the initial surge made him think that within a year, there might be as many as two dozen groups working to solve community problems, but that didn't happen. Group members began to realize that projects like *The public agenda* will take longer to nurture the public to change (*The public agenda*, 1995).

WCTV6 recognized the potential of the project and assigned a reporter to do 90-second weekly updates. News and production director Mike Smith was surprised how well the project caught on, noting that the other local television stations not affiliated with the project started doing news stories about it. General manager Dave Olmstead liked the idea that the newsroom was put in closer touch with the people's issues, saying, "It's a rare opportunity when you can be associated with a cause that affects the entire community. This belongs to the community. All we do is facilitate the dialogue" (*The public agenda*, 1995, paragraph 19).

Charity (1995) wrote that the *Democrat* can point to the increased citizen involvement in the community and higher reader approval ratings as an indication of the project's success. The project executed several public journalism concepts very well: created public discussion, got people involved in community, and gave prominent media play to the ideas of ordinary citizens. Rosen (1994b) suggested that what set the project apart was its emphasis on public deliberation, close cooperation among participants, and long-term commitment. However, there were some unanticipated challenges. After creating the small groups, both the *Democrat* and WCTV6 found resistance to the media's desire to cover the discussions, as some group members thought media coverage would inhibit what members would say. And among *Democrat* journalists, *The public agenda* generated little interest, prompting managing editor Bob Shaw to say, "I think it's seen by the staff as a two-reporter project. I don't think it's really sunk in. I've been disappointed at how few reporters have bothered to show up at (Public Agenda) meetings" (*The public agenda*, 1995, paragraph 63).

KVUE (AUSTIN, TX) AND THE NATIONAL ISSUES CONVENTION

Several scholars link the 1990s growth of public journalism with the growth of citizen activist groups whose goals, unlike specific-issue interest groups, are more communal, emphasizing public deliberation and consensus building (Friedland, Sotirovic, & Daily, 1998; Merritt, 1998; Charity, 1995). A number of foundations are active supporting such organizations as the National Issues Forum, the National Civic League, and Study Circles Resource Center. A large-scale example of public deliberation was the National Issues Convention in Austin in 1996, where 459 citizens from across the country were convened for a 4-day exercise in public dialogue and a national community conversation. The citizens were randomly chosen, and they included wealthy business people, teachers, rock musicians, and welfare recipients. The convention paid the expenses: the main requirements of the participants were to submit to two lengthy surveys (one before and one after the convention) and to attend 3 days of public discussions on issues such as education, welfare, family, and foreign aid.

The convention afforded local media an excellent opportunity to experiment with public journalism. Nearly all attempts at public journalism had been newspaper-driven; as we have seen, television stations have partnered with newspapers, but the public journalism initiative has its roots in newspapers. Prior to the convention, however, one Austin television station, ABC affiliate KVUE-24, had begun to implement some public journalism techniques without the help of a newspaper. The affiliate decided it wanted to improve its crime reporting and assembled members of the community into focus groups, asking the groups how this could be done. The station also held staff meetings to discuss strengths and weaknesses of its crime coverage. The groups concluded that the key to reporting crime was "responsibility." Acting on this conclusion, the station began a 6-week campaign, "KVUE Listens to You on Crime," that included broadcasting a checklist of guidelines for crime coverage. KVUE also aired longer packages that featured its staff discussing crime coverage and included sound bites from the community members who participated in the focus groups. The station also began an exercise that included following every crime story with an explanation of how the story met the station's responsibility guidelines; it also urged viewers to phone or e-mail to express their ideas about how well the stories met the station's pledge of responsible crime coverage (Reynolds, 1999, pp. 117–118).

Building from this initiative, KVUE decided to practice public journalism while covering the 1996 presidential election. The National Issues Convention in Austin was a logical starting point. The station sent a news anchor and reporter to the public journalism sessions at the NIC hosted by the Poynter Institute and began airing commericals promoting its pledge to focus on the issues during the campaign. KVUE also began airing stories on the accuracy of political advertisements, called the "Truth Test."

Meanwhile, the NIC was organized around issues that citizens identified on the survey they completed on their arrival. The participants were provided with factual information packets assembled by a bipartisan committee and placed in groups of about 20 people, and discussions were moderated by trained staff. After 3 days of discussion, the second survey was taken. The results indicated that many people changed their opinions, but their more basic values were largely unaffected. Merritt (1998) noted that the important result was that when given the opportunity for public deliberation, backed by relevant information, citizens found they could agree on many issues and move beyond merely having opinions to developing more thoughtful, public judgments.

Reynolds (1999), in one of the few research projects on a television public journalism effort, conducted a content analysis that compared KVUE's coverage of the NIC and 1996 primaries to that of another Austin station, NBC affiliate KXAN, which she expected would take a more traditional political reporting approach. In the NIC reporting, she expected to find that the framing of KVUE's public journalism reporting would be more on issues (as opposed to the event) and more on positive news. In reporting on both the NIC and the primary campaign, she expected KVUE to focus less on polls and horse-race coverage, and KVUE's "sourcing" would include more informed public sources (citizens, candidates, and experts as opposed to political partisans and random people in the street) than the traditional station, KXAN. She found that the public journalism station, KVUE, did frame a higher percentage of NIC stories on issues and ran longer stories than KXAN; however, the traditional station (KXAN) reported a larger number of NIC stories (13 to 9) with more story frames (5 to 3). Concerning positive NIC news, public journalism station KVUE did not air any stories with a negative tone, whereas 44% of its stories were coded as positive and 56% neutral; traditional station KXAN had 8% negative stories, 15% positive, and 77% neutral. As expected, Reynolds found that KVUE focused less on horse-race coverage in its NIC and campaign reporting, as the public journalism station aired 3 of 31 stories with this as a dominant frame, whereas KXAN ran 9 of its 37 stories framed on this aspect. In terms of sourcing, she found that types of on-air sources used by both stations were virtually identical. Reynolds warned that the results need to be taken with caution because they are based on a small sample of stories. However, she concluded:

> Need for orientation applies not only to voters, but also in this case to the Austin media. All of the stations were uncertain about how to handle the NIC because it was a new and different kind of event. Because KVUE was greatly interested in the NIC, and because it had a firm grasp of the public journalism concept, it was better prepared to explain the convention's importance to viewers. KVUE's coverage was not only different than KXAN's, as this case study/content analysis shows, by most accounts was better because it was more useful to the public." (p. 129)

ASNE CHANGE COMMITTEE
AND "PROJECT RECONNECT"

Concerned about the shrinking base of newspaper readers and the uncertainties caused by the growth of the Internet, the American Society of Newspaper Editors in 1994 created a Change Committee that included editors and publishers interested in developing and experimenting with change initiatives that would ensure the long-term viability of the industry (McGuire, 1994). The committee focused on ways that news executives could reorganize their newsrooms for better efficiency, and realign their staff's news values to resemble more closely those of readers and citizens. The cultural transformation at the Norfolk *Virginian-Pilot* discussed earlier is one example of the dozens of newspapers that used newsroom reorganization as a method to redefine news values in a more public frame. The ASNE Change Committee found that its interest in changing newspapers paralleled many of the goals of public journalism. In the committee's 1997 report, Rosen wrote the centerpiece article, an essay that reinforced the newspaper industry's need to change. Rosen believed part of the "institutional failure of journalism" is characterized by newspaper journalists resisting outside criticism, working in an environment that has been conditioned not to learn, and a failing of the industry to challenge the wisdom of its elite members. He called newspaper editors and journalists a "herd of independent minds" who are afraid to shed their objectivity and independence to solve the problems of journalism. Finally, he suggested that the reason journalists are so reluctant to change is that change requires "losing the thing you love. Which is journalism" (p. 9).

To address the need for change and pair newspapers with prominent journalism schools in the practice and teaching of public journalism, the Change Committee announced "Project Reconnect." The initiative teamed newspaper editors with faculty and students from journalism schools to design projects "to re-connect [sic] each newspaper with a specific group in its community that had become disaffected and disenchanted with how the newspaper covered its community" (Project Reconnect, 1997, p. 28). The teams were assigned to research disaffected audiences and then reach out to them through community forums, focus groups, moderated discussions with opinion leaders, one-on-one interviews with citizens and community leaders, and surveys. The project received a 2-year, $80,000 funding commitment from the Pew Center for Civic Journalism. The staffs in each newsroom were to participate in discussions focusing on how the paper had been framing stories of interest to the disaffected groups and come up with ideas about coverage that might reconnect to that public. Among the participants and their projects:

- *The* (Fredericksburg, VA) *Free Lance-Star* and Howard University, addressing the disconnect between African Americans and coverage of Civil War topics;
- *Raleigh News & Observer* and the University of North Carolina, addressing coverage of blue-collar neighborhoods;
- *The Oregonian* and the University of Oregon, working with environmental groups and environmental businesses and industry;
- *The* (Colorado Springs) *Gazette* and the University of Colorado, addressing the disconnect over the coverage of business;
- *The* (Columbia) *State* and the University of South Carolina, focusing on the disconnect between conservative Christians and people of religious faith.

IMAGINE AT THE *ST. LOUIS POST-DISPATCH*

While editor of the *St. Louis Post-Dispatch*, Cole Campbell slowly moved the paper toward a public journalism model similar to the one he initiated in Norfolk. As discussed in the previous chapter, Campbell asked journalists to consider what would happen if they envisioned their roles less in terms of describing the present and more toward the imagination of a better alternative. Imagination brings people together and nurtures empathy. With these ideas in mind, the *Post-Dispatch* in 1999 redesigned its Sunday news analysis section into a section called *Imagine St. Louis.*

Each week, the front page of the section leads with a story about an issue identified as one of the city's pressing priorities, defining the problem and its scope. The lead is accompanied by a *Conversations* column, featuring reader comments and letters, as well as announcements of organizations and events that are associated with the issue. Below the fold on the front page is a weekly feature of one citizen's personal experience with the issue. The topics addressed by the *Imagine* sections include illiteracy, immigration, the St. Louis arts community, and plans for a new bridge across the Mississippi River. For the illiteracy edition, section editor Mike Duffy worked with area literacy and education organizations to schedule speakers and meetings in conjunction with the paper's coverage of the issue. Radio and television stations also planned call-in shows on the topic. The scheduled events were then printed in the section's *Conversations* column. Duffy said the local media are attracted to the cross-promotion the section offers (Ford, 1999). On inside pages, information is packaged in an "issues map," with graphics and key questions related to the issue and several citizen perspectives about how those questions might be answered. Another section feature, *Who calls the shots*, includes a list of decision-makers and policy leaders, a bibliography of where to get more information, and a directory of agencies where people can get help or volunteer to give it.

Duffy said the section has been well-received by St. Louis groups associated with issues the section has addressed. "This region is so fragmented, unless some strong institution comes to the fore to talk to people, to find common cause, acknowledge a common destiny and make real strong structural improvements in the region, we'll be in trouble in the next century" (p. 15).

Campbell set out his vision for *Imagine St. Louis* on the front page of the inaugural section, focusing on the value of a community having a shared sense of what is important, especially in an era where much of the public debate dodges issues and fails to provide help for people to work through problems and solve them. Campbell (1999) wrote:

> We hope this new Sunday section, Imagine St. Louis, will help all of metropolitan St. Louis—black and white, native and newcomer, rich and poor, city and suburb, Missouri side and Illinois side—engage in serious discussion of our most pressing priorities. We hope these will become continuing conversations, because what you say will affect how we explore each issue. Over time, we hope, all this talk and news coverage will set the stage for action. (p. B1)

AWARDING CIVIC JOURNALISM

Many editors, including Davis Merritt, point to former Knight-Ridder CEO James Batten as the first newspaper executive to value the ideas that have come to embody civic journalism. The Pew Center for Civic Journalism, in memory of Batten's contribution to the growth of the idea and its practice, gives a $25,000 annual James K. Batten Award for Excellence in Civic Journalism. Schaffer (1999a), director of the Pew Center for Civic Journalism, wrote, "Unlike other journalism contests, the Batten awards are distinguished from heralding work that not only moves the needle in the community—but also moves journalism to new places" (p. 2).

The Pew Center for Civic Journalism described some of the Batten Award winning projects as follows (Schaffer, 1999a; "Why the Informed Citizen," 1999):

• *The Portland Press Herald/Maine Sunday Telegram,* "The Deadliest Drug: Maine's Addiction to Alcohol." This eight-part series was "a courageous effort that listened to the silences in the community." The report put human faces on the startling statistics that showed the true cost to citizens of the use and abuse of alcohol. The newspaper agreed to help citizens form study circles, and more than 70 communities created groups that involved more than 2,000 citizens. The action plans created by the groups were complied into a book as well as published in the paper.

- KRON-TV, San Francisco, "About Race." An exploration into how race and ethnicity shape the Bay Area that was broadcast on the nightly news during February 1998 sweeps. The initial series, a five-story package, reviewed the genetics of race, diversity in the workplace and schools, talking about race, and how to bridge racial differences. The station invited the public to participate in on-line conversations, and over the course of a year produced 18 stories, including an hour-long special that was provided to more than 90 local schools.

- *St. Paul Pioneer Press,* "Poverty Among Us." The paper chronicled once a month for 7 months what it was like to be poor in Minnesota at a time when welfare reform was replacing the welfare safety net with welfare-to-work requirements. Stories were told through the eyes of working poor, school children, and immigrants. The paper conducted a poll about attitudes toward poverty, and the public was asked to participate in the project by forming groups in association with St. Paul public libraries that read literature on poverty. The paper also published a guide and "tool kit" to help people set up discussion groups. More than 2,500 people got involved in the project.

The Batten awards are given at an annual symposium that brings editors, journalists, scholars, and foundation directors together to recognize civic journalism efforts and chart the course for the movement's future. Speaking at the 1999 Batten symposium titled "A Citizens'-Eye View: Civic Journalism, Civic Engagement," sociologist Michael Schudson, a scholar well-known in the public journalism movement, seemingly restated one of the theses of this book:

> Civic journalism will be making a mistake if it opts for a kind of sloppy populism: Anything the experts do must be tainted. Anything that happens at the grassroots receives the benefit of the doubt. That, I think, is the wrong impulse. I think we have to rely on expert knowledge. (Why the Informed Citizen . . ., 1999, p. 9)

We would edit Schudson's admonition to say that much of what passes for civic journalism has already opted for a type of sloppy populism. His advice, however, is particularly relevant to the growing number of journalists who enthrone public opinion simply because it is public.

The last decade of the 20th century saw the birth and growth of civic (or public) journalism. Although still in its adolescence, the idea has appealed to journalists sensitive to critics who contend the media is too detached, elitist, sensational, conflict oriented, or profit driven. Hearing this cacophony of criticism, many journalists are questioning their own values, becoming "outer-directed" and empowered by the mandate of the people that public journalism gives them. The power of the press, in a traditional sense, is seen as a journalistic and democratic problem. The press, corrupted by its First

Amendment freedom, has behaved irresponsibly, and the remedy is to rein in freedom and reinvest it in the name of the people. These beliefs underscore public journalism, and although the practice is still evolving, it has matured to the extent that it can be said to be characterized by:

- More thorough and systematic attempts to listen to the public. Polling, focus groups, town hall meetings, and community conversations—some scientific, others sophomoric—are used to give the public the opportunity to set the media's news agenda.

- Pooled media resources and cross-media cooperation and promotion that creates a larger audience for public journalism initiatives. The goals are to broaden the appeal of public journalism and increase media effects.

- More emphasis on citizen participation in the media. Members of the public are invited to attend news planning meetings, asked to supply questions for journalists to ask official sources and candidates, and urged to speak up at media-sponsored community conversations where their discussions are recorded by journalists and reported as news.

- Efforts by public-minded editors and academicians to move the practice of public journalism out of the newsroom and into the university classroom, thus placing on public journalism a stamp of professional accreditation for future generations of journalists.

Together, these practices self-impose on the media an active responsibility for reengaging people into public life and making public life work. The media works to meet this responsibility by: (a) revitalizing democracy, championing public issues, and encouraging voting, (b) bringing people together to recognize a stronger sense of community and nurturing development of shared interests, values, goals, and dreams of a better life, and (c) encouraging the public to participate in the media and, accordingly, see the media as a larger part of their lives—as a social and political facilitator, an instrument of community well-being, and a promoter of populist causes.

9

The Waning of
Press Autonomy

Operators of the media, whoever they are, must always resist the temptation to capture the media they operate. They can do this by recognizing that it is beyond their power to always depict American society accurately from their own limited viewpoints. They must be willing to share that portrayal among warring groups and constituencies, who alone can show how things appear to them. The media must play host in a more dramatic and representative way than ever before to the variety and conflict in the nation. Every group must feel that it has an opportunity to plead its own cause in its own way and its own voice. To insist on such participation should be the task of media criticism.

—Jerome A. Barron

We saw in the last two chapters who the public journalism leaders are and what various newspapers are doing to implement the new model in their daily practice. There seems little doubt that the press is slowly losing its editorial autonomy, giving it up out of a sense of public consciousness and a desire to democratize journalism. Public journalism has simply been one of the forces (maybe the main one) to prick the tough skin of the institutional press and make it aware of its public responsibilities. It is always possible, of course, that this shift from press freedom to press responsibility—from press autonomy to public involvement—will be only temporary. However, it is our contention that this change will be more than a momentary whim and will grow constantly in the 21st century until America has a truly populist press.

Throughout the 20th century, even when strong public sentiments were buffeting the American media, the traditional Enlightenment principle of editorial autonomy of the press held tight. Slowly it was being eroded, however, and more and more emphasis was put on the public and its rights and less on freedom of the press. Many examples can be given to support this contention, and in this chapter we provide some of these. We have already discussed the impact of the Hutchins Commission in the 1940s and the grow-

170

ing influence of communitarianism and public journalism. It seems that for some time now, the elitism that held tight during the Enlightenment and continued through the 20th century has lost its grip, and the spirit of egalitarianism and democracy—of letting the people speak—has gained the upper hand. What is happening to the press illustrates this shift from autocratic journalism of the elite to democratic journalism of the people.

Many critics feel that media managers largely determine what is news and that even the journalists in the trenches have little to say about it. "News has become largely a management product," wrote Canadian journalism educator James Winter (1998, p. 139). From hiring and promotion to assignment, framing, sourcing, and editing, management makes the decisions, he added (p. 139): "Far from being independent-minded professionals, most journalists are employees who do the job the boss wants in return for a pay cheque." Therefore, Winter said, "the resultant news product is not monolithic in nature, but is overwhelmingly narrow in terms of its range and focus." He quoted Otis Chandler of the *Los Angeles Times* as saying, "I'm not going to surround myself with people who disagree with me" (p. 140).

THE MUTING OF THE PRESS

It should be stressed, however, that what is happening to the press is not due entirely to a new moral consciousness that has somehow fallen over the world of journalism. Although the spirit of community has indeed invaded portions of the press and has spread a sense of responsibility, it has far from revolutionized press practices. and although democracy and egalitarianism are joining hands to push back press autonomy, great segments of the press are as autocratic as ever. Little doubt exists, however, that strong moral forces are at work on the press, and a growing sense of responsibility, together with public concern and a heightened social consciousness, are muting the shrill voice of the press.

Added to this internal reformation, the press is losing its institutional freedom because of other not so altruistic factors. It is a fact that at the end of the 20th century, the press alienated the people by its excesses, its negativism, its invasion of privacy, and its growing detachment from the community. Absentee owners and multimedia conglomerates were growing rapidly, adding to this alienation. The public became increasingly restless and critical. It was time for a change. It started with a challenge to journalistic theory, that very Enlightenment-based theory that spawned the free press. Such a change in theory, still evolving, has made its impact in practice.

Court mandates reflecting citizen opinion increased and the press gave up more freedom. The press felt the blows of huge libel actions and its timidity increased. In addition, plaintiffs had begun using civil laws to get around

First Amendment protection. Now the focus was not on the content or accuracy of the messages, but on the manner in which the information was gathered. These legal actions, called *trash torts,* include nuisance, unjust enrichment, assault, stalking, negligence, trespass, intrusion on seclusion, and invasion of privacy. Codes of ethics proliferated as citizen complaints grew, further muting the press' voice.

Other pressures on the press came from communitarians and public journalists whose insistence on community-building and responsibility was slowly sinking into media consciousness. Along with this communitarianism, the press sustained general public pressure to be more positive, more moderate, more socially helpful in its news and opinion.

Advertising pressures on the media, although not new, proceeded unimpeded. In fact, by the end of the 20th century, advertising was getting so dominant in the media as to distract the audience from the purported editorial content. There was an observable increase in concern for the "bottom line," and profits tended to crowd out a concern for the public good. This ultra-capitalistic grab for maximum profits had been the main target of the critical theorists of the 1970s and 1980s who lambasted the greedy self-centered Western press. Perhaps they were too extreme and too far to the left to have much impact, but they were soon (in the early 1990s) joined by a host of counter-Enlightenment postmodernists, communitarians, and public journalists—representing not only the political left, but the middle and right—who now have mounted a sustained attack on the money-spirited press.

The audiences (the publics) have, at the same time, increased their criticism of the press. Polls have shown the unpopularity of the press. Various segments of the population were demanding greater access to the press and even a voice in its policy and decision making. Along with all of this came the mushrooming impact of the Internet that siphoned off previous press power and shattered the press's news–opinion monopoly. If this were not enough, there were voices questioning the very core of American press theory—the value of freedom itself. There were even those insisting that the First Amendment gave the press too much power and placed the public in a helpless position where their desires and welfare were largely ignored. In short, the press was undemocratic. Besides, it was virtually lawless, not controlled by legal norms as were other institutions.

The litany of criticisms of the press is almost endless. Some of it is relatively mild. Much of it is extremely harsh, and getting harsher. Listen to journalist Jim Squires, former political writer and editor of the *Chicago Tribune:* "What could be more unfair to citizens than the outright corruption of journalism, which takes place daily in all quarters of the so-called news media?" Believing that standards of journalism are presently nonexistent, Squires (1998, p. 68) saw news being merged with entertainment and concerned mainly with sex and crime and prominent people. As to press freedom, Squires (p. 70) maintained that the press "has enjoyed special privileges because it was a special business with a unique goal of serving the public interest." But, he added, "Journalism can't make that claim anymore."

Many journalists say that the low status of the press can be improved by the press itself, through the professionalizing of journalism. They believe that if journalism had higher standards for entry, more rigid educational requirements, a commonly accepted code of professional ethics, and a system for "disbarring" ("depressing"?) irresponsible journalists, the press would improve very quickly and retain its favored spot under the First Amendment.

Most critics seem to doubt this. Professionalization would not solve the basic problems. The press would still be exempt from laws. It would still make editorial decisions that affect the public. It would still have its great power. In fact, say the critics of professionalizing journalism, the press would be even more of an elite institution than it has been because it would be an exclusionary group, being able to keep certain people out of journalism. And, say the critics, look at the legal profession. Is it any more ethical and socially responsible than journalism? Professionalization has not done much to dissipate the generally negative image of lawyers.

FREEING THE VOX POPULI

Since the beginning of the American republic, the voice of the people has been enthroned as ultimately important, at least in theory, but it has always been the voice of only a small number of the people—the powerful, the rich, and the intellectuals that pushed the country forward. Democracy has been of a minimalist kind and excluded huge portions of the population. The politicians, the industrial tycoons and big businessmen, the publishers and radio–television personalities, the religious and educational establishment, the movie and entertainment celebrities—these are the people whose voices have largely shaped the country.

William Greider, a former editor of *The Washington Post,* has written much (1993) about this "mock democracy," as he calls it. In the field of politics alone, he said, the people have neither the personal ability nor the wherewithal to participate meaningfully. Except for a well-educated, sophisticated segment of media-wise citizens who know how to play the game and gain entry to the areas of power, the American public is politically impotent and virtually uninformed about what is really happening. Listen to Greider:

> Beyond the fact of unequal resources . . . lies a more troubling proposition: that democracy is now held captive by the mystique of 'rational' policymaking, narrow assumptions about what constitutes legitimate political evidence. It is

a barrier of privilege because it effectively discounts authentic political expressions from citizens and elevates the biases and opinions of the elites. (p. 36)

Authentic political expressions from citizens do get some hearing, of
course—in the home, the office, the restaurants and bars, and at parties
where the uninformed swap biases with each other. This may be a kind of
informal vox populi, but it is not the kind of informed dialogue that has any
real impact on the reality of the political world. Why? Because it is not
plugged into the places of power. It could be that many Americans think this
is how the system is supposed to work, directed by the elite few who have the
knowledge and expertise. The general expectation seems to be that this
imbalance is quite natural. Citizens, however, are assigned an inferior status.
If knowledge-based expertise and communication skills are needed to
influence governmental decisions, it is obvious that most citizens will be
powerless. How, then, can this be called democracy?

The communitarians and public journalists saw the exclusion of the
masses of Americans from the political arena, and set out to better the situation. Among other things, they seem committed to the goal of developing
and nurturing equality in political expression. This, of course, is difficult.
Where private wealth and power is unequal, people will be unequal in their
political influence. Although the ideal reform would be to level the playing
field as much as possible, many communitarians see the present political system tilting the other way, with those already having the advantage gaining
more and more power. A good example of this, said Greider, is the subsidy
the rich get through the federal tax code in the form of allowable tax deduc-
tions—"tax breaks that, practically speaking, are only available to corporations and people with substantial surplus wealth" (p. 51).

Another press critic, Dennis Mazzocco (1994) placed the blame for press
intransigence to a large extent on corporate control of the media. He believed that more than ever before, media executives and their corporations
"are able to hide behind their first amendment rights in order to prevent
greater citizen participation in their affairs" (p. 143). The current situation
cannot be reduced, he said, until government is forced, through political
action, to shift the balance of media power in favor of common people. Otherwise, so far as communication is concerned, we will continue to have a
kind of mock democracy.

The press, of course, plays a big part in this mock democracy. What the
press chooses to tell the people, the politicians must respond to. What the
press ignores, the politicians can ignore also. It is obvious that the press has
tremendous power and is, in fact, a primary player in the elite power game of
politics. Greider (1993, p. 287) asked these telling questions: "Who elected
the reporters and editors? Why should they be able to set the political
agenda according to their own peculiar tastes and interests?" What has hap-

pened is that the press has virtually abandoned the people and is catering increasingly to the elite and their interests. Journalists have joined the ranks of politicians on talk shows and in public forums and, in effect, have become autocrats. Instead of supporting democracy, the American press has turned its back on it, opting to align itself with the government more often than with the nonelite portions of the citizenry.

Alexis de Tocqueville warned early in America's development that democracy could suffocate itself (Revel, 1985, p. 12) and in its final stage could be little more than a dictatorship of public opinion. And the formulator of this public opinion, the stirrer of the democratic pot—the press—could itself become an elite institutional authority, thereby frustrating the fragile power of the democratic ideal. The masses of people, by being passive and not speaking up against press and other abuses, could blame themselves and their lack of involvement for the coming of this new authoritarianism (of a small group of *active elitists*). This may be called democracy, but really it is pseudodemocracy where no more than half the people (and large portions of them ignorant and disinterested) even vote, much less actively participate in democratic dialogue and debate.

Today's public journalists, among others, see this very situation developing. They are attempting to create a real democracy in America, one in which there is actually a majority government and where people's voices can be heard to a much greater degree. This is perhaps the primary motivation to reform the press so as to spread its power and freedom to the people. Let us now look at some related factors that have contributed, and are contributing, to the new paradigm shift of freedom to the people and away from the press—from the concept of press autonomy to one of public involvement and empowerment.

THE PEOPLE'S RIGHT TO KNOW

What the press, and certainly the government, seems to forget is that a free press is supposed to exist for the benefit of the people. The press is more than a profit-making business; it is a public institution given special privileges under the Constitution so that it can provide information needed by a sovereign people. It is true that the people do not have a Constitutional right to know, but they have a philosophical right to know. Why else would the First Amendment grant the press such an important gift as freedom? The Founding Fathers hardly had that much love for the press.

Press people generally justify their messages by appealing to the public's right to know. Nonpress people increasingly are challenging such a rationale, saying in effect that there is no such right to know, and even if there were, it would not mean that the people have a right to know everything. The libertarians, it seems to us, are caught in their own trap. They insist on a people's right to know and at the same time tout their right to press freedom. If the people do have such a right to know, the press is thereby relieved of its freedom because press freedom includes the freedom *not* to let the people know.

However, let us assume that the public does have a right to know. That means that the government and/or the press has the obligation to fulfill that right—to let the people know. The government, of course, does not do it. And the press, often blaming the government or other institutions for their secrecy or censorship, does not do it. So the right, if it exists, is an unfulfilled right, a phantom right that sounds good but signifies little or nothing.

Do the people have a right to know information that might harm government negotiations with other nations? To know about the private lives of others? To know about details of criminal acts? We could go on and on with such questions. The fact is that we really know that such a "right to know" is rather nebulous, even meaningless. The reality at present is that the people have only a right to get the information that the press (along with the government and other institutions) wants the people to get. Here is the way Canadian journalism educator James Winter put it (1998, p. 140) regarding the role of the press in letting the people know:

> The media are a delivery system for the policies favoured by the corporate elite who own them, and their brethren. Although the media *survive* by making a profit, and delivering audiences to advertisers, they *exist* in order to impart selected information, ideas, opinions, and values to their audiences.

Slowly but surely, various public and government pressures are changing this picture. Public journalists, for example, are insisting that much information the public does get is harmful and that the press is irresponsible in publishing it, that the people (or the majority of them) really do not want to get such information. Of course, as the public makes its voice known to the press leaders and these leaders act on it, the traditional autonomy of the journalism institution is eroded.

Increasingly, not only in the United States, press autonomy is being challenged. The people and their rights and freedom are being enthroned. For example, The World Association of Press Councils meeting in Istanbul in September 1998 declared that "freedom of the press is recognized not simply as a freedom for journalists, editors or proprietors but rather as a right of all citizens to be informed on all matters of public interest." The group also declared that it is implicit and inherent in a free press that it exercise its powers and duties in a responsible manner, and that the press must be accountable to the public, not the government.

Le Monde of Paris, commenting on this declaration in Istanbul, noted (Vernet, 1998, p. 24) that the intention was praiseworthy, involving setting rules to which the journalists and the media would voluntarily subscribe—

responsible information, respect for privacy, etc. In an editorial in *The Times* of London at about the same time (Sept. 26, 1998), the writer was critical of the WAPC's Ankara declaration, calling its demand for a global code of ethics a "bad order" and saying that it "would be impossible in practice to devise a global code acceptable to all societies that would not curtail the freedoms essential to good reporting."

In the 20th century such proposals as that of the WAPC seemed doomed to failure. As the new century begins, however, it becomes clearer that man v parts of the world are ready for more responsibility and credibility of the press and are willing to see press freedom restricted if that is what is necessary. At the United Nations, for example, there has been a proposal for a "jam squad," a special U.N. team that could be sent quickly to any crisis spot in the world carrying equipment to jam, or block, "harmful radio and TV broadcasts" (Mann, 1997, p. A5). This team could jam any broadcasts that it would consider dangerous or that could incite people to violence. Rep. Edward Royce (R-California) called this team "a worthy idea." Such activities are not uncommon, although they have been conducted on an ad hoc basis. For example, the United States and its allies have conducted similar operations in Yugoslavia since 1997.

Regardless of the problems with such a "right," most public-spirited commentators believe in it. Lord Francis Williams of Britain, in his *The Right to Know* (1969, p. 36), proclaimed the benefits of such a right but recognized that it is constantly challenged. "It is rare," he wrote, "for this function [permitting the people to know] to be exercised without challenge." Why? "The secrecies of governments, the self-preserving mechanisms of bureaucracies, the pressures of great interests, the compulsions of political ideologies, stand in its way."

In another book (1994) with a similar title (*The People's Right to Know*), edited by Williams and Pavlik of the Freedom Forum Media Studies Center in New York City, various authors extolled the virtues of letting the public know, but pointed out problems with the concept. Williams asserted (p. 85) that the discrepancy between those with access to information-age service and those without it "can well be interpreted as a threat to First Amendment guarantees of our Constitution." Such a statement seems to us rather extreme inasmuch as the First Amendment says absolutely nothing about equal access for all people to information. However, it does show the concern that many people have about the inability of citizens to know.

THE PEOPLE'S RIGHT OF PRESS ACCESS

This is another right that press libertarians say does not exist, and, again, they are right in a legal sense. News media are private businesses and laws that would force them to accept for publication offerings from citizens would undoubtedly be called unconstitutional.

This is exactly what happened in the Florida case of Tornillo v. The Miami Herald. In 1972 Pat Tornillo was running for the Florida House of Representatives. He was criticized in the *Miami Herald*, and Tornillo wanted space to answer the criticism. It was denied by the *Herald*. Tornillo took the case to the Florida courts and he was upheld. The *Herald* then appealed to the U.S. Supreme Court where the case was heard in 1974. Jerome Barron, a Washington lawyer, represented Tornillo. The issue considered by the Supreme Court (*Media Law Reports*, 1978, p. 1898): "whether a state statute granting a political candidate a right to equal space to reply to criticism and attacks on his record by a newspaper violates the guarantees of a free press." The case was decided in favor of the newspaper, with Justice Byron White writing (p. 1905): "The Court today said that the First Amendment bars a state from requiring a newspaper to print the reply of a candidate for public office whose personal character has been criticized by that newspaper's editorials."

In spite of this decision, the issue has been kept alive, and there is no doubt that in the 21st century, some kind of *rapprochment* will be made so that unrepresented persons and groups can participate in the mainstream press. A precedent has been set with the broadcast media, with the Federal Communication Commission as its monitor. There is no logical reason why such a commission cannot regulate the print media. If the concept of fairness is sound for the broadcast industry, why not for the newspaper and magazine industries? Of course, there is the free press clause of the First Amendment—but it can be changed as we suggested earlier. Or it can be interpreted by the Supreme Court in ways that will open the press to more populist involvement.

Perhaps the leading advocate of a people's right of access to the media has been Barron, the lawyer–professor who called media practices "private censorship" and controlling opinions of the public that should be exposed. Barron (1973, p. xiv) wrote that "the First Amendment should be restored to its true proprietors—the reader, the viewer, the listener." He added: "Freedom of the press must be something more than a guarantee of the property rights of media owners." So far the courts have thwarted attempts to provide individuals and groups access to the press, but as Barron said, the fight is not over. This issue will not die, and Barron was optimistic, saying in the final sentence of his book, "Attention is at last being given to the idea that the First Amendment grants protection to others in the opinion-making process besides those who own the media of communication" (p. 343).

The idea of public access to the press is nothing new. Actually as far back as 1947, the Hutchins Commission in its report (Commission on Freedom of the Press, 1947, p. 13) said that the press "must be free to all who have something worth saying to the public, since the essential object for which a free press is valued is that ideas deserving a public hearing shall have a public hearing." It is obvious that when the time is ripe for such access to take place, the press will certainly lose much of its autonomy and have some outside force (such as the courts) participating in the editing process.

PRESS COUNCILS AND OMBUDSPERSONS

Although press councils have not caught on in an important way in the United States, they have been rather successful in other countries. At least their presence indicates that the press is being watched, evaluated, and criticized for certain irresponsible acts. These councils, voluntary and unofficial in the open societies of the West, do have a salutary effect on press activities. Although several states have such councils, the experiment with an American national press council was not successful. The National News Council lasted for 11 years, from 1973 to 1984.

Funded largely by the Twentieth Century Fund, a New York research foundation, it lacked widespread support and continuing financial resources. From the beginning, the NNC faced vigorous opposition from most of journalism. Newspaper executives felt that the council impugned their virtue and threatened their autonomy and, of course, they invoked the First Amendment. However, as Brogan (1985) said, in his story of the council, "The American Constitution was not divinely inspired. The people of the United States enacted it, and as Thomas Jefferson himself observed, the people have the right to change or reinterpret it whenever they so desire" (p. 4).

The council had no powers of enforcement. It simply looked into citizen complaints, made suggestions, and counted on publicity to bring about changes. Norman Isaacs of the *Louisville Courier-Journal* was perhaps its chief supporter, and A. M. Rosenthal of the *New York Times* its main opponent. The council had little press or public support and, when it ran out of money at the end of 1983, voted to suspend operation in early 1984. Some of the founding members of the NNC were (Brogan, 1985, p. 113) William Rusher, publisher of *National Review;* Loren Ghiglione, editor of the Southbridge, MA, *Evening News;* Irving Dilliard, former editorial page editor of the *St. Louis Post-Dispatch;* and Ralph Otwell, managing editor of the *Chicago Sun-Times.* Such councils had worked well in some other countries, particularly in Sweden and Britain, but it could never catch on in the United States, although a few state councils (e.g., in Minnesota) did continue.

The idea of press (news) councils is consistent with the goals of public journalists and those who want greater participation of the public in news decisions, but, by and large, it does not resonate with most journalists (at least executives). This is ironic, wrote Gilson (1999), because news media insist that all institutions they cover admit their sins, apologize, and carry out immediate reform. "Yet those same news outlets," said Gilson, "refuse to do so when their own work is called to account and found wanting" (p. 7).

In the 20th century the idea of press councils languished except in a few countries. Certainly it did in the United States, the keystone of individualism and Enlightenment freedom. The press council idea is not dead, however, and in this new century there is the growing concern that the press needs somebody or some group to watch and have an impact on its activities. Some sort of monitoring authority will likely arise again, and when it does, it may very well be a nonjournalistic group that this time will have some enforcement powers. No institution should be beyond public control, although the press comes close. Here we have a press that wants to be a check on government and on other public institutions, but does not want anyone checking it. This is true even when those watching it and criticizing it (as with the National News Council) would not be government officials. The rationale for news councils is that the press will correct some of its mistakes and be more responsible if subjected to public exposure. The idea of press councils has been with us since mid-20th century, and even if not generally successful as yet, does indicate a shift in emphasis from freedom to responsibility.

Another sign of journalism's "people-concern" has been the rise of ombudsmen (or ombudspersons). They have appeared in many parts of the world where the press is relatively free. These persons usually work for the media they represent but they are the people's representatives, the persons to whom citizens can complain when they see what they consider injustices in editorial content. On many newspapers that have ombudspersons, these readers' representatives are also critics of the newspaper's practices. It is common for them to have a column in which they appraise the working of the newspaper. In spite of some obvious weaknesses, the concept of the ombudsperson is one that contributes to the citizens' voice in journalism and does its part to decrease the autonomy of the newspaper's authorities.

THE INTERNET

We have already dealt to some extent with the Internet. Certainly it is one of the main ways press autonomy may be threatened in the 21st century. The press must take the Internet seriously and try to adapt its institutional practices to the great competition presented by cyberspace. By the end of the 20th century, more than 10 million computers had access to about 60,000 interconnected computer networks (Trager & Dickerson, 1999, p. 160). In the first decade of the 21st century, those numbers will probably double or triple. The institutionalized press is quite likely to be split asunder by the Internet, its traditional power diverted into millions of communications outlets operating in the hands of the people. As governments (or the people) see the danger generated by this megapluralism or cacophony of uncontrolled voices, laws will emerge to control them. In the process, such legal restraints will lap over onto the traditional and institutional media such as newspapers and magazines. What this means is that traditional media autonomy that the American press has enjoyed will come to an end. The rationale: the need for order, responsibility, and social harmony.

The Internet, in its haste to democratize journalism, will have, in effect, destroyed the institutional autonomy of the press. Such legal restraint on the Internet in the United States began back in 1996 when Congress passed the Child Pornography Prevention Act to protect minors from pornography through use of the computer technology. The act clearly advanced government interest in protecting children from the harms of pornography. Without a doubt, an increasing number of restraints will be placed on the Internet.

These restraints will be welcomed by many Americans. The idea that people are "naturally rational, moral creatures, without the need for strong external restraints has been exploded by experience," as Bork wrote (1997, p. 138). There is not much resistance, according to Bork, to the "propaganda for every perversion and obscenity" that is flooding America. What little opposition there is, he says, "comes from people living on the moral capital accumulated by prior generations" (p. 139). In spite of the negativism of such critics as Bork as they ponder the Internet and other mass technologies of communication, there are those who see this electronic revolution as promising the citizen a real chance at democratic involvement.

A new term, in fact, has arisen to indicate the expansion of the enlarged potential for communication offered by the Internet—the *electronic citizen* (Davidson & Rees-Mogg, 1997, p. 315). These authors believe that the technology of the Information Age will give rise to new forms of governance; certainly such technology can make possible truly representative government, injecting into our pseudodemocracy real and direct participation in political action by the citizens. This term points out the growing significance of free speech through the electronic media. It is clear that the new electronic technologies are powerful new media that have introduced new means for information dissemination for all citizens.

The whole concept of communication ethics will be greatly impacted by this vast extension of unmediated message sending and receiving. Ethicists will have to deal with the behavior of individuals who will be able to find and build on the ideas of others. It will be all too easy for the ideas and works of others to be unethically appropriated without proper attribution. Procedures for defining and identifying Internet abuses and for proposing punishments will be one of the consuming tasks of the 21st century.

In Germany (Geldner, 1977, p. 37) the Internet has already proved to be a danger to national stability, and perhaps even to security. Prosecutor Manfred von Hagen of Berlin is offended by a home page of a young radical socialist telling how to blow up trains, information that the prosecutor sees as endangering law and order. He calls the material on the web site "terrorist propaganda." Although Von Hagen's legal efforts failed to shut the site down, the case does point up the problems facing the Internet in many countries.

A well-organized central web site for right-wingers also exists in Germany; the so-called *Thule-Netz* provides some 200 links to the pages of many other neo-Nazi groups in Germany. The Thule Society, based in Munich, was perhaps the foremost supporter of Hitler and the Nazis in the 1930s and 1940s, and the Internet site or net (*Thule-Netz*) carries on its name today. Its pages carry platforms advocating reclaiming eastern territories for Germany, anti-Semitic chat groups, pages for skinheads, and links to organizations in other countries (Geldner, 1997, p. 37).

Some nations—such as Ethiopia, Libya, Sudan, Iraq, Yemen, Cambodia, and North Korea—are controlling access to the Internet by not connecting to the network (Trager & Dickerson, 1999, p. 161). Other governments are imposing controls by dominating the hardware necessary for sending and receiving messages, and still other countries—Myanmar and Singapore are good examples—are controlling the Internet by using any means possible including outright censorship (p. 161). China has "computer security units" patrolling the Internet in search of "dangerous information" (Bell, 1999, p. 21) and has tough regulations that will lead to imprisonment for Internet users subverting "state secrets." Freedom for Internet users, it seems, is in for a long struggle.

Pessimists among newspaper people see the Internet as dooming the newspaper. We think this is unjustified and, although it may greatly expand the potential for citizen communication, it is doubtful that it will eliminate the newspaper—or the book. Even William Gates, chairman and CEO of Microsoft, confessed in a speech in 1999 that he preferred to read from paper than from a computer screen. He stated:

> Reading off the screen is still vastly inferior to reading off of paper. Even I, who have these expensive screens and fancy myself as a pioneer of this Web Lifestyle, when it comes to something over about four or five pages, I print it out and I like to carry it around with me and annotate. And it's quite a hurdle for technology to achieve to match that level of usability. (Darnton, 1999, p. 5)

Many social critics—on the left and right—are far from enamored of the Internet. Chomsky, for example, said (Barsamian, 1994, p. 51) that one has "a different relationship to somebody when you're looking at them than you do when you're punching away at a key-board and some symbols come back." He preferred (p. 51) "direct, personal contact" and suspected that the Internet relationship is too abstract and remote and that it will have unpleasant effects on what people are like. "It will," he believed, "diminish their humanity."

Bork may well outdo Chomsky in his denigration of the Internet. Bork sees the Internet as beguilingly attractive and far more dangerous than most people realize. He is especially concerned about socially harmful material on the Internet such as plans for making bombs, plans for painless suicide, racist diatribes, and sexual perversion. In his best-selling book, *Slouching Towards Gomorrah,* Bork (1996) documented (p. 138) how one can find the most perverted, bestial, lewd, obscene, filthy, and indecent material on the Internet. He warned that if there is not a counterattack against these excesses (by resorting to legal as well as moral sanctions) "the prospects are for a chaotic and unhappy society, followed, perhaps, by an authoritarian and unhappy society" (p. 139).

LAW AND THE DEMISE OF PRESS FREEDOM

It has been said, half in jest, that lawyers now run the newspapers. Although this is not literally true, there is plenty of evidence that concern with libel and other legal matters is consuming more and more of the newspapers' time, effort, and finances. It is surely having a chilling effect on editorial decision making. When confronted with a decision as to whether to publish a certain story, the first inclination of editors is to get a legal opinion. This is a great change from the free-wheeling days of American journalism when publishers and editors made these decisions themselves.

Press autonomy and freedom may be relatively safe from legislative control, but certainly not from judicial restrictions. As the 20th century came to an end, the press was losing more and more of its freedom and as the 21st century began, the trend showed no sign of ceasing or reversing. The First Amendment protects the press from legislative constriction of its freedom, but it does nothing to keep the executive and judicial branches from taking away press freedom. Executive orders can control the press and have been used from time to time, and the courts are constantly meddling in press affairs, usually with the result of restricting press freedom.

It is evident why newspaper editors, instead of making autonomous news decisions, are seeking advice from their lawyers. From just one issue of the journal *The News Media & The Law* (1998, Fall) came the following headlines that point up the impact of court decisions on the press:

- "Court upholds contempt order against NBC" (p. 3)
- "Prosecutors 'due process' right overcomes reporter's privilege" (p. 6)
- "Wrestling producer's reporter not covered by reporters' privilege" (p. 7)

- "State high court upholds prior restraint on videotaped talks" (p. 11)
- "High court won't hear media appeal on access to Starr investigation records" (p. 10)
- "Court Denies Review of Reporter's Suit" (p. 10)
- "Access to Gates deposition blocked by appellate court stay" (p. 13)
- "Newspaper restrained from publishing story for 12 days" (p. 14)
- "Media denied access to attorney's interim expense records" (p. 15)
- "Cameras banned from school shooting trial" (p. 20)
- "New Internet law intended to restrict minors' access to 'harmful' material" (p. 20)
- "Families win right to sue over use of autopsy photos" (p. 36)
- "Photographers arrested while covering riots" (p. 40)
- "Radio Free Asia Team Bumped from China Trip" (p. 41)
- "CBS Freelance Producer Detained in China" (p. 41)

MAKING THE MEDIA PAY

In 1998 several court cases pointed out the rather new and serious legal ways the press is losing its freedom. An NBC news magazine promised a trucking company in Maine that it would get a glowing portrayal on the show; "Dateline NBC" gave the company a very negative roasting. *The Cincinnati Enquirer* published a hard-hitting piece on questionable business practices of Chiquita Brands International in which the reporter got some of his facts by stealing thousands of voice mail messages. In California, a television cameraman jumped aboard a helicopter and videotaped a victim's conversation with a paramedic; it was broadcast by CBS on its show "On Scene: Emergency Response." Enterprising reporting? Not at all. Each of these cases landed reporters and their bosses in court, defending not the truth of the stories, but how the information was gathered. Margaret Gorzkowski (1998), writing in *Quill,* believed that what media executives and reporters must realize is that "the public, as represented by recent juries, has chosen to punish journalistic violations of civil law as severely as it punishes journalists who defame" (p. 25).

In the Chiquita case, the Gannett Co. paid Chiquita Brands an extremely large sum and "renounced" its story in order to avert extended litigation. Lawyer Bruce W. Sanford of Washington, DC, asked an important question in the September 1998 *American Editor:* "What does it say about the American press or the condition of First Amendment law at the turn of the century that the Gannett Co. has paid Chiquita Brands more than $10 million and renounced a lengthy investigative report, substantial parts of which may have been true?" (p. 17).

Earlier (in 1992) there was the famous Food Lion case where ABC "Prime Time" broadcast that the food chain was selling rotting meat, fish dipped in bleach to hide its smell, cheese nibbled on by rats, and other unsavory practices. Food Lion did not sue for libel and claim that the charges were false. It charged that ABC staffers trespassed when they used hidden cameras on the premises and committed fraud by lying about their previous work experience. So even as early as 1992, the plaintiff was asking the jury to decide the case, not on the truth of the story, but on what it called deceptive newsgathering techniques. The jury ruled for Food Lion and awarded the grocery chain $5.5 million in punitive damages. Jane Kirtley, executive director of the Reporters Committee for Freedom of the Press, wrote (1997) that if "the laws of trespass and fraud can be used against journalists without the leavening influence of the First Amendment, all investigative reporting is at risk" (p. 48).

What all this says about the press is that it is coming under increasing pressure from governmental statutes such as disorderly conduct, assault and obstruction of justice, trespass, and impersonation. As Bruce Sanford (1998) noted, in addition to the courts' antagonism to press freedom, "the academic community has turned away from expansionist views of the First Amendment to an emphasis on 'media responsibility.' Scholarship has experienced a noticeable shift in focus from privileges [of the press] to obligations" (p. 18) The growth in the number of "nondefamatory torts" (legal wrongs caused by the press that have nothing to do with injuring reputation, as in the classic libel suit) places a substantial pressure on the press and erodes its traditional shelter under the First Amendment.

CODES OF ETHICS: NORMATIVITY

Ethical codes are growing in number and impact. Discussions in and out of newspapers about ethics have increased substantially since the 1980s. Students in journalism schools read them, discuss them, and ingest their principles. What this means is that journalists are increasingly obtaining a monolithic set of ethical principles. Whereas in the past every newspaper might have its own policies on ethics, thereby giving a moral pluralism to the press system, increasingly they are sharing the same basic journalism ethics. This is what the public journalists want, for it reduces the impact on society of individualist ethics and gives some predictability to press actions.

Not only are journalism codes of ethics getting more attention in the United States, but around the world they are appearing increasingly. Associations of journalists and individual media have ethical codes. In the United Nations there have been repeated calls for an international code of media ethics, and such recommendations have found favor with many journalism scholars around the world. It seems certain that some such instrument will be developed in the next few years. In 1999 such a global code was discussed in the U.N. with a "transnational complaint mechanism" to enforce it. Another U.N. proposal has been a "Universal Declaration of Human Responsibilities" that would declare that media freedom must "be used with responsibility" and that reporting that "degrades the human person or dignity" must be avoided (*World Press Freedom Committee Newsletter,* Dec. 21, 1998, p. 5).

Public journalists and other assorted communitarians are especially fond of ethical codes. For people wanting to see smooth-running, predictable, normative community codes of ethics leading to a kind of moral conformity and predictability, codes are essential. A moral framework is assumed to be a condition of community. Therefore, said Christians, "social institutions such as . . . the press must empower the public sphere by breathing air into the collapsed lungs of the spirit" (Nerone, 1995, p. 70). Christians seemed to be advocating an ethics of engagement and community conversation, noting that the press "has bigger fish to fry" than merely improving technology and performance. "In the communitarian worldview," he said (Nerone, p. 70), "the news media should seek to engender a like-minded philosophy among the public." If this is be done, journalists would have to have a common ethics themselves before they could engender a like-minded philosophy in the public.

ENLARGING JOURNALISM'S SCOPE

As the concept of journalism expands and as the definition of "a journalist" fades into semantic obscurity, the power and the freedom of the institutionalized press are diminished. Actually, we have never really been sure just who is a journalist, but with the coming of public relations, then radio, then television, and now the Internet, determining just who is a journalist becomes next to impossible. Journalism schools and organizations have faced this problem. Most schools are now "mass communications schools" or some such names that evidence the synthesis of nonjournalism activities with various kinds of communication activities. The main academic association of journalism teachers, which until the 1990s was the Association for Education in Journalism (AEJ), is now the Association for Education in Journalism and Mass Communication (AEJMC). "Journalism" is fading; "communication" is coming to the forefront, depreciating the older narrowly conceptualized *journalistic activities.*

The concept of journalism is much more specific and institutionally related than the term communication, which is so broad that it is almost meaningless. James W. Carey, a leader in cultural studies, would not agree, for he has suggested a definition of communication "of disarming simplicity."

Drawing on such sources as Kenneth Burke, Thomas Kuhn, Peter Berger, and Clifford Geertz, Carey presented (1989) this definition: "Communication is a symbolic process whereby reality is produced, maintained, repaired, and transformed" (p. 23).

We wonder if Carey's definition is really disarmingly simple. We disagree with his core contention, although we concur that communication is a symbolic process. But does communication *produce* reality? We think not. Does it *maintain* reality? We think not. Does it *repair* reality? We think not. And does it *transform* reality? We think it does to the degree that it provides an abstracted or distorted picture of reality. We agree with Korzybski and the general semanticists who would compare communication to a map—a map, they insist, "is not the territory" or that it is not reality. Even Carey, later in his book (1989, p. 167) seemed to agree with Harold Innis, the Canadian communications scholar, who "argued that *any* form of communication possesses a bias. . . ." It would appear to us that a more useful definition of communication, certainly a more realistic one, might be this: *Communication is a process through which reality is transformed by human beings into symbols that depict many of the characteristics of that reality.*

Just who is a journalist? Nobody we know can really give an answer anymore. Strict definitions collide with liberal definitions and the latter appear to be winning the day. An example of a strict definition: A journalist is a full-time worker for a traditional news medium—such as a newspaper or magazine—whose chief duties are writing or editing news and editorial content. An example of a liberal definition: A journalist is a person who provides news, analysis, and other material to a specialized or mass audience. There are, of course, degrees of strictness and liberalism in other definitions falling between such extremes.

A good example of a country with a strict or narrow concept of a journalist is Germany. According to the Association of German Journalists (*Deutsche Journalisten-Verband*), only fulltime editorial employees qualify as journalists although this severely restricts the population of "journalism" (Kunczik, 1988, p. 2). Such a narrow definition is the subject of much critical comment in Germany. Wanting a more liberal definition, many critics (usually academics) would infuse entertainment into the concept of journalism in addition to news/interpretation. Some would consider all public communicators as journalists. Splichal and Sparks (1994, p. 227) said that at least one German scholar has contended that such communicators are, in fact, journalists and says that everybody plays the role of communicator (*Jedermann die Rolle des Kommunikators spielt*). This would imply that everybody is a journalist, although perhaps not a full-time one. Therefore, would this not mean that the concept of journalist is rendered meaningless in its older sense?

In the United States it would necessitate the First Amendment free-press clause being extended to include everybody who communicates to or with a public (inasmuch as he or she is a journalist and presumably part of the press). Surely it would include the millions of Americans who send messages through the Internet, those who mail newsletters to various publics, those who are advertisers and public relations people, those who speak to huge audiences (such as mass rallies), and those who speak to specialized audiences (such as religious congregations or academic classes). So we can see that many new sectors of journalists are coming into being: teachers, preachers, actors, politicians, entertainers—and perhaps even musicians.

As the definition of "journalists" grows in scope, perhaps to become synonymous with "communicators," we can see that the concept of the *press* disappears. With its disappearance will go the institutional power and freedom that once was associated with it.

IDEOLOGICAL DETERMINISM

The ideology of America is capitalism. It seeps through the walls of culture, determining almost everything, casting its gold and silver patina over the institutions of mass communication as it envelops journalism. Karl Jaspers (1957, p. 136) saw the press falling prey to economic forces and thereby losing its freedom. He wrote of the press being in an institutionalized cage guarded by the political and economic powers.

Under such controls, he maintained that press people "cultivate the art of lying and indulge in propaganda on behalf of matters repugnant to their higher selves" (p. 136). They have to write in keeping with the basic economic philosophy that they embrace—and this philosophy is capitalism. Capitalism is the engine that pulls a long train of ideological coaches, all filled with cultural cargo compatible with financial profit. One of these coaches is the press, a big business enterprise that confines journalism and determines its total configuration.

The one-time newsroom has now become an adjunct of the business office. Although the business office has always been important in journalism, it has taken on a special power in the last 50 years. Editors and other journalists are made acutely aware of the impact of their stories on circulation figures and on advertisers. Journalistic autonomy is therefore eroded, generally without public notice, by the concern for ever greater profits.

Americans are so accustomed to seeing capitalism writ large across the pages of newspapers and television screens that they hardly notice the enslaved status of their press. As they search with ever more difficulty for oases of news in the vast deserts of advertising, they have slowly adapted to the new business-oriented advertising media that are taking the place of the news media. In a sense, it is dishonest to call a *newspaper* by that name. Money, not news, is the new driving force in journalism. Such beliefs, based squarely on anticapitalism, elicit among critics of public journalism such questions as this, posed by Dennis (1995a): "To what extent is public journalism a triumph of critical theory and neo-Marxist critiques of the media on the one hand, or similar to 'developmental journalism' advocated by Asian leaders?" (p. 48). The basic question might well be: Do the press critics, underneath their rhetoric, really want to do away with capitalism?

Journalism education, by and large, reflects the values of journalism and comports with its ideological bias. Increasingly it, too, is falling prey to the lure of money and is tying itself in with the big media groups. From these vast profit-making concerns, journalism education receives endowed professorships, research funds, new buildings, and equipment. Growing streams of media professionals are sharing their ideological war stories with generations of journalism students. It does seem rather strange that public journalists have welcomed funds for their projects from big media groups. Might not this prove just as harmful to their public emphasis as if they were receiving funds from the government?

Seldom if ever does one hear the big media groups being criticized by mainstream journalism academics. After all, one cannot bite the hand that feeds it. Journalism education is part of the media system that is part of the capitalistic enterprise. Little wonder that American journalism tends to perpetuate the status quo, offers little or no criticism of the big media groups, and largely prepares students for the ideologically enslaved world of bottom-line journalism that awaits them. Dennis (1995a) posed this question: "Why do critics, who have historically warned that chain newspapers would lead to a homogenized press, praise solid corporate support for public journalism?"

Standardization of journalists seems to be the goal, and the standards to which they must conform are community building, group solidarity, and profit enhancement (still considered important). Traditional libertarians see this trend as sapping journalistic freedom and autonomy and depreciating the individual. They note that in journalism education, students are hearing less about freedom and more about press obligations to the public, less about writing and editing and more about management techniques, less about correct grammar and precise writing and more about political correctness and personal appearance, less about public service and more about advertising and business office practices.

Libertarianism, that infused journalism courses with the value of freedom and media diversity from the earliest days through the 1960s and put a premium on meritocracy, was being virtually replaced by century's end by an emphasis on media accountability, management, and corporate monopolies. News was de-emphasized in the classroom and personality profiles and features, packaged in splashy boxes and clever headlines in blues and reds, dominated newspaper pages. Television courses had "gone Hollywood" in their attempt to entertain. A spate of courses such as Multiculturalism had begun to replace traditional courses like History of American Journalism. Textbooks, of course, followed suit with a proliferation of esoteric and specialized publications. A brief glance at the titles of journalism books for the last few decades illustrates this shift in emphasis, and a look at journalism curricula is even more eye-opening.

EGALITARIANISM

The recent emphasis on egalitarianism in journalism is somewhat puzzling, but it is being supported by public journalists and communitarians, and therefore it must be taken seriously. It is strange because libertarianism still plays an important part in press matters, and libertarianism spawns meritocracy, and meritocracy is an enemy of egalitarianism. It seems that the concept of egalitarianism is arising along with the idea of professionalization of journalism—another strange pair. A profession's elite and exclusive status would seem to militate against journalistic equality.

But democracy, Greider believed, "should at least be permanently committed to the goal of nurturing and defending equality . . . even if everyone concedes that private wealth and power will always be unequal and that individuals thus will always be unequal in their ability to exert influence" (p. 51). Why should journalism go on as before? ask the public journalists. Why should we continue to think that the wealthy few at the top of the media pyramid know what is best for us to receive as journalism? The answer is usually that such an elite have the experience, the knowledge, and intelligence not available to the average citizen. However, it may just be that, as Greider stated (p. 407), the basic skepticism the people have of elites is justified, and that "if the real inside story were known," the elites would prove to be "as recklessly human as the rest of us."

Equality, especially equality in social or public institutions, has become the postmodern watchword, and it has invaded the press, where it is giving rise to a kind of democratic style of management. Many writers have predicted the death of democracy, and here are the public journalists trying to reconstruct it in journalism. The public journalists want to refute such writers as Revel (1983) who refers to democracy as "an accident" that has ended, a "brief parenthesis that is closing before our eyes" (p. 4). If a kind of egalitarianism based on a restored democracy comes to journalism, it would drain the autocratic energy and decision making and spread it around the media staffs—and even into the ranks of nonpress people. This egalitarian impulse is having its impact on libertarian press freedom, tied as it is to the capitalistic vertical hierarchy with its strong chain of command.

Jane Doe, the audience member, is envisioned as "equal" to the editor of the newspaper and her voice should be listened to seriously in respect to edi-

torial decisions. Public journalists contend that the First Amendment protects the freedom of the editor or publisher and ignores Jane Doe. What is
needed is a greater sense of egalitarianism, where the citizens, the reporters,
and other journalists are on equal footing with editors and publishers. Unrealistic, naïve, idealistic? Perhaps—but realism and hard-nosed capitalistic
pragmatism, contend the public journalists, has been tried in journalism
and found wanting.

Libertarians respond to such a statement by noting that the assumption
that egalitarianism will improve journalism is unsubstantiated. When, they
ask, is egalitarianism in the management of any private or public institution,
from a grocery store to the military, considered the best policy? Are all people equally prepared to be journalists? Certainly they are presumed equal to
try to become journalists, but as experience tells us, there is not really equality among journalists so far as quality is concerned, and surely there is no
equality between journalists and nonjournalists. If there is, then perhaps we
should shut down all the journalism schools, media conferences, and media
in-house training programs.

Public journalists are convinced that citizen participation can help journalism. They see the press principally as having a mission to form communities that will bring harmony and stability, not friction. Public journalism
offers hope for democratization in communication and a greater equality
among community members. What public journalists seem to realize is this:
When the press has much freedom, equality diminishes inasmuch as various
individuals will be free to excel over others. This would imply social control
(some elite authority) in the newsrooms (or any community) to produce a
kind of equality. Thus the quandary, for public journalists seem not to like
such social control in newsroom or community. Public journalists do not
seem to realize that unless there is some authority to force egalitarianism, it
will not exist. Therefore, as we go into the 21st century, the spirit of press
responsibility and egalitarianism will lead to a natural decrease of journalistic freedom and autonomy.

Citizen involvement is closely tied to equality and to democracy. The public journalists know this and are trying to develop new ways to enhance such
involvement. The Jeffersonian concept of the engaged citizens does, however, assume qualities of citizenship that perhaps are not to be found in all
people. Public journalists think that people want to be engaged and that all
that is needed is the press to stimulate them, to guide them and support
them, and to provide them with common aspirations of the community.

Perhaps the public journalists are correct: The inertia that seems to pervade the citizenry has never really been challenged effectively by journalism.
The seeming indifference of citizens—some 50% to 60% of registered voters do not vote—may well stem from the fact that the news media do not
really try to engage them. Engaging is more than informing, and the old lib-

ertarian press policy of information must change to one of engagement, contend the public journalists, so that the public is stimulated to action.

If the journalistic program of the public journalists is successful, and it likely will be, this situation of people's passivity will change. The more the people are involved in journalism, the less autonomy the press will have. Ideally, members of the public will engage one another and institutions that surround them in a more knowledgeable and active manner. This is all part of the democratizing process pushed by the public journalists and presages the evolution of the press into one that belongs to, or at least encompasses, the people and not simply the media elite.

Epilogue:
A Brief View Into the Future

Slowly but inexorably the communitarian worldview is unfolding. Order and community spirit are taking over from social chaos and individualism. Out of the disorder that threatened to turn the 20th century into a vast wasteland is evolving a cautious and pluralist world of tribalized societies seeking stability and safety. Freedom is being sacrificed to order. Individualism is being sacrificed to social responsibility. Although a utopian hope for many communitarian one-worlders, the future does not promise a global community. Instead what are developing are many small, homogeneous communities composed of ideological, religious, economic, or ethnic groupings with members sharing basic values, seeking group support and loyalty, and desiring considerable segregation from incompatible groups.

Hayek pointed out (1944, p. 222) that in small communities there will be common views on projected tasks, standards of value, and a great many subjects. These common views, however, will become increasingly fewer the wider the community net is thrown, and, he said, when there "is less community of views, the necessity to rely on force and coercion increases." So it is to be expected that within megacommunities like the European Union, the Arab world, the ASEAN nations, and the United States of America, mini-communities are forming as people try to find a living place under common standards of value.

Fukuyama (1999), writing in *Atlantic Monthly,* joined the communitarians by pointing out the weaknesses of individualism, which he believes is at the heart of what he calls "the great disruption" in society. In recent years, he said, the cult of individualism has spilled over into the area of social norms where it has "eroded virtually all forms of authority and weakened the bonds holding families, neighborhoods, and nations together" (p. 56). He was convinced that we can expect a new social order because human beings are by nature social creatures whose instincts cause them to join together in communities. Fukuyama believed that the culture of individualism, so beloved by libertarians, "ends up being bereft of community" (p. 59).

Fukuyama, like the public journalists, recognizes the importance of social order and believes that such order emerges from below—from the people —and not from above. In an optimistic shift in *The Great Disruption,* he said that Hobbes was wrong about man's natural state being one of war. Rather, said Fukuyama (Wolfe, 1999, p. 43), it is a "civil society made orderly by the presence of a host of moral rules." Government, Fukuyama thought (p. 45) should stand aside and permit people to find their own ways to revitalize their communities. Public policy will thus crystallize through community conversation and action, and a kind of democratic order will emerge.

FAREWELL TO LOCKEAN MAN

As the Enlightenment Individual is replaced by the Communitarian Group, the future world will comprise a diversity of self-perpetuating collectivities to replace the individualism of the past few centuries. This may not bode well for worldwide peace and harmony, but it does mean that within the various communities there will be a sense of safety, order, agreement and common morality. A return to tribalism, perhaps, but such a return will afford like-minded individuals a renewed sense of brotherhood and solidarity.

As Fukuyama tells us, Enlightenment liberalism has led to an individualism in which the human being is "narrowly consumed with his own immediate self-preservation and material well being, interested in the community around him only to the extent that it fosters or is a means of achieving his private good." This is the kind of person the communitarians of today refer to negatively as the atomistic individual. Fukuyama continued: "Lockean man did not need to be public-spirited, patriotic, or concerned for the welfare of those around him, rather as Kant suggested, a liberal society could be made up of devils, provided they were rational."

No doubt the future communities will have collective affinities with Fukuyama's Lockean individual. Group selfishness and pride may very well replace individual selfishness and pride. However, future communities will surely provide a greater degree of democratic participation and the sharing of commonly held values; such a participation in a common cause found in the community will bring to the person enhanced dignity. Group loyalty and pride will be paramount.

The kind of recognition a communitarian seeks is as a good, functioning, contributing member of the group. It is thus that the communitarian acquires dignity. Fukuyama held that the cause of anger or shame for the group-oriented person is not that others fail to recognize his or her own worth, but when their groups are slighted or disparaged. Conversely, the greatest sense of pride or happiness arises not as a matter of personal success, but because of the success of the group. This can easily be seen in Japan particularly and in Oriental societies generally. Community spirit found in most of Asia is long-standing and growing. One criticism Asians have long had of the United States is its lack of community. Fukuyama (1992) wrote about this lack of community:

> The breakdown of community life in the United States begins with the family, which has been steadily fractured and atomised over the past couple of generations in ways that are thoroughly familiar to all Americans. But it is evident as well in the absence of any meaningful sense of local attachment for many Americans, and the disappearance of outlets for sociability beyond the immediate family. Yet it is precisely a sense of community that is offered by Asian societies, and for many of those growing up in that culture, social conformity and constraints on individualism seem a small price to pay. (p. 242)

It appears that what the communitarians want is a kind of Far Eastern spirit of community. Perhaps they even desire a return to the harmonious and conformist communities of ancient China, which were for several thousand years based either on the philosophy of Confucius and Mencius or on the strict legal codes of the Ch'in and Han dynasties. There was a collective responsibility (e.g., families were responsible for the conduct of their members), and it was impossible for individual freedom to make much headway. What was important was duty, loyalty to the group, and a spirit of solidarity. To a significant degree, these traits still exist throughout the Orient.

This Asian concept of social stability, consensus, and respect for authority is not a popular one for many Western journalists. For example, Johann P. Fritz, director of the International Press Institute, thinks this upbeat "responsibility" type of journalism valued in China and other parts of the Orient is wrong. Writing in *IPI Report* (1999, p. 32), he said that truth, not responsibility, is the best path. He claimed that Asians have a notion of journalism that promotes stability and harmony, but does not mirror reality. He wrote that in order for the Asians to benefit society, they must not deal in patriotism or social responsibility, but in truth. He further maintained that instead of the Asian model, we need a press that "functions as a vociferous public watchdog" and "operates as an essential counterweight to those in power."

Public journalists in America would most likely respond to Fritz in this way: What is wrong with socially responsible journalism that contributes to stability and order? They would insist that *all* versions of reality are distorted, not just those in Asia. No press system provides complete news, and always some truth is lost. As to "those in power"—are not the free-press journalists endorsed by the IPI and most Western journalism *those in power?* The public journalists would say that Fritz makes the mistake of all Enlightenment-inspired libertarian journalists: thinking that freedom is more important than anything else—even more important than patriotism and social responsibility. A spirit of solidarity, public journalists contend, is a good thing, and often disclosing the "truth" can be very irresponsible. So they have considerable sympathy with the Oriental journalistic values, especially the spirit of solidarity and the desire to think of the group, not the individual.

What is needed for America in order to have such a spirit of solidarity, say the communitarians, is an open and ever available potential for interaction among community members, or to have what public journalists call *community conversations* that can take place when needed. Technology will permit this to happen. What we need, as Habermas said, is a sphere of public discourse that resembles a basic speech situation, and with the technology at hand, this kind of personal of communication can take place. Communication forms community. Mere physical or geographical association is not enough; a sharing of ideas, feelings, information, opinions is what is needed for community—a sense of "commonness" among persons. This does not mean that there will be no elite representatives to facilitate this democratic community.

Mihailo Markovic, a Yugoslavian philosopher, wrote (1974, pp. 86–87) that there must be a "moral and intellectual elite" in any progressive and humanist society. But such people will consider their leadership "no more than an honor, and use force only against those who break democratically established norms of social behavior." Markovic envisioned a day when there will be no need for a group of professional politicians. Various deputies, gifted people from various professions, would hold office for a limited time and would receive no more pay than any other creative worker.

This idea would fit into the basic message of the communitarians and public journalists, but there are many people, journalists among them, who take issue with such an idea, believing it naïve and utopian and that open and free communication often alienates people, causes friction and factions, and leads to social disharmony. Walls, not communication, they say, make good neighbors. At least, they believe that often what causes social or community problems is too much public interaction and too much knowledge about your neighbors.

However, this is no either–or situation, and the wise person wants to keep some private space and also be able to move at will into a community or public space. As Habermas and others pointed out, the "public sphere" is essential to good communication and to the sustenance of community values and progress. But it should be remembered, however, that the "private sphere"—which seems to us as elusive as the public one—is what gives us the chance to calmly consider our personal progress and values and to renew our spiritual and psychological energy.

TOWARD A NORMATIVE, DEMOCRATIC PRESS

How does the press fit into all this? It seems obvious that a community of aims and interests requires social communication that instills a great degree of common outlook and thought. This can come about only through a group-oriented press that provides informational and ideational solidarity for the specific communities served. The mass communication outlets have not built community; they have been too broad, too distant, too cosmopolitan, too unfocused, and too impersonal.

What will be needed in the 21st century are localized media, interacting constantly with the community members, and reinforcing group values and norms. A complete ethical code for journalists, that all-encompassing system of values that is implicit in a community-based system, does not and has not existed in a libertarian press system. Normativity in the press, something that really has not existed, will be the defining characteristic of future communitarian or public journalism. And it will be largely a citizen-directed normed press, eliminating the possibility of elitist dominance of journalism, as it has been the absence of such a public participatory normativity that led to the present communication disorder and irresponsibility.

The media in these homogeneous communities, supported by the loyalty of their citizens and the leadership of moral leaders, will know what to publish and not to publish. As the press becomes increasingly a "people's press," the duties of the traditional editorial gate-keepers (editors, news directors, publishers, et al.) will be transferred to the citizens themselves. At least, they will have continual and direct entre to their representatives who serve as media functionaries. This seems to be what the public journalists and communitarians of today want and this is likely what they will get—growing citizen participation in press decision making in a real democratic press.

A BOLD, NEW MEDIA WORLD

Projecting the present public journalism philosophy into the new century, we can see a bold new step toward a more democratic press system, at least in the West. This, of course, probably would have happened anyway even under our more traditional media structure, but there is a real possibility that it will go beyond the present concern with focus groups, audience interviews, and polls. If the people (the public) are to have real influence and power with the press, they have to have some more substantial voice in its operation. This will likely go beyond providing feedback and even serving as shareholders in media companies. The people cannot be alienated from the machinery of information.

The people must break the press's monopoly on communication that gives it control over the ideological way of thinking and the view of the world. In short, the press's power must be spread to the people. As Markovic (1974) said, "A permanent concentration of power in the hands of any particular social group would be an essential limiting factor of the whole further development" (p. 226).

The various communities that will spring up within nations, at least if the communitarians' dream comes true, should have a say in who makes the editorial decisions that affect them every day. So what is the logical solution? A democratic community press. In other words, the citizens of a community would elect the editors of their newspaper or newspapers. The editor would serve for a certain term just as do elected political officials, and if the citizens do not feel that the paper is fulfilling their expectations, then a new editor could be elected. As with political elections, the people would then have journalistic representatives who are truly responsible to them.

Because in America we do have a capitalistic press system, such an idea of elected editors and news directors seems utopian and even naïve. But we also believe in democracy, or say we do. Does it not make sense to want the press, our "fourth branch of government"—certainly a most influential social institution—to be under the citizens' control? Is it unreasonable to want the press to be "of the people, by the people, and for the people"?

It could be that community-oriented "people's newspapers" of the future would be privately financed, either by community taxes or from gifts or subsidies from wealthy community members or businesses. Of course, advertising could still be used, but in smaller quantity and more community-relevant. At any rate, it would be a drastic change, one that would put journalism more in the hands of the people and shift the editorial emphasis from the values and prejudices of the elite media managers of today to the values and prejudices of the community. Along with the possibility of amending the First Amendment's free-press clause, which was suggested earlier in this book, such a "citizen press" would not only put the press system under law but would also democratize it, making it a vital part of the community.

COMMUNAL BOOSTERISM

Such a community system would definitely change the essence of news media. Just how such a democratic media would work for radio and television is something that future communitarians must solve. Actually, as in the case of newspapers, broadcast and cable stations may be regulated by their own communities and basically financed as they have been. Information harmful to the common good would be handled very carefully, if at all. The emphasis would shift from negativism to positivism, entertainment to education, irrelevancy to relevancy, discordance to cooperation, and despair to hope. The focus would be on group interest, not on private interest. Certainly it would be on responsibility, not on media-controlled freedom. Why, asks the communitarian, should we risk social, emotional, and moral harm for the sake of some abstract press freedom?

Two American academic researchers, Sharon Dunwoody and Robert Griffin, dealt (1999) with the basic comportment of media found in smaller, homogeneous communities. They told us that:

> Media organizations in homogeneous community structures must treat conflict within their geographic borders gingerly, as a public airing could threaten the existing power structure. Reporting that would point fingers at individual or institutional members of the community, that would expose local wrongdoing among the powerful or that would raise sensitive issues would not be consistent with a consensual role. (p. 142)

Dunwoody and Griffin further maintained that the role of a news medium in a nonpluralistic community is to help maintain the status quo and to keep order. The press would give legitimacy to the prevailing power structure and "would play an active role in the maintenance of community stability," endeavoring to prevent or lessen tension. Such a press is a kind of "community booster," they said (p. 142), and would "emphasize the good developments over the bad." Such an ideal of a press that is a cheerleader for community progress is certainly consistent with the desires of public journalists and communitarians. It could be that such idealistic objectives for the community press, reinforced by the kind of public-powered press suggested earlier, would revolutionize the news media in the new century and make them truly community-responsive.

FROM FREEDOM TO RESPONSIBILITY

For American journalists, press autonomy will die hard. The Enlightenment had a deep impact on them, even more than on their European counterparts. Even though freedom has really extended to only a small number of media executives and owners, the average journalist reveled in the idea of a free American press. In spite of constant lip service to democracy, American journalists find it hard to relinquish their powerful perogatives to the public, but that is what they are doing and will do increasingly in the 21st century.

We saw earlier that the ideas and practices of the public journalists are recasting the press into a community-related enterprise. Institutional press freedom, with its virtual ignoring of the public, is fading away. We hope that in this book we have given the reader ample indications and reasons for the press's loss of institutional freedom. More freedom can be expected to be lost as the new century progresses. Evidence exists everywhere that society is becoming more community-oriented, not only in the mass media. As to journalism itself, there are several important signs of freedom loss. For one thing, there is ever more conformist—and technological—journalism education where students are becoming community-minded and team-oriented. Various forms of sensationalism and negativism are being discouraged in journalism.

People's access to the media is being encouraged and enlarged. Not only is the people's "right to know" being championed, but their right to express themselves in the media is being urged. All sorts of techniques are being used to find out what the public wants from the media, to bring more of the people into the editorial action, and to turn the media into people's forums. Lawyers and MBAs are increasingly determining the direction of the mass media, and journalists and editors are shrinking into the background.

The press in the 21st century will have reached the point where it recognizes that its basic role is to serve the public, to stimulate democratic participation, to foster harmony and cooperation. Without such a communitarian press, the future would suggest that journalists risk becoming what Fukuyama (1992) called "secure and self-absorbed last men . . . striving for high goals in the pursuit of private comforts" (p. 328).

Sometime before the middle of the 21st century, Fukuyama's "last men" will be standing apart outside the borders of a multitude of communities, seemingly smug in their individualism and affluence and unaware that the world has passed them by. Inside the enclaves, the communitarians will be singing their paeans to order and waving their flags of harmony and cooperation.

Order for the most part has at last come out of chaos, solidarity out of personal effort and competition. No more social friction severing the bonds of group progress; no more individualistic acts that break the spirit of common striving; no more relative morality permitting all kinds of contradictory social action. All is now a kind of happy conformity, group loyalty, and a feeling of personal security. At last a community of communities: the communitarian dream come true.

And what about the "last men" standing aloof from communities? In spite of their individualistic bravado as their numbers shrink, it is quite likely that most will be shouting into the lonely vastness that surrounds them, "Woe, O woe is me! Where is my support? Where are my comrades? Why am I alone with this awful sense of angst spawned by my false self-reliance?"

They are indeed alone, recognizing reluctantly that in their isolation they are nothing. Their spirit is split asunder and they are the most lonely and miserable of creatures. A few of these individualists, to be sure, will persevere in their atomistic courage and resolve to spurn human entanglements and continue to defy community, but it is probable that even these, in spite of their outward manifestations of satisfaction, will capitulate to their sense of estrangement and finally recognize the need for companionship and solidarity. They will at least seek a group of like-minded egocentric materialists with whom to associate. However, they will find that in the twilight zone of freedom as they search frantically for a home, like Don Quixote tilting at windmills, they will be pursuing an impossible dream—a community of individualists.

References

Abel, H., & Woodward, T. (1999, March 24). Pew's news. *San Francisco Bay Guardian*, p. 8.

Achbar, M. (Ed.). (1994). *Manufacturing consent: Noam Chomsky and the media*. Montreal: Black Rose Books.

Alaily, J. (1999, June 19). Democracies are emerging, but not media freedom. *IPI Report*, 15–26.

Albert, E., Denise, T., & Peterfreund, S. (1969). *Great traditions in ethics*. New York: American Book.

Altschull, J. H. (1990). *From Milton to McLuhan*. New York: Longman.

Altschull, J. H. (1995). *Agents of power*. New York: Longman.

Anderson, C. W. (1990). *Pragmatic liberalism*. Chicago: University of Chicago Press.

Arkoun, M. (1994). *Rethinking Islam*. Boulder: Westview Press.

Ashmore, H. S. (1989). *Unreasonable truths: The life of Robert Maynard Hutchins*. Boston: Little, Brown.

Associated Press v. National Labor Relations Board, 301 U.S. 103 (1937).

The Associated Press et al. v. United States, 326 U.S. 1 (1945).

Attarian, J. (1997, Fall). Edmund Burke: Champion of ordered liberty, *The Intercollegiate Review*, 37.

Bagdikian, B. (1992a, May–June). Journalism of joy. *Mother Jones*, 48–51.

Bagdikian, B. (1992b). *The media monopoly*. Boston: Beacon Press.

Baran, S. J., & Davis, D. K. (1995). *Mass communication theory: Foundations, ferment, and future*. Belmont, CA: Wadsworth Publishing.

Bare, J. (1992, Fall). Case study—Witchita and Charlotte: The leap of a passive press to activism. *Media Studies Journal*, 149–160.

Barney, R. (1997). A dangerous drift? The sirens' call to collectivism. In J. Black (Ed.), *Mixed news: The public/civic/communitarian debate*. Mahwah, NJ: Lawrence Erlbaum Associates.

Barron, J. (1973). *Freedom of the press: For whom? The right of access to mass media*. Bloomington: University of Indiana Press.

Barsamian, D. (1994). *Secrets, lies and democracy*. Chicago: Common Image Press.

Becker, C. (1945). *Freedom and responsibility in the American way of life*. Westport, CT: Greenwood Press.

Beiser, F. (1996). *The sovereignty of reason*. Princeton, NJ: Princeton University Press.

Bell, S. (1999, Summer). Global media revolution. *Global Media News*, p. 21.

Bellah, R. (1986). *Habits of the heart*. New York: Harper & Row.

Berlin, I. (1969). *Four essays on liberty*. London: Oxford University Press.

Best, S., & Kellner, D. (1997). *The postmodern turn*. New York: Guilford Press.

Bishop, E. (1999, June). *St. Louis Journalism Review*.

Blanchard, M. A. (1977). *The Hutchins commission, the press and the responsibility concept*. (Journalism Monographs).

Blevens, F. R. (1995). *Gentility and quiet aggression: A cultural history of the commission on freedom of the press.* Unpublished doctoral dissertation, University of Missouri.

Boaz, D. (1997). *Libertarianism: A primer.* New York: The Free Press.

Bollinger, L. C. (1998, Spring/Summer). The Hutchins Commission, half a century on—III. *Media Studies Journal.*

Bork, R. (1996). *Slouching toward gomorrah.* New York: HarperCollins.

Bottomore, T. B. (1968). *Critics of society: Radical thought in North America.* New York: Pantheon Books.

Brogan, P. (1985). *Spiked: The short life and death of the National News Council.* New York: Priority Press.

Buckner, J. (1996, October 19). Public journalism: Good or bad news? *The Charlotte Observer,* p. 19A.

Buckner, J., & Gartner, M. (1998). Public journalism in the 1996 elections. In E. Lambeth, P. Meyer, & E. Thorson (Eds.), *Assessing public journalism* (pp. 223–231). Columbia: University of Missouri Press.

Bull, H. (1977). *The anarchical society: The study of order in world politics.* New York: Columbia University Press.

Campbell, C. (1999). Journalism as a democratic art. In T. Glasser (Ed.), *The idea of public journalism* (pp xiii–xxix). New York: Guilford Press.

Carey, G. W. (1984). *Freedom and virtue: The Conservative/Libertarian debate.* Lanham, MD: University Press of America.

Carey, J. W. (1987). The press and public discourse. *The Center Magazine, 20,* 4–16.

Carey, J. W. (1989). *Communication as culture: Essays on media and society.* Boston: Unwin-Hyman.

Carey, J. W. (1998, March/April). The decline of democratic institutions. *Columbia Journalism Review,* 6.

Carey, J. W. (1999, Summer). Newspapers at the crossroads. *Nieman Reports (Special Issue).*

Carter, S. (1993). *The culture of disbelief.* New York: HarperCollins.

Chafee, Z. (1928). Liberty and law. In H. M. Kallen (Ed.), *Freedom in the modern world.* New York: Coward-McCann.

Chafee, Z. (1941, August 9). Free speech in America, *The Saturday Review of Literature,* 3–4, 16–17.

Chafee, Z. (1947). *Government and mass communications.* Chicago: University of Chicago Press.

Charity, A. (1995). *Doing public journalism.* New York: Guilford Press.

Christians, C., Ferre, J., & Fackler, M. (1993). *Good news: Social ethics and the press.* New York: Oxford University Press.

Chomsky, N. (1987). *On power and ideology.* Boston: South End Press.

Civic journalism: From citizens up. (1996, July). *Civic Catalyst,* 9.

Clark, J. M. (1926). *Social control of business.* Chicago: University of Chicago Press.

Cohen, E. D. (1992). *Philosophical issues in journalism.* New York: Oxford University Press.

Coleman, R. (1997). The intellectual antecedents of public journalism, *Journal of Communications Inquiry, 21*(2), 61.

Collinson, D. (1987). *Fifty major philosophers.* London: Routledge.

Colson, C. (1989). *Against the night: Living in the new dark age.* Ann Arbor, MI: Servant Books.

Commission on Freedom of the Press. (1947). *A free and responsible press.* Chicago: University of Chicago Press.

Commission to make 2-year study of all phases of press freedom. (1944, February 24). *The New York Times,* p. A11.

The Committee to Frame a World Constitution. (1948, April 3). Preliminary draft for global federation. *The Saturday Reveiw,* 7–11.

Conte, C. (1996, September 20). Civic journalism. *CQ Researcher, 6,* 819–839.

Cooper, T., Christians, C., Plude, F., & White, R. (1989). *Communication ethics and global change.* New York: Longman.

Corrigan, D. (1999). *The public journalism movement in America: Evangelists in the newsroom.* Westport, CT: Greenwood Publishing Group.

Dali, S. (1942). *Essays of Michel de Montaigne.* New York: Doubleday.

Darnton, R. (1999, March 13). The new age of the books. *The New York Times Book Review.*

Davidson, J. D., & Rees-Mogg, W. (1997). *The sovereign individual.* New York: Simon & Schuster.

Daviss, B. (1997, March). Of the people, by the people, for the people. *Ambassador Magazine.*

Day, L. (1997). *Ethics in media communication.* Belmont, CA: Wadsworth.

Dennis, E. (1995a, July 29). Raising questions about civic or public journalism. *Editor & Publisher,* 48.

Dennis, E. (1995b, September 13). *Wait a minute, Chicken Little!* Speech at the Pew Center for Civic Journalism, Washington, DC.

Denton, F., & Thorson, E. (1998). Effects of a multimedia public journalism project on political knowledge and attitudes. In E. Lambeth, P. Meyer, & E. Thorson (Eds.), *Assessing public journalism* (pp. 143–157). Columbia: University of Missouri Press.

Denton, T. (1994, January 16). *Ft. Worth Star-Telegram,* pp. 6, 11.

Dewey, J. (1927). *The public and its problems.* Denver, CO: Swallow Press.

Dewey, J. (1963). *Liberalism and social action.* New York: Capricorn.

Diamond, E. (1997, August). Civic journalism. *Columbia Journalism Review,* 11–12.

Diamond, L. (1996). Democracy in Latin America. In T. Farer (Ed.), *Beyond sovereignty* (pp. 52–104). Baltimore: Johns Hopkins University Press.

Dickinson, J. (1944). The old political philosophy and the new. In *Thomas Jefferson: Proceedings of the American Philosophical Society, April 22–24, 1943* (pp. 246–247). New York: West Publishing.

DiNunzio, M. (1987). *American democracy and the authoritarian tradition of the west.* Lanham, MD: University Press of America.

Donaldson, S. (1992). *Archibald MacLeish: An American life.* New York: Houghton Mifflin.

Drucker, P. F. (1999, October). The information revolution. *The Atlantic Monthly,* 47–57.

Drury, M. (1943, April 12). Ruml. *Life,* 35–38.

Dunwoody, S., & Griffin, R. (1999). Structural pluralism and media accounts of risk. In D. Demers & V. K. Viswanath (Eds.), *Mass media, social control and social change* (pp. 139–158). Ames: Iowa State University Press.

Durant, W. (1966). *The story of philosophy.* New York: Washington Square Press.

Dykers, C. R. (1998). Assessing Davis Merritt's public journalism. In E. Lambeth, P. Meyer, & E. Thorson (Eds.), *Assessing public journalism* (pp. 57–82). Columbia: University of Missouri Press.

Edgerton, R. (1985). *Rules, exceptions, and social order.* Berkeley: University of California Press.

Elections '96: From citizens up. (1996, July). *Civic Catalyst,* 9.

Elshtain, J. B. (1995). *Democracy on trial.* New York: Basic Books.

Etzioni, A. (1993). *The spirit of community.* New York: Crown Publishers.

Etzioni, A. (1996). *The new golden rule.* New York: Basic Books.

Fallows, J. (1996). *Breaking the news: How the media undermine American democracy.* New York: Pantheon Books.

Fascetto, J. (1999, October 12). *Issues in the Latin American news business today.* Speech at the University of Missouri School of Journalism, Columbia.

Feinstein, A. (1995, September/October). Media under pressure in newer democracies. *IPI Report,* 16–18.

Fishkin, J. S. (1991). *Democracy and deliberation: New directions for democratic reform.* New Haven, CT: Yale University Press.

Flink, S. E. (1997). *Sentinel under siege: The triumphs and troubles of America's free press*. New York: Westview Press.

Ford, P. (1999, Summer). Shining a light in dark corners. *Civic Catalyst, 4,* 15.

Fouhy, E., & Schaffer, J. (1995, Spring). Civic journalism—Growing and evolving. *Nieman Reports,* 16–18.

Frankel, M. (1995, Fall). Journalists should leave reform to the reformers. *The Masthead,* 21–22.

Freire, P. (1989). *Pedogogy of the oppressed*. New York: Continuum.

Friedland, L., Sotirovic, M., & Daily, K. (1998). Public journalism and social capital. In E. Lambeth, P. Meyer, & E. Thorson (Eds.), *Assessing public journalism* (pp. 191–220). Columbia: University of Missouri Press.

Fritz, J. (1999). Upbeat reporting distorts quality. *IPI Report,* 2nd quarter, 2.

Frohnen, B. (1997, Spring). Does Robert Bellah care about history? *Intercollegiate Review,* 19.

Frohnmeyer, J. (1995). *Out of tune: Listening to the first amendment*. Golden, CO: North American.

Fromm, E. (1941). *Escape from freedom*. New York: Rinehart.

Fromm, E. (1955). *The sane society*. New York: Rinehart.

Fukuyama, F. (1992). *The end of history and the last man*. New York: Avon Books.

Fukuyama, F. (1999, May). The great disruption: Human nature and the reconstitution of social order. *The Atlantic Monthly,* 55–80.

Gans, H. J. (1998, Fall). What can journalists actually do for American democracy? *Harvard International Journal of Press/Politics,* 6–12.

Gartner, M. (1997, April 14). *Joe Creason lecture*. University of Kentucky, Lexington.

Gay, P. (1973). *The Enlightenment: A comprehensive anthology*. New York: Simon & Schuster.

Geldner, A. (1997, August 6). Das cyberpatrol. *Stuttgarter Zeitung,* reprinted in the *San Francisco Bay Guardian,* p. 37.

Gellner, E. (1996). *Conditions of liberty: Civil society and its rivals*. London: Penguin Books.

Gilson, G. (1999, Winter). On resistance to news councils. *Harvard International Journal of Press/Politics,* 5–10.

Ginsberg, B. (1986). *The captive public*. New York: Basic Books.

Glasser, T. (1999). *The idea of public journalism*. New York: Guilford Press.

Gonzales, S. S. (1992, August). *The American pattern of the press: A model to follow?* Shorenstein Barone Center discussion paper D.

Gordon, A. D., & Kittross, J. M. (1999). *Controversies in media ethics*. New York: Longman.

Gorzkowski, M. (1998, December). Focus on news-gathering. *The Quill,* 5.

Gray, J. (1996). *Isaiah Berlin*. Princeton: Princeton University Press.

Greider, W. (1993). *Who will tell the people: The betrayal of American democracy*. New York: Simon & Schuster.

Grosswiler, P. (1998). *Method is the message: Rethinking McLuhan through critical theory*. Montreal: Black Rose Books.

Guroian, V. (1998, Fall). The moral imagination in an age of sentiments. *The Intercollegiate Review,* 10.

Habermas, J. (1975). *Legitimation crisis*. Boston: Beacon Press.

Habermas, J. (1991). *Critic in the public sphere*. London: Routledge.

Habermas, J. (1996). *Moral consciousness and communicative action*. Cambridge, MA: MIT Press.

Hachten, W. (1996). *The world news prism*. Ames: Iowa State University Press.

Hamelink, C. (1983). *Cultural autonomy in global communications*. New York: Longman.

Harwood, R. (1996, March 8). The legitimacy of "civic journalism." *The Washington Post,* p. A21.

Hay, G. (1970). *An essay on the liberty of the press*. New York: Arno Press.

Hayek, F. A. (1944). *Road to serfdom*. Chicago: University of Chicago Press.

Henry, C. F. H. (1996). *Has democracy had its day?* Nashville: ERLC Publications.

Hocking, W. E. (1942, February). What man can make of man. *Fortune,* 90–93.

Hoffer, E. (1956). *The true believer*. New York: Mentor Books.

Holmes, S. T. (1993). *The anatomy of antiliberalism.* Cambridge, MA: Harvard University Press.

Hoyt, M. (1995, September/October). Are you now, or will you ever be, a civic journalist? *Columbia Journalism Review,* 27–33.

Hughes, F. (1950). *Prejudice and the press.* New York: Devin-Adair Co.

Humboldt, W. von. (1993). *On the limits of state action.* Indianapolis: Liberty Fund.

The Hutchins Report—A twenty-year view. (1967, Summer). *Columbia Journalism Review,* 8–20.

Hutchins, R. M. (1942, January). The university at war. *University of Chicago Magazine,* 1–7.

Hutchins, R. M. (1945, August 12). *Atomic force: Its meaning for mankind.* Radio address under the auspices of the National Broadcasting Company and the University of Chicago.

Jackson, W. (1996, Oct. 7). The press cops out. *The New York Times,* p. A17.

Jameson, F. (1988). *The ideologies of theory.* Minneapolis: University of Minnesota Press.

Jaspers, K. (1957). *Man in the modern age.* Garden City, NY: Doubleday.

Jensen, J. (1962). Freedom of the press: A concept in search of a philosophy. In *Social responsibility of the newspress* (pp. 75–88). Milwaukee: Marquette University Press.

Johnson, P. (1988). *Intellectuals.* New York: Harper & Row.

Johnson, S. (1998). Public journalism and newsroom structure. In E. Lambeth, P. Meyer, & E. Thorsen, *Assessing public journalism* (pp. 123–142). Columbia: University of Missouri Press.

Jonas, H. (1984). *The imperative of responsibility.* Chicago: University of Chicago Press.

Jung, C. C. (1924). *Psychological types.* New York: Harcourt, Brace.

Kaplan, R. (1994, February). The coming anarchy. *The Atlantic Monthly,* 44–76.

Kaplan, R. (1997, December). Was democracy just a moment? *The Atlantic Monthly,* 55–80.

Kelly, M. (1996, November 4). Media culpa. *The New Yorker,* 45–49.

Kendall, W., & Carey, G. W. (Eds.). (1966). *The Federalist Papers by James Madison, Alexander Hamilton and John Jay.* New Rochelle, NY: Arlington House.

Kirtley, J. (1997, March). Getting mauled in Food Lion's den. *American Journalism Review,* 48.

Knecht, G. B. (1996, October 17). Why a big foundation gives newspapers cash to change their ways. *The Wall Street Journal,* p. A1.

Knutson, A. L. (1948). The commission and its critics. *Public Opinion Quarterly, 2,* 130–135.

Kunczik, M. (1988). *Journalism als Beruf.* Cologne: Boehlau.

Lambeth, E., Meyer, P., & Thorson, E. (1998). *Assessing public journalism.* Columbia: University of Missouri Press.

Lambeth, E. B. (1992). *Committed journalism: An ethic for the profession.* Bloomington and Indianapolis: Indiana University Press.

Lappe, F. M., & DuBois, P. M. (1994). *The quickening of America: Building our nation, remaking our lives.* San Francisco: Jossey-Bass.

Laquer, W. (1996). *Fascism, past, future.* New York: Oxford University Press.

Lasch, C. (1995). *The revolt of the elites and the betrayal of democracy.* New York: Norton.

Lasswell, H. (1941). The structure and function of communication in society. In L. Bryson (Ed.), *The communication of ideas* (pp. 37–38). New York: Harper & Brothers.

Lasswell, H. (1948). The achievement standards of a democratic press. In H. L. Ickes (Ed.), *Freedom of the press today: A clinical examination by 28 specialists* (pp. 171–178). New York: Vanguard.

Lau, D. C. (1970). *Mencius.* New York: Penguin.

Lazare, D. (1996). *The frozen republic: How the constitution is paralyzing democracy.* New York: Harcourt Brace.

Lee, A. M. (1937). *The daily newspaper in America.* New York: Macmillan.

Leslie, C. (1976). The hedgehog and the fox in Robert Redfield's work and career. In J. V. Murra (Ed.), *American anthropology: The early years: 1974 proceedings of the American Ethnological Society* (pp. 146–166). New York: West Publishing.

Leslie, L. Z. (2000). *Mass communication ethics: Decision making in postmodern culture*. Boston: Houghton Mifflin.

Levy, L. W. (1985). *Emergence of a free press*. New York: Oxford University Press.

Lichter, S. R., Rothman, S., & Lichter, L. S. (1986). *The media elite: America's new powerbrokers*. Bethesda, MD: Adler & Adler.

Lipow, A. (1982). *Authoritarian socialism in America & the national movement*. Berkeley: University of California Press.

Lippmann, W. (1922). *Public opinion*. New York: Harcourt Brace.

Lyons, L. M. (1947, April). A free and responsible press: A review of free press report. *Nieman Reports*. 1–3.

MacIntyre, A. (1984). *After virtue*. Notre Dame, IN: Notre Dame University Press.

MacIntyre, A. (1990). *Philosophy East and West, 40*(4), 489–497.

MacLeish, A. (1941). The Duty of freedom. In H. L. Ickes (Ed.), *Freedom of the press today*. New York: Vanguard Press.

Magee, B. (1988). *The story of philosophy*. New York: DK Publishing.

Mann, J. (1997, December 3). International outlook. *Los Angeles Times*, p. A5.

Markovic, M. (1972/1974). *From affluence to praxis*. Ann Arbor: University of Michigan Press.

Mattelart, A. (1979). *Multicultural corporations and the control of culture*. Sussex, NJ: Harvester Press.

Mayer, M. S. (1969). *On liberty: Man v. the state*. Santa Barbara, CA: Center for the Study of Democratic Institutions.

Mayer, M., & Hicks, J. H. (Eds.). (1993). *Robert Maynard Hutchins: A memoir*. Berkeley: University of California Press.

Mazzocco, D. W. (1994). *Networks of power: Corporate TV's threat to democracy*. Boston: South End Press.

McChesney, R. (1997). *Corporate media and the threat to democracy*. New York: Seven Stories Press.

McGuire, T. (1994, October). Sharing the excitement of newspaper change. *ASNE Bulletin*, 5.

McIntyre, J. S. (1979). Hutchins Commission's search for a moral framework. *Journalism History*, 6.

McIntyre, J. S. (1987). Repositioning a landmark: The Hutchins Commission and freedom of the press. *Critical Studies in Mass Communication*, 4.

McLuhan, M. (1965). *Understanding media*. New York: McGraw-Hill.

McManus, J. H. (1994). *Market-driven journalism: Let the citizen beware*. Thousand Oaks, CA: Sage Publications.

McNair, B. (1998). *The sociology of journalism*. London: Arnold.

Meiklejohn, A. (1948). *Free speech and its relation to self-government*. New York: Harper.

Merriam, C. E. (1939). *The new democracy and the new despotism*. New York: Macmillan.

Merrill, J. C. (1974). *The imperative of freedom*. New York: Hastings House.

Merrill, J. C. (1994). *Legacy of wisdom: Great thinkers and journalism*. Ames: Iowa State University Press.

Merrill, J. C. (1998). *The princely press: Machiavelli on American journalism*. Lanham, MD: University Press of America.

Merritt, D. (1990, September 9). Here's our election bias. *Wichita Eagle*, p. 13A.

Merritt, D. (1996, July/August). Missing the point. *American Journalism Review*, 29–31.

Merritt, D. (1997). Public journalism, independence, and civic capital . . . Three ideas in complete harmony. In J. Black (Ed.), *Mixed news: The public/civic/communitarian journalism debate* (pp. 180–187). Mahwah, NJ: Lawrence Erlbaum Associates.

Merritt, D. (1998). *Public journalism and public life: Why telling the news is not enough* (2nd ed.). Mahwah, NJ: Lawrence Erlbaum Associates.

Merritt, D., & Rosen, J. (1998). Imagining public journalism. In E. Lambeth, P. Meyer, &

E. Thorson (Eds.), *Assessing public journalism* (pp. 36–56). Columbia: University of Missouri Press.

Meyer, D. H. (1976). *The democratic enlightenment.* New York: G. P. Putnam's Sons.

Mill, J. S. (1986). *On liberty.* New York: Macmillan. (Original work published 1861)

Molnar, T. (1967). *Utopia, the perennial heresy.* New York: Sheed and Ward.

Molnar, T. (1998). *Twin powers: Politics and the sacred.* Grand Rapids, MI: Eerdmans.

Munson, E. S., & Warren, C. (1997) *James Carey: A critical reader.* Minneapolis: University of Minnesota Press.

Needham, J. (1943). *Time: The refreshing river.* New York: Macmillan.

Nelson, D. (1955). *After authoritarianism: Democracy or disorder?* Westport, CT: Greenwood Press.

Nerone, J. C. (1995). *Last rights: Revisiting four theories of the press.* Urbana: University of Illinois Press.

Newfield, J. (1974). Journalism: Old, new and corporate. In R. Weber (Ed.), *The reporter as artist: A look at the new journalism* (pp. 54–65). New York: Hastings House.

Newman, J. (1989). *The journalist in Plato's cave.* Cranbury, NJ: Associated University Presses.

New voter education project reaches one in four North Carolina voters, and impresses 82% favorably. (1996, December). *A press release by the Pew Center for Civic Journalism* [Online]. Available: http://www.pewcenter.org/doingcj/research/r_voters.html

The News Media and the Law. (1998, Fall).

Niebuhr, R. (1946, October). The fight for Germany. *Life,* 64–72.

Niebuhr, R. (1960). *Moral man and immoral society.* New York: Scribner's. (Original work published 1932)

Nietzsche, F. (1966). *Beyond good and evil.* New York: Random House.

Nisbet, R. (1980). *History of the idea of progress.* New York: Basic Books.

Nisbet, R. (1990). *The quest for community.* San Francisco: ICS Press.

Noack, D. (1999, February 20). Opening up the story meeting: Readers and noneditorial staffers join discussions. *Editor & Publisher,* 26–30.

Packard, A. (1998, December). Infringement or impingement. *Communication monograph No. 168.* Columbia, SC: Association for Education in Journalism and Mass Communication.

Parenti, M. (1995). *Against empire.* San Francisco: City Lights Books.

Parry, K. (1999, Winter). A view from the civic journalism trenches. *Civic Catalyst, 1,* 12–13.

Peikoff, L. (1982). *Ominous parallels: The end of freedom in America.* New York: New American Library.

Peterson, M. (1976). *Adams and Jefferson: A revolutionary dialogue.* Oxford, MS: Oxford University Press.

Peterson, T. (1963). The social responsibility theory of the press. In F. Siebert, T. Peterson, & W. Schramm, *Four theories of the press* (pp. 73–103). Urbana and Chicago: University of Illinois Press.

Pew Center is renewed. (1999, Summer). *Civic Catalyst,* 9.

Picard, R. (1985). *The press and the decline of democracy.* Westport, CT: Greenwood Press.

Pool, I. (1983). *Technologies of freedom.* Cambridge, MA: Harvard University Press.

Project Reconnect. (1997). *Change: Living it, embracing it, measuring it,* 28. A report by the American Society of Newspaper Editors Change Committee.

The public agenda. (1995). A report published by the Pew Center for Civic Journalism and The Poynter Institute for Media Studies [Online]. Available: http://www.journalism.wisc.edu/cpn/sections/topics/journalism/stories-studies/pew&poynter-tallahassee.html

Reddin van Tuyll, D. (1998, October). *Public journalism as postmodern phenomenon.* Paper presented at the Conference on Public Journalism, University of South Carolina.

Revel, J. F. (1978). *The totalitarian temptation.* New York: Penguin Books.

Revel, J. F. (1985). *How democracies perish.* New York: Harper & Row.

Reynolds, A. (1999). Local television coverage of the NIC. In M. Macombs & A. Reynolds (Eds.), *The poll with a human face* (pp. 113–131). Mahwah, NJ: Lawrence Erlbaum Associates.

Riesman, D. (1959). *The lonely crowd.* New Haven, CT: Yale University Press.

Rorty, R. (1995, January 30). Two cheers for elitism. *New Yorker,* 86–89.

Rosen, J. (1994a, June 13). *Getting the connections right: What public journalism might be.* Presentation to Project on Public Life and the Press, First Summer Institute, American Press Institute.

Rosen, J. (1994b). *Public journalism: A progress report.* A report published by the Project on Public Life and the Press.

Rosen, J. (1995, May/June). Public journalism: A case for public scholarship. *Change,* 34–38.

Rosen, J. (1996). *Getting the connections right: Public journalism and the troubles in the press.* New York: Twentieth Century Fund Press.

Rosen, J. (1997). Losing the thing you love. *Change: Living it, embracing it, measuring it,* 8–13. A report by the American Society of Newspaper Editors Change Committee.

Rosen, J. (1999). The action of the idea: Public journalism in built form. In T. Glasser (Ed.), *The idea of public journalism* (pp. 21–48). New York: Guilford Press.

Rosen, J., & Merritt, D. (1994). *Public journalism: Theory and practice.* Dayton, OH: Kettering Foundation.

Rosen, J., & Taylor, P. (1992). *The new news v. the old news.* New York: Twentieth Century Fund.

Roszak, T. (1986). *The cult of information.* New York: Pantheon Books.

Said, E. (1981). *Covering Islam: How the media and the experts determine how we see the rest of the world.* New York: Pantheon Books.

Sandel, M. J. (1996). *Democracy's discontent.* Cambridge, MA: Harvard University Press.

Sanford, B. (1998, September). Chiquita lesson: Libel isn't weapon of choice. *American Editor,* 17–19.

Schaffer, J. (1996a). *Civic journalism Washington style: Reporting beyond the Beltway.* Pew Center for Civic Journalism [Online]. Available: http//www.pewcenter.org/doingcj/speeches/index.html

Schaffer, J. (1996b). *Tapping the hidden sources in your community.* Pew Center for Civic Journalism. [Online]. Available: http//www.pewcenter.org/doingcj/speeches/index.html

Schaffer, J. (1997a). *Civic journalism: The idea, the evolution, the impact.* Pew Center for Civic Journalism. [Online]. Available: http//www.pewcenter.org/doingcj/speeches/index.html

Schaffer, J. (1997b). *Is it possible to do significant journalism in an era of botton-line concerns and technological change?* Pew Center for Civic Journalism. [Online]. Available: http//www.pewcenter.org/doingcj/speeches/index.html

Schaffer, J. (1998). *Civic journalism: Redefining news, engaging readers, making a difference.* Pew Center for Civic Journalism. [Online]. Available: http//www.pewcenter.org/doingcj/speeches/index.html

Schaffer, J. (1999a, Summer). The Batten winners: Journalism that took risks. *Civic Catalyst,* 2.

Schaffer, J. (1999b). *The media and civic engagement.* Pew Center for Civic Journalism. [Online]. Available: http//www.pewcenter.org/doing cj/speeches/index.html

Schlesinger, A. (1963). *In retrospect: The history of a historian.* New York: Harcourt, Brace & World.

Schouls, P. A. (1989). *Descartes and the Enlightenment.* Montreal: McGill-Queen's University Press.

Schudson, M. (1978). *Discovering the news.* New York: Basic Books.

Seidenberg, R. (1974). *Posthistoric man.* New York: Viking Press.

Shepard, A. (1994, September). The gospel of public journalism. *American Journalism Review,* 28–34.

Shuster, A. (1995, September/October), Democracies are emerging, but not media freedom. *IPI Report,* 19.

Shuster, G. N. (1929, June 19). Letters and censorship. *Commonweal,* 176–178.

Slater, P. (1976). *The pursuit of loneliness: American culture at the breaking point.* Boston: Beacon Press.

Smith, D. (1986), *Zechariah Chafee, Jr.: Defender of liberty and law.* Cambridge, MA: Harvard University Press.

Splichal, S., & Sparks, C. (1994). *Journalism for the 21st century.* Norwood, NJ: Ablex.

Squires, J. (1998, Spring/Summer). The impossibility of fairness. *Media Studies Journal,* 66–71.

Stephen, J. F. (1982). *Liberty, equality, fraternity.* New York: Henry Holt. (1993) Indianapolis: Liberty Fund.

Stevenson, L., & Haberman, D. L. (1998). *Ten theories of human nature.* New York: Oxford.

Storin, M. (1996, July). Civic journalism: Part of the solution. *Civic Catalyst,* 8, 11–12.

Survey: First amendment taking a beating with public. (1999, July 4). Columbia, MO: *Daily Tribune.*

Thames, R. (1998). Public journalism in the 1992 elections. In E. Lambeth, P. Meyer, & E. Thorson (Eds.), *Assessing public journalism* (pp. 111–122). Columbia: University of Missouri Press.

Tillich, P. (1957). *The Protestant era.* Chicago: University of Chicago Press.

Tinder, G. (1993, October). Liberalism and its enemies. *The Atlantic Monthly,* 116–122.

Tocqueville, A. de. (1966). *Democracy in America.* New York: Harper & Row. (Original work published 1838)

Torrey, N. L. (1960). *Les philosophes.* New York: Capricorn Books.

Trager, R., & Dickerson, D. (1999). *Freedom of expression in the 21st century.* Thousand Oaks, CA: Pine Forge Press.

Tucker, R. W., & Hendrickson, D. C. (1990). *Empire of liberty: The statecraft of Thomas Jefferson.* New York: Oxford University Press.

Tunstall, J. (1977). *The media are American.* New York: Columbia University Press.

United States v. Associated Press, 62F. Supp. 362 (1943).

Vernet, D. (1998, Septebmer 24). The return of the new world information order. *Le Monde,* 24.

Weaver, P. (1994). *News and the culture of lying.* New York: Free Press.

Why "the informed citizen" is too much to ask—and not enough. (1999, Summer). *Civic Catalyst,* 8–9.

Wiener, N. (1950). *The human use of human beings.* Boston: Houghton Mifflin.

Wilkinson, R. (1972). *The broken rebel: A study in culture, politics, and authoritarian character.* New York: Harper & Row.

Will, G. F. (1995, December 6). The Francis Boyer lecture. Paper presented at the American Enterprise Institute, Washington, DC.

Williams, C. J. (1995, September/October). Russians' choice: Mental junk food. *IPI Report,* 23.

Williams, F. (1969). *The right to know: The rise of the world press.* London: Longmans.

Williams, F., & Pavlik, J. V. (1994). *The people's right to know: Media, democracy, and the information highway.* Hillsdale, NJ: Lawrence Erlbaum Associates.

Wilson, E. O., (1998, March). Back from chaos. *The Atlantic Monthly,* 41–62.

Winter, J. (1998). *Democracy's oxygen: How corporations control the news.* Montreal: Black Rose.

Wolfe, A. (1999, August 2). The shock of the old. *The New Republic,* 42–45.

Woo, W. F. (1995, July/August). Should the press be an observer or an actor in public affairs? *St. Louis Journalism Review,* 10.

World press freedom committee newsletter. (1998, December).

Wrong, D. (1994). *The problem of order.* New York: The Free Press.

Zakaria, F. (1994, March/April). A conversation with Lee Kuan Yew. *Foreign Affairs,* 73(2), 109–127.

Zhao, Y. (1998). *Media, market, and democracy.* Urbana: University of Illinois Press.

Author Index

Subject Index

About the Authors

John C. Merrill is professor emeritus of journalism at the University of Missouri. In 2000, he completed 50 years of teaching, 25 of them at Missouri. His BA is in English and history. He has two master's degrees, one in journalism and one in philosophy, and a PhD in mass communication from the University of Iowa. He has worked on newspapers in four states, and has taught in Kansas, Louisiana, California, Virginia, Maryland, and Missouri, as well as in Spain, Egypt, and Taiwan. He has lectured and held journalism workshops in some 80 countries and is the author or editor of 30 books, most of them on international communication and journalism philosophy.

Peter J. Gade is assistant professor at the H. H. Herbert School of Journalism and Mass Communication at the University of Oklahoma. He holds a BS in history from the State University of New York at Brockport, an MA in journalism from Louisiana State University, and a PhD from the University of Missouri. His newspaper experience is with the Elmira (NY) *Star Gazette* and *The* (Corning, NY) *Leader.* He has been a research consultant for the *St. Louis Post-Dispatch.* Gade has worked in documentary films, and has taught at Mansfield University in Pennsylvania, Keuka College in New York, the University of Missouri, and the University of Oklahoma.

Frederick R. Blevens is associate professor of mass communication at Southwest Texas State University. He has a BS and MA in journalism from Ball State University, and a PhD in journalism from the University of Missouri. He has been a reporter for the *Tampa Tribune* and the *Camden Courier-Post,* a reporter/editor for the *Philadelphia Bulletin,* and city editor of the *San Antonio Light.* He has also been deputy metro editor for the *Ft. Worth Star–Telegram,* state editor of the *Houston Chronicle,* and editor of *Missouri Magazine.* Blevens has taught at Ball State, San Antonio College, the University of Missouri, Texas A&M University, and Southwest Texas State University.